HALF
THE
HOUSE

BOOKS BY HERBERT KOHL

Half the House
Reading, How To
Age of Complexity
Language and Education of the Deaf
Teaching the Unteachable
36 Children
The Open Classroom
Anthony Cool as Golden Boy
Writing, Math, and Games in the
Open Classroom

HALF
THE
HOUSE

Herbert
Kohl

E. P. DUTTON & CO., INC.
New York / 1974

Copyright © 1974 by Herbert Kohl
All rights reserved. Printed in the U.S.A.
First Edition

10 9 8 7 6 5 4 3 2 1

Published simultaneously in Canada by Clarke,
Irwin & Company Limited, Toronto and Vancouver

Library of Congress Cataloging in Publication Data

Kohl, Herbert R
     Half the house.

     1. Kohl, Herbert R. 2. Teaching, Freedom of.
3. Conduct of life. 4. Negroes—Education. I. Title.
LA2317.K64A34   371.1'0092'4   74-1472
ISBN 0-525-12030-0

Designed by Lucy Fehr

"Growing in Spirit" from *C. P. Cavafy: Collected Poems,* to
be published by Princeton University Press, fall 1974.

To Akmir, also known as Leroy Carter,
and to Hal Scharlatt

Contents

Preface

There are two questions that press themselves on adults in this culture at this moment: Is it possible to live a healthy life in an unhealthy society? and Is it possible to change oneself in midlife despite one's education and the practical pressures to survive? In this book I've focused a lot on schools because teaching is at the center of my life. However, the school is my personal metaphor—it is possible to say the same things about business, industry, law, medicine, art, athletics. We all have to face ourselves and decide whether we'll continue to function in familiar though destructive ways or learn how to learn as adults.

While writing this book many people have helped and often pushed me. Marcie MacGaugh, Kathy Sloane, Orlando and Lisa Ortiz, Cynthia Brown, Margot Nanny, Hilary Bendich, Hal Scharlatt, Bob and Susan Lescher, Lee and Carol Swenson, Alice Trillin and Miranda Knickerbocker have read the many drafts of the manuscript and gave me courage to finish it. My wife, Judy, lived through the writing and read, reread, and helped think through every aspect of the book. There are other people to thank—everyone at Other Ways, my parents and children, the students at P.S. 105 and 79. Many of the ideas of Claude Lévi-Strauss, Carl Jung, M. C. Richards, John Carpenter, John Harwayne, Daniel Peck, David and Dee Dee Spencer and Ludwig Wittgenstein have informed my thought and have provided a framework upon which to develop ideas and make sense out of experiences. They are not of course responsible for the use I have made of their ideas.

GROWING IN SPIRIT

He who hopes to grow in spirit
will have to transcend obedience and respect.
He'll hold to some laws
but he'll mostly violate
both law and custom, and go beyond
the established, inadequate norm.
Sensual pleasures will have much to teach him.
He won't be afraid of the destructive act:
half the house will have to come down.
This way he'll grow virtuously into wisdom.

C. V. CAVAFY

I

Approximations

[1]

Twelve years ago I set out to be a good public school class-room teacher. My focus was on what could be done in one classroom with a small number of young people. Quite unexpectedly work in the classroom led me to political and social conflict as well as to struggle within myself.

Initially I defined my role exclusively in terms of the students in my class. I abandoned traditional ways of being a teacher, although they suited me quite well, because my students didn't respond to them. I locked my classroom door from the inside, put black paper over the window in the door, and isolated my class from the rest of the school. After several years within that limited world I learned how to respond to my students' needs, to listen to their voices, to understand how they perceived the world. I also learned how to develop a learning environment in which they flowered. Most of my students were black and by the time they reached the fifth and sixth grades had been designated failures by the school. However, I saw the kids' faces, listened to them talk, and watched them play outside of school and couldn't perceive any failure. In the confines of my classroom I witnessed my students learn and create, become excited by the intellectual and artistic power they developed, and I sensed that there was some-thing deeply wrong in the whole school. For a while, however, I shut off questions that dealt with the school as a whole or the competencies and attitudes of the other teachers. I believed that it was possible to confine my role as a teacher and a person to my classroom.

3

My relationships with other teachers and the administration while we were at work were formalized and predictable. Most of the time we had nothing to do with one
another. Once a month there was a staff meeting during
which the principal and assistant principal made announcements. There was never any discussion, and dissent
within the staff or the school community was never dealt
with publicly.

I nodded to other teachers in the halls; we occasionally
discussed union business (meaning salaries, of course) or
shared information on how to get around the bureaucracy.
We never visited one another's classrooms and avoided
talking about our successes and failures. I had a few friends
who taught in the same school and we tried to work together, but everything about the institution pulled us
apart. We each had our own rooms, our own students, our
own books, our own supervisors.

No matter how much I objected to these arrangements
superficially, it was comfortable to have relationships managed that way. No conflict was ever expressed openly on
the staff, and people who hated one another lived an
uncomfortable truce for years without revealing their feelings. All of the disagreements, arguments, questions, at-
tractions, and repulsions that develop when people live
with one another face to face and express their feelings
were sanitized by the strtucture of our lives within the
school. Of course, cliques formed and gossip proliferated
under these conditions, but nothing was ever expressed
in the open. It was considered bad form for one adult to
oppose another publicly or even express affection during
the school day. We were expected to act like professionals
and not like people. A year before, I had naively opposed
the principal of the first school I taught at during a
faculty meeting. Everyone in the room looked shocked,
but no one said a word to me. Several months later I received a letter from the Central Administrative Office

transferring me to another school. I was stunned, since the principal had already assigned me to a class for the next year. He denied knowing anything about the transfer. An older teacher to whom I showed the letter, however, reminded me of the faculty meeting, told me I was asking for trouble, and indicated that problems were always dealt with indirectly, leaving the individual bewildered and with no recourse—and she shrugged and added that if I couldn't get used to the nature of the institution I would never survive in my new school.

This sanitation of personal life is not peculiar to schools. Most large bureaucracies and many businesses also formalize the relationships of adults to one another. I have talked to probation officers, welfare workers, hospital employees, policemen, members of federal and state bureaucracies, corporate functionaries, secretaries, janitors, store managers—and they have all experienced the same impoverishment of life at work. Despite the rhetoric of people working as a team or cooperating for the good of the students, the company, the clients, the patients, and so forth, most people feel isolated at work and unable to express disagreement or deal openly with their feelings about people they work with. And most people also seem relieved, for the unpleasantness of conflict is avoided.

My students forced me out of isolation and right into the midst of a battle I am still engaged in fighting twelve years later. As some of the students began to trust me, they told me how they felt about the school and the other teachers. One of the third-grade teachers was a particularly brutal racist. He hated black kids, perhaps hated all kids, but since there were only black kids at the school the hatred came out in overtly racist forms. He beat kids, shoved them against the wall, called them all kinds of nigger. There was no shame in his actions, either. The more people who witnessed his actions the better he felt. His idea was that you had to show "them" how tough you were in order to create discipline. Only later did I realize how frightened he must have been of those little children.

For a year I avoided thinking about him. However, my students kept bringing up the issue and finally put it to me directly: do something about him or you're the same as he is, as brutal and racist and willing to let us be hurt.

There was no talking to this particular person. I spoke to the principal, who informed me that this teacher was tenured and that, besides, it was none of my business. The students pressed the issue, insisted I intervene in public and prevent their friends from being brutalized. This was the first time in my life I had to act on my moral belief or change my whole image of myself.

In the culture of teachers the worst sin you can commit is opposing another teacher in front of the students. In many cases it will get you fired or transferred immediately while years of incompetency with the students will be overlooked. I desperately didn't want to be fired, needed to teach, liked the comfort and success of my classroom. I had just emerged from years of turmoil and confusion and had begun to feel rooted and strong. Nothing in me at that point wanted conflict and uncertainty, yet I had to oppose that person, to risk being fired, to commit myself to battling the principal and the whole system that supported such hatred and oppression. There was no way for me to turn away from the situation and still maintain the trust of my students. Either I opposed racism and brutality or I was racist and brutal. There was no liberal middle position to take; so, full of anxiety and fear and uncertainty, I tried to stop the teacher and oppose the principal. At that point I learned how unprepared I was for conflict.

I wanted things to change at the school painlessly and rationally. Although I stopped the teacher from hitting a child once or twice and he avoided me and was quiet in my presence, there were unexpected consequences of my actions. The other teachers began to treat me hostilely—I was considered a traitor to my profession and unethical. The principal classified me as a troublemaker, although he left me alone because he was afraid I might create a scandal.

Although these incidents with the other teacher were never dealt with publicly, I had emerged from my classroom and began to look more closely at the school. Things I had avoided thinking about—the lack of books, the repulsive lunches served, the hatred and failure most of the students experienced every day, the sheer overwhelming misery of daily life at the school—began to obsess me. I had to do something about everything even if no other adult cared. In despair at having complied with such cruelty for so long, with no knowledge of politics or strategy, and with no sense of how I would act under pressure, I decided to go to people in the community and try to force the principal out. I had no program or plan for change and my main impulse was to destroy, but I wasn't even prepared to do that effectively.

The principal was a nice liberal man who spent all of his time covering up problems and pretending he was leading a good school for "difficult" children. He saw no problems unless they were forced on him. My wife, Judy, who was also teaching at the school, and I went to the Harlem Parents Committee, a group of parents who were attempting to force the schools in Harlem to meet the needs of black youngsters, and we told them about conditions at P.S. 79. The committee agreed to confront the principal with the information we gave them in an open meeting. Judy and I managed to obtain the students' address lists from the principal's office and together with members of the H.P.C. we composed a fact sheet on the school, which we mailed to all the parents and teachers involved in the school. The circular called for parents to come out to the next Parents Association meeting and let their anger be known.

The teachers at the school were scared and defensive. The principal fluttered about nervously during the days before the meeting. He knew that Judy and I were responsible for the circular but avoided direct contact with us.

There was a strategy meeting at Isaiah Robinson's house. At that time he was the leader of the H.P.C. I had given the committee names of incompetent and racist teachers as well as documentary evidence of their behavior. Members of the committee wanted to attack individual teachers and the principal. I responded to their plans for confrontation in a way I hadn't expected. In my mind for the first time I saw the principal and teachers as scared people, as warm and funny with their families, as unable to get other jobs; I identified with them and told the committee that nobody really needed to be hurt, that the meeting could deal with the issues without dealing with specific individuals. I was acting just like the principal, trying to avoid conflict as much as possible. The committee respected my wishes, although Isaiah told me that nothing would happen but talk unless there was a direct confrontation. He also reminded me that the children were in pain, that that was the whole reason for their and my concern, and finally that there was no way to avoid some pain in the situation. He was right; the meeting was nothing but talk, the principal and teachers remained at school for several more years until people from the community without the questionable assistance of soft-hearted liberals like myself forced them out and began to make a decent school for their children. I was afraid to destroy and therefore what needed to be built in the school had to wait.

I see now that we should have confronted those teachers and the principal no matter how much pain and anxiety were involved. That doesn't mean that they shouldn't have been given their chance to respond to the needs of the students. However, if they refused to change, they had to be forced out of the school by whatever means possible. It was the children's lives or theirs. That doesn't mean I should have wasted energy hating or resenting them, or thought of them as less than human. I could retain my identification and compassion—however, they had to go.

But at that time I wasn't ready to deal with the consequences of my awareness. Teaching at the school became an increasingly painful and depressing phenomenon. After the abortive confrontation I continued my work in general isolation from the rest of the staff. Judy left the school because she couldn't handle the pressure.

I was faced with a serious dilemma. Life within my classroom was fine. The students worked with amazing joy and energy. We got along fine, spent time before school talking and after school dancing or playing basketball. If only I could have blinded myself to the rest of the school, could have witnessed without sorrow former students reverting to old self-destructive ways of functioning or being punished for being too clever or articulate, then I could have become an accepted eccentric recluse within the school. But I couldn't—my own backing out of the confrontation bothered me. I knew the community frightened me as much as it did other teachers and that I was somewhat bolder than most but cut from the same middle-class fabric. I also knew that as soon as I stepped out of my classroom and tried to act again that was the end of my job.

I took a middle-class way out—Judy and I saved some money and took a year off. We went to Spain, fully realizing that neither the kids nor their parents could take any time away from their lives. In Spain I wrote, did some thinking, chopped a lot of wood, dreamed, read, wrote a bad novel about my childhood, corresponded with some of my former students, and, at the end of the year returned to New York City resolved to get involved with the kids and with teaching in some new way.

Along with Betty Rawls, a gifted, sensitive Black woman

whom I met at Teachers College, Columbia, I taught several classes in psychology and reading for high schools, primarily the older brothers and sisters of former students. We used people's apartments or empty rooms at Teachers College, Columbia. The kids came because they wanted to—it was wholly different from public school. There was no mandatory attendance, no set curriculum (although Betty and I worked hard on putting material together we hoped the students would respond to), no hostile teachers or administrators to bother with. I didn't have the feeling that used to nag at me in public school that we had to be "working" all the time, and I became more relaxed with the kids than ever. Before that I had still been a teacher, not a traditional lecturer but still an adult among thirty-six or twenty-seven young people. I had set the environment, provided the learning options, mediated fights, taken attendance, filled out evaluation sheets. It was different when Betty and I worked together. The students listened to us, but more often they determined the direction of the class, raised questions, decided to shift the issues altogether or talk about personal rather than academic issues.

At the same time this was happening I exercised another traditional option and returned to graduate school at Teachers College while Judy supported us by teaching at the Manhattan School for the Severely Disturbed. I took classes in anthropology, psychiatry, and education and managed to sustain interest for one semester. Halfway through the year I began looking around for ways to get more deeply involved with the kids and to teach more. Graduate school was a boring, bitchy, political game and since I didn't want to become a professor it left me cold.

At this time I became involved with the federal government. Nelson Aldrich, an old friend from Harvard who had also taught in Harlem with me at P.S. 79, invited me to attend a Columbia University meeting on the teaching of writing. He also suggested I bring along some of my fifth- and sixth-grade students' writing. My own despair and confusion about not knowing how to connect with a place that would allow me to teach and at the same time be committed to dealing with the social and economic realities of the kids' lives made me extremely aggressive, bitter, and often loud and obnoxious. At the meeting I was ready to tell every one of the writers and professors (whose work I really didn't know) that they were full of shit when Nelson suggested I precede my tirade by reading some of the students' writing.

The response amazed me—the people were interested in the kids' voices, in their ideas, thoughts, perceptions. They were curious about how the kids came to write, what I had said or done. I needed that validation of my work and responded to the praise by allowing myself, foolishly perhaps, to be convinced to run another conference on writing and to put together a group that would bring teachers and writers together in the classroom. The group, to be called the Teachers and Writers Collaborative, was to be based at Teachers College, Columbia, and funded by the U.S. Office of Education.

There was a meeting at East Hampton, Long Island. There were a number of superstars in education and literature present, as well as observers from the Office of Education and the Office of Science and Technology. I brought along a group of teachers who were doing exciting work in Harlem and the Bronx. The paper I wrote for the meeting was published by *The New York Review of Books,* and after the conference I emerged as director, organizer, and proposal writer for the Teachers and Writers Collaborative. A small room at Teachers College was assigned to me.

I got carried away by the promises and never realized that it would take a year of proposal writing, gaming, and prostituting to squeeze some money out of the Office of Education. By the time the Teachers and Writers Col-

laborative received money and became somewhat operable
I was neither teaching nor writing but, instead, hustling
money and doing politics.

What mainly redeemed my life in those days was that
I met David Spencer and other members of the Harlem
community who were leading the struggle for community
control of Intermediate School 201 and its five feeder
elementary schools.

Occasionally I have come upon teachers—people with
greater wisdom, understanding, strength, and experience
than I have—and I follow them, observing and learning.
David was and is such a person. He sees right into people,
understands their motives and feelings, grasps all the complex interrelationships between good and evil intents in
people's souls. He is not fooled by people, sees his friends
and enemies clearly, and yet he is not cluttered by hatred
or resentment.

I found myself working for David and the rest of the
I.S. 201 Community Planning Board while playing around
with proposals at the Teachers and Writers Collaborative.
201 was a new intermediate school that the New York City
School Board promised would provide a model of quality
integrated education. For five years members of the community pleaded with the school district to build a new
school on the border of black and white communities
rather than in the middle of a community of 450,000 black
and 250,000 Puerto Rican people. The educational experts
paid no attention to community people and for years assured them they knew how to integrate the school even
though it was located on 127th St. and Madison Ave.
The community people still believed the pious promises of
the professionals right until the moment the integration
plan for 201 was announced by Bernard Donovan, who
was Superintendent of Schools at that time—201 was to be
50 percent black and 50 percent Puerto Rican.

I was at the meeting when that plan was announced to
members of the community, and I remember the shocked

silence of the audience and then the almost spontaneous outburst of anger and frustration that led the community to embark on the struggle to control their schools. Those people had had enough of promises and they realized that if their children were not to be destroyed it would be only through their doing.

201 was not very far from P.S. 103 and 79, where I had taught. I had met people involved in the struggle there through Isaiah Robinson and the Harlem Parents Committee. I had a key that opened up our office at Teachers College at night, a mimeograph machine, paper, and access to many young people—former students and their friends—from the community who had artistic and literary skills that could be used in the service of the community planning board. I had also recently acquired some proposal writing skills as well as an understanding of how proposals can seem to say one thing and actually mean another.

I offered my skills and the facilities and resources I had available to members of the community planning board and they made use of them. It was a dream coming to life —the fight with the school system I couldn't sustain, in the service of the children, now coming from their parents, who had been made stronger by Malcolm X, by the riots, by a deeper understanding of the beauty and power of their own blackness and brownness.

I served an apprenticeship at I.S. 201. There was overwhelming opposition to the community's goals. The Teachers Union called the parents anti-Semitic, an irony I, a Jew born and schooled in the Bronx, couldn't let pass. Police were posted outside the school to prevent violence between teachers and parents; the central school administration did everything it could to undermine community control of schools. Yet through all this trouble the members of the community held together, defined roles for one another, and built out of nothing the reality (if only temporarily) of poor people taking control of a major institution that controlled their lives,

The energy and intensity of people like Dave Spencer and Bob Nicol and Babette Edwards frightened and fascinated me. I was just learning how to take risks and they were all the way there; I was scared and they were too, but it was their community and their children. I was still an outsider to the struggle.

After a year's battle at 201, after raising money for the Collaborative and then being told at the end of one year that the hustle had to begin all over again to raise money for the second year Judy and I decided to leave New York. I had had a serious automobile accident, we had a child, Antonia; the battle at 201 seemed won at that time, and the Planning Board, having received recognition and been promised money, was becoming a Community Governing Board. I couldn't spend another year administrating and playing games with government administrators. I had to develop focus and some long-term work that would be both rewarding to me and of value to others. Larry Ziff, one of the members of the Board of Advisors of the Collaborative, suggested I come to Berkeley and teach at the University of California for six months. Having no other offers, Judy, Tonia, and I left for California.

My six months at U.C. Berkeley were boring. I missed the excitement of working with younger people, missed the diversity, craziness, and energy of my former students. The students at Cal were in the top 12 percent of their high school classes, were the "good" students who spent more time figuring out what their teachers wanted than learning for themselves. I have always felt more comfortable with the "bad" students, the loud, defiant, questioning, angry ones.

By this time *36 Children,* an account of one of the years I spent teaching in Harlem, appeared and all of a sudden I found myself an educational expert. The Carnegie Corporation of New York even offered Allan Kaprow, the art historian and creator of happenings, and myself money to develop a teacher training program. I was reluctant to do teacher training, which struck me as even more boring than teaching at U.C. Berkeley, but Kaprow and I took the money anyway, got ourselves affiliated with the Berkeley Unified School District and assigned to an empty storefront at 2556 Grove Street in Berkeley. We called ourselves Other Ways.

At that point I wasn't sure what strategy to use to change the public schools in Berkeley—in fact, didn't know for sure that change was needed. There were some things I resolved not to do, however, based on my past experiences. I did not want to be a teacher in an isolated classroom. I wanted to work closely with other people, with peers who were willing to fight the same battles and take the same risks, to relate whatever work was done to the community, to parents and students, and shift as much power as possible away from a centralized administration. I wanted to help develop a fine place of learning where young people and adults could come together and work collectively to free themselves of traditional American ideas and attitudes right in the middle of a public school system with the goal of eventually claiming public money. In retrospect, I think I plunged into Other Ways blindly and naively. I had no idea of the nature and intensity of the battles it would involve. Perhaps that naivete was necessary, because knowing what I now know I am not sure I even would have begun the battle.

There were many battles for survival during the three years I was involved in Other Ways. Some of the external problems were expected—the battles with a liberal school board and a hostile school administration, as well as those with cynical parents and righteous police officers who felt that young people had no right to be on the streets during the day or travel through the community without supervision. However, the internal battles between the staff and students and especially among the staff members themselves were unexpected.

We could have done anything we wanted for and with

the kids. We were free to cooperate with one another, work together, deal directly with our disagreements, share our successes and failures. We also knew that we wanted to work together, be open and honest and trusting. We thought that if any trouble developed it would be because the kids weren't ready for openness. We were wrong. Many of the kids were ready; it was the adults who didn't know how to be trusting or cooperative with one another. Our first year was hell. We became sneaky, bitchy, gossipy, competitive, self-righteous, blind in every way. We had all been schooled in the U.S.A. and had learned our lessons well. We could talk about alternative life styles but essentially we didn't know how to be any different from our parents and teachers.

The experience was not what I had expected. In my isolated classroom I had no trouble relating to my students in open and honest ways. All of a sudden, however, I had to deal with peers, not kids, and it was much more difficult. For the past three years I have been involved in a process of unlearning, decontaminating, restructuring, rethinking, and refeeling my own life. I have been learning new ways to deal with my fears, with my nastiness and competitiveness, and with my difficulty in cooperating with others in common work.

Adults can come together. The process I have lived through in the last few years seems to be occurring in a much broader context than that of schools. There are people in collectives, communes, community corporations, businesses, and professions who are attempting to live less competitive, more communal and humane lives. Many of them encounter the same problems in themselves that we did at Other Ways. These problems are not unsolvable —we are not condemned to be the individuals we were schooled to be. Re-education is a possibility; but it is a painful process, for if we accept the need to undo our training, we have to accept the fact that we are all contaminated, and often in ways we are not aware of. It is dangerous to attempt to change oneself, especially when there are no rules or guarantees, no therapist to protect you, no clear map of the future. At every step of the voyage one is responsible. And one has to survive during the process. The world does not stop or become indulgent to people who are developing new forms of life.

[2]

Five years ago some friends of mine left Berkeley to start a commune in the state of Washington. There were three couples and two young babies. Bob had just finished his Masters of Fine Arts in painting and Carolyn had done some organic gardening. Annika, their child, was one year old. Richard and Susan were both graduate students in biology and their daughter, Jane, was also one. John was a sociologist and Sara a musician.

Richard owned three hundred acres on the Washington coast and their plan was to live in tents the first year while they cleared the land and began to farm and put up permanent dwellings.

After six months on the land everyone returned to Berkeley. It was cold and rainy in Washington. The tents didn't provide enough shelter, the people were tired of one another, no one knew what to do about sewage or how to clear the land efficiently, their few neighbors were hostile, they hadn't brought the right tools, they ran out of food, their babies were unhappy. They didn't have the skills necessary to survive away from the university. Bob didn't have enough time or privacy to do his painting; Richard and Susan couldn't connect their knowledge of biology to the group's biological needs. John's sociology didn't help him deal with the tension that isolation created and Sara's music began to get on the others' nerves.

After a few weeks of avoiding one another in Berkeley, the group came together again. The bitter feelings and sense of defeat that they felt the last month in Washington disappeared and they discovered again that they liked one another and wanted to live together on the land again. They just hadn't been prepared the first time. If they wanted to return to the land and survive, they had to learn how to farm and build and clear land. They also had to learn to share work, to live in relative solitude, to slow down and develop the patience necessary to build a new life. They had to learn to deal with conflict, to stop hurting one another, to toughen themselves up. There was no use going right back to Washington, for they knew they would fail again. So they split up for six months. Bob and Carolyn became apprentice carpenters, Richard and Susan enrolled in an agricultural college, and John became involved in a free school as well as several encounter groups. Sara began to make instruments as well as teach music.

They came together periodically to share their thoughts, which began to develop into a self-criticism session. They tried to tell the truth, as they perceived it, about themselves and others in the group, and develop internal means of dealing with criticism. A solidarity emerged from these meetings that never existed in Washington.

I sat in on one of their sessions. It was painful watching them struggle with expressing their feelings directly while trying to stop worrying about whether they were being approved. They wanted to be honest and they also wanted to be liked. They were afraid to incur one another's wrath, and there was a lot of swallowed anger. Bob was trying to tell Richard that he felt Richard wasn't sincere in sharing the land fully with the others. However, Bob was afraid that Richard would reject him if he sounded as cynical as he felt, so his words merely hinted at his meaning and Richard misunderstood. After a while Bob exploded and blurted out his mistrust. Richard was visibly relieved. He was angry with Bob but open enough to admit his own mixed feelings about the land. Nothing was resolved during that session, but a problem was articulated, and therefore the group could focus on its resolution rather than waste energy avoiding the issue.

After six months they made another attempt to settle the land. This time it was much better. They knew something about building and farming, were more tolerant of one another, and managed to put up two cabins and plant a small vegetable garden. Richard got to know the neighbors and shared some of the information he had picked up at agricultural college with them. Still, the group had serious problems. Bob was bored, wanted to paint and not build cabins. Carolyn was restless but she didn't know why. John and Sara wanted more people to join them, but Richard felt that was stupid, since they hadn't even worked out the problems of communal living with the small number of people they already had. After six months on the land Bob, Carolyn, and Annika split. Several other people arrived. Some fit in; others hung around for a while, then moved on. John left to join a free school and Sara joined him after a few months. After five years only Richard, Susan, and Jane remain of the original group, and they are getting restless now that the routine of farming is no longer fun. It is their land, however, and they have to decide what to do about the newcomers who want to remain. Richard is not prepared to turn the deed over to the commune. He refers to himself as a hip capitalist these days and is quite honest about his desire to hold on to the land.

Bob is doing happenings and teaching painting somewhere on the East Coast. He and Carolyn just split up. I talked to him recently about the failure of their commune. He said the experience hadn't been one of failure at all. None of the people involved had expected to spend the rest of their lives on the land in Washington and they had all realized it the second time. Their commitment hadn't been to developing a permanent new settlement but rather to learning things about themselves and about living with others. All of the original members had grown up in the suburbs and had felt isolated. They had never lived in extended families, hadn't known what it was like to relate constantly to many different people, to share facilities. and depend upon themselves. Bob felt that the commune had been for a short time a family for them and that it was only natural to move out of the family once he had grown up.

Over the year and a half they spent together the eight people involved learned a great deal about their own strengths and weaknesses. They all gained skills; learned to use their hands and bodies, to live with uncertainty and conflict, to be less competitive. They educated themselves and somewhat compensated for the poverty of their upbringing and formal schooling.

I know another person who is also going through great changes in his life and can't deal with them yet. Stu Welch is a computer scientist who works for a large computer research center. Stu and his wife, Susan, came from lower-middle-class homes in New York City. They never knew what it was to live in a house of their own, had never experienced the suburbs. After thirteen years of public schools, four years at college, four more years of achieving a doctorate, and two years of doing post-doctoral work—that is twenty-three years of formal school—Stu was finally ready to work on his own. He decided to take the highest paying job he was offered. That's how he got to work for the corporation, where he has been very successful.

Stu and Susan bought a three-bedroom tract house in an upper-middle-class suburb, dressed it with carpets and stuffed chairs, a large TV and hi-fi—all the things they had denied themselves during six grubby years as graduate students. After a few years those fancied rewards of hard labor become boring and meaningless. The company was a cold, competitive place and even though Stu's work was interesting, he began to realize that he wanted to know more than computer research. There was the Vietnam War to worry about, the education of his sons, the development of a life in which Susan and he and others they cared about could live cooperatively, learn about one another and stand together instead of always competing.

For a while Stu began to change. He became involved in developing free schools, was thinking of moving into an older, more modest house. He and Susan began to explore alternatives to his work and he became involved in community and school affairs.

However, it isn't that easy. The corporation needs Stu's ingenuity and intelligence. Some of the executives have sensed Stu's restlessness and so recently he has been given an elaborate facility to manage by himself, is allowed to spend some time on community projects and some time on "ecologically sound" research. The corporation is giving a little bit to make him more comfortable, to ease the guilt and seduce him into feeling relevant. He loves the lab he works in, is almost married to it. He doesn't mind the raises he keeps on getting while other people are being let go all the time. The Vietnam War is over, the horror has abated somewhat, and the urgency for change blunted. Stu talks about his work in kinder, more resigned terms than before, although periodically he feels like kicking the whole thing. He is aware of the contradictory pulls in his life and yet is too comfortable to decide to confront the company or leave. He lives right in the middle of the diseased institution, benefitting from his service to it and fantasizing its demise. At some point he will have to choose whether to oppose the corporation or leave.

It is difficult to live a healthy life in this culture, since we are all in complicity with it's worst aspects. Paying taxes, using the freeways, buying more than we need, tolerating someone else's poverty, saving for our personal futures, worrying exclusively about our own children—all are acts of complicity. This is true for Art at Shell, but also for me in my home in the Berkeley Hills, and for people in communes, collectives, alternative institutions of any sort. The sustained and responsible attempt to change aspects of this culture leads us into inconsistencies, into supporting what we want to destroy in many subtle and unexpected ways. However, assuming responsibility for this complicity and for our own failures is the only way I know to develop sustained action that might eventually lead to a humane society. This brings a lot of unexpected pain and uncertainty, especially if one is involved in alternative institutions.

For a while at Other Ways we believed that we were pure and different from the rest of the school district because we said so. We adopted a revolutionary stance and mistook that style for substance. We tried to create new forms without knowing how to sort out the old ones. It took many crises and confrontations to acknowledge our failures and begin to build a new way of learning based on a tough and complex analysis of the way in which we were contaminated by what we were trying to destroy.

[3]

A few years ago the cryptic message "Build=Destroy" was painted on walls throughout central Harlem. I asked some teenagers what the inscription meant and they explained that it was a message from Allah delivered to the Blood Brothers, a Muslim-oriented group. It meant that an action, in order to effect change, must have elements of both creativity and destructiveness. Neither creativity nor destructiveness is effective by itself. I didn't immediately understand the explanation, but I do now.

There are some destructive acts that have no creative content. The feeling of being abused or frustrated or oppressed can lead people to act in order to "get even." On a personal level, burning down a school because a teacher failed you, or slashing the car tires of someone you don't like leads nowhere beyond momentary satisfaction. The same is true for revenge on a political level. Burning down a bank or killing a cop out of anger and frustration produces no fundamental economic or political restructuring of society. Destroying a school without a vision of and plan for new forms of learning does not lead beyond the destructive act itself: one is left with charred ruins and the ability to do no more than reconstruct a patched-up version of the old institution.

In a similar way the attempt to avoid conflict and destruction while creating new forms of living is ineffective. People move to the hills to create communes away from the pressures of the city and find the city comes to them in the form of hostile neighbors, building inspectors, land speculators, police, and their own needs to consume and compete.

Some people prefer to develop free schools completely outside the public school system rather than challenge the existing bureaucracy, and they find themselves in the midst of legal hassles, constant hustling for money, and the inability to free themselves from the paradigms their own schooling has imposed upon them.

Others try to create alternatives within the public schools without destroying the bureaucracy itself and find themselves absorbed, diluted, co-opted, and generally assimilated by the institution without producing significant change.

Food conspiracies try to get around the economic system without confronting it. However, when they become successful, they have to confront retail businesses they are ruining as well as incipient capitalist greed in their own people.

As long as people involved in alternatives believe they are pure and can live without pain and destruction, they will have no way to deal with the conflicts that actually arise.

The need to destroy is not a happy phenomenon and when it becomes a value in itself it destroys the destroyer by dehumanizing him or her. I recently heard a story about a group of American students who went to cut sugar cane with the Venceremos Brigade in Cuba. The American students were accompanied on the two-day trip to the cane fields by some Cubans. One evening the Cubans showed the film *Battle of Algiers,* which portrays the victory of the National Liberation Front of Algeria over the French. There are many scenes of violence in the film and every time a Frenchman was killed or maimed, the American students applauded and cheered. After the film the Cubans started getting on the American students for being inhuman enough to enjoy violence. Many of the Cubans had been involved in the revolution, had fought and killed. They hated violence, although they knew it was necessary at the time. They were angered by the American students' obsession with revolutionary violence rather than with the building of a new world after the violence or, if possible, without it. The student who told me this story was there. He said it changed his way of thinking and feeling. He felt that when he had arrived in Cuba, he had been an angry, rebellious child playing at revolution and when he had left he had learned he could never love violence even if he was forced to act violently in what he felt was the services of humanizing this society. And he told me he also wouldn't forget how corrupting and dehumanizing violence could be even if done for the best of reasons. He wanted to build, but accepted the fact that he might have to destroy as well.

Some people become countercultural or revolutionary overnight. They take acid; blow pot; make love freely for the first time; go on a protest march and get their heads busted; spend a night in jail; read a book that makes sense of their lives for the first time. The next day they let their hair grow or let it down, change their clothes, smoke dope, and feel free and fugitive. They buy the whole package in the way I imagine some people buy Ultrabright, believing it will actually give their mouths sex appeal. They also forget that what they have bought is precisely a package and that the substance of change is quite other than the external appearance of change. The package might be countercultural, but the belief in packages puts them right in the mainstream of American culture.

This phenomenon reminds me of what happened to my oldest child, Antonia, when she became four years old. She imagined that as soon as she became four she would become as tall as all the older children at her nursery school. She also imagined that she would know how to read, be able to take care of herself without a babysitter, and cook her own dinner. The day after her birthday she was disappointed because she wasn't taller, couldn't read, still was a little girl. But she wasn't completely disappointed, because, wanting to be more independent, and believing that being four gave her the license to act independently, she discovered that she could do many things she previously feared. She could jump down four steps and cook an egg and begin to learn how to read and play with the older kids.

It is the same with passing into a more open style—it doesn't produce all the changes converts expect, but it does give them some impetus to act differently. If they then act in new ways, others will respond to them as if changes have occurred, and this in turn can reinforce the conversion. With some additional strength it becomes easier to confront one's past as well as deal with present oppression—to build and to destroy.

There have been some attempts to build new forms of living simultaneously with the destruction of old ones. When the Weathermen formed themselves into collectives, they tried to prepare for communal living and battling through the violent uprooting of their personal pasts (attachments to parents, to favorite objects, and many other things) as well as their culturally determined responses (heterosexual love, male dominance, obsessive cleanliness, and so forth).

A Weatherperson, signing herself "a daughter of the American Revolution," described some of the struggle (*Berkeley Tribe,* May 29, 1970; *Weatherman,* pp. 452-3):

Once people start living collectively, real changes start to come down. One of the first things we got into in my group was a trip about women's liberation, male chauvinism, and monogamy. Most of the women in the group had come in as the other half of a guy—in other words, they related to the movement and the collective through their old men. Monogamy held us back in all sorts of ways. A revolutionary has to be a strong, self-reliant person, not totally dependent on another individual or group for their personal sanity. Monogamy was in direct opposition to this. Also, it divided women from each other . . . when you have a boyfriend, every other woman close to him is a direct threat.

Monogamy held members of the collective back from relating to each other fully, because we always felt obliged to relate primarily to that one person, and everyone else was secondary. We couldn't relate politically, personally, or sexually to anyone else without feeling guilty about it.

So we smashed monogamy—everyone broke up their monogamous relationships. At first, there were all kinds of crises around it. People made it on the sly, and then didn't make it at all for fear of being male chauvinists. That was clearly a bummer and couldn't last for long, but we did kind of a flip-flop from celibacy to a near orgy state. Fucking became pretty impersonal—if someone was a revolutionary, that was a good enough reason to make it, never mind if you dug the person or not. That didn't work either, because there is something special about making it, and the orgy stage was just too much of a "macho," "I don't give a shit" trip.

Looking over all those trips we went through, some of them seem a bit crazed. Although the bourgeois hang-ups about possessiveness and dependency have to be smashed, there is nothing wrong with loving someone, and giving and gaining strength from a relationship. What we gotta do is take that love and build it with other people that we know—spread it thick, not thin, with men and women.

The Weatherpeople tried to uproot the past violently and quickly. I don't know the outcome of their personal efforts, but there are obvious dangers. No one knows the consequences of violence done to the self, the vestiges of hatred and hostility the act of purification leaves. Furthermore, it is not easy to know when new forms of behavior become the symbolic equivalent of the old ones that have supposedly been rooted out. Blowing up a bank can be the symbolic equivalent of attacking one's father; it can also be a political act that has little psychological contamination but is part of a larger plan for social revolution. The contaminated and uncontaminated act may be externally identical. However, the former, because not fully conscious, can lead to self-destructive behavior quite separate from any vision of making a new world.

There are other dangers. People attempting to change under stress always go through periods of regressing to old forms of behavior. New forms of acting need constant testing and reinforcing. The Weatherpeople's impatience doesn't tolerate regression and therefore they may not have given much thought to ways of supporting people who have regressed.

In addition, the sudden uprooting of the past by a small, tight group can lead to extreme dependency. As the past is destroyed, the present group can assume the function of neutralizing anxieties, and becoming the focus for all people's needs. Autonomy cannot begin to develop under such circumstances, and the possibility exists that people in such tight groups will become unable to function outside the group.

[4]

The past cannot be wiped out in one fell swoop, and it cannot be denied. However, it need not trap us. As W. V. O. Quine said in another context (*From a Logical Point of View,* Harper Torchbook, p. 79, 1963):

> . . . we must not leap to the fatalistic conclusion that we are stuck with the conceptual scheme that we grew up on. We can change it bit by bit, plank by plank, though meanwhile there is nothing to carry us along but the evolving conceptual scheme itself. The philosopher's task was well compared . . . to that of a mariner who must rebuild his ship on the open sea.

The task that Quine describes is not restricted to the philosopher's life. Anyone who is involved in remaking his or her life has to rebuild on the open sea. And to pursue the mariner's image, we can only rebuild the ship with the material we have on board (or with things we can ingeniously fetch out of the ocean). Plank by plank our ship can be reconstructed until it looks different, sails differently, until no board or bolt remains where it used to be. However, if we rebuild too suddenly or too ambitiously, if we try to rebuild the bottom of the boat without waterproofing it, we might sink ourselves. And if we rebuild without thought, we might discover that we have created a modern version of the ship of fools.

I know a lonely, scared woman who has been trying to rebuild her life for the last few years. She lives in a suburb of New York with her husband and three teenaged children. The family is wealthy; their life together is tense, often violent. The five people can't stand one another, yet they depend upon one another. They do not live in community with any other people, although they see friends on formal occasions. The children will be leaving home during the next three years and their parents are getting nervous about living together without the kids to provide buffers between them. Lorraine told me that she is beginning to hate her house, and feels physically ill when she looks at all of her possessions. The counter-culture tempts her. She would like to move out, join a commune or become connected to some form of relevant work. She would also like to become more open physically, to relax in the presence of other adults, to be able to touch them and be touched without cringing.

For the last few years she has taken to attending en-counter groups, hoping they would provide her with phys-ical ease and a more relaxed life. She really doesn't want to give up her home or her things, although she knows she should and feels sick about them. She wants to change her life without giving up anything. As long as there is a therapist to lean on or a group leader to accept her ac-tions, she will allow herself to change a bit. But she's scared of "going too far."

At first the groups had a good effect on her, which transferred to the life of her family and made it less tense. Recently, the change has leveled off. One group seems like another. Occasionally she has a particularly good group session and talks about it for weeks. She has become a con-noisseur of groups rather than a participant in them. She removes herself from the experience and judges the group leaders' ingenuity, mastery of group techniques, and other skills. She watches the other participants to see the dy-namics of the group and no longer gets involved. She is beginning to be bored with these games and has recently fallen into a deep depression. Everything seems hopeless; she has even forgotten why she became involved in groups in the first place. She is becoming bitter and conservative. She feels that the counterculture is a lie, that things aren't all that bad at home. But she doesn't fully buy her own rationalizations and is very much in mid-passage, confused about her goals, afraid to try to change once more, yet unable to return fully to her old life. At present she is contemplating becoming involved in a women's group, but she is frightened. The group is not at all like the ones

she has experienced in the past—there is no therapist involved, no time limit on the group's existence, no money
involved. If she goes, it is her choice, and if she decides
to leave, that is also her choice. And her encounter with
the other women will not be couched in pseudo-medical
or psychological terms. She will not be a patient but an
adult who has decided to take responsibility for her own
life—and this scares the hell out of her.

There are other people who embraced demonstrations, marches, protests of one form or the other for
social or personal reasons and who ended up connois-
seurs. I remember people talking about how good or bad
the latest peace march was. They weren't talking about
whether peace had been achieved, but rather how festive
the occasion was, how many people turned out, how good
the music or speeches were, how they felt. The issues
were forgotten and the question of whether peace could
be obtained through peaceful demonstration avoided.
Many of these people began dropping out of marches and
demonstrations not because the goals were achieved but
because they became bored. The issues were forgotten
because people's expectations for their own liberation
through public participation were disappointed.

It is easy to drop out, to abandon the attempt to make
one's life more humane and less competitive. Long hair
doesn't change one's personality. Therefore one can take
the attitude that long hair doesn't work. The same is
true for other attempts at reconstruction—working in the
ghetto, living in a commune, leaving the suburbs and
living in self-enforced poverty. When these actions lead to
no answers but only greater questioning of oneself and
the society and therefore greater and more dangerous rebuilding of the entire society, it is easy to retreat to the
suburbs or disappear into dope. Many people who have
ventured briefly into the so-called counterculture or the
more revolutionary underground have pulled back. They
had not built any base in their personal or social life to

sustain conflict, had not sufficient confidence in themselves to find new ways of using their own psychological and physical resources.

I have often been tempted to pull out myself; period- ically feel so drained, exhausted, and isolated that quitting or conforming seem the only sane alternatives. My dreams at those times transport me to Paris or Spain, to faraway magical places where I can live free of pain and conflict. Often I am full of fantasies of escape or withdrawal and desperately need renewed energy and support from others who are less down. Only recently I have learned to ask friends for help, to feel trusting enough of a small number of other people to ask for and offer love, share resources, and feel strengths in common and extended commitment.

None of us knew what we were getting into when we started out to change this society. It seemed simple—we were right, therefore things would have to change. The unexpected dangers and difficulty of our voyage have posed a whole series of new problems in our lives. We set out with supposed clear objectives—to change a school or confront racism in a community or humanize a profession like law or medicine—and we ended up on an open-ended journey into ourselves. It became clear that we had to learn how to change ourselves, and that psychiatrists, psy- chologists, university professors, parents, teachers—all of the people whose role was to lead, or teach—embodied the principles of the culture we were revolting against. The cure the professionals and sanctioned authority held out was conformity with and acceptance of a world we knew was cruel, inhuman, and not inevitable.

However, there was a more important discovery: that none of us had been prepared to take power over our own lives and learn new ways of feeling and responding to each other. We did not know how to deal with the pain, conflict, anxiety, and uncertainty that result in cutting one's self loose from the culture one grows up in no matter how awful that culture might be. It was like being cut loose at sea without a compass, ignorant of how to read the stars, and with no clearly defined destination.

Learning how to learn, how to deal with new and un-expected experiences, how to deal with familiar experi-ences in new ways is essential for anyone who is crazy enough to try to build a new culture while confronting the old one.

The desire to change and the acquisition of new, more humane ideas do not perform a magical transformation on the self. We must learn how we learn best; must learn about absorbing things silently, about responding to dreams and fantasies, about observing others with a mini-mum of ego, about developing intuition, perception, trust, about taking chances and dealing directly with conflict. We must develop an anarchist sensibility so that we can respond to the unknown, unexpected, changing aspects of a life in transition. We must learn how to stop trying to make our lives and dealings with other people predictable, and we must learn how to find teachers and allow our-selves to be taught.

It is crucial for each of us to understand ourselves as learners and therefore to deal with experience as the material out of which we will constantly build and rebuild our world. It is not unusual for people to learn nothing from their experience; to, for example, consider them-selves as failures in business or love or art rather than as people who are just learning how to sell or love or create. Because they learn nothing and think of their actions in absolute terms of success and failure, many people neurotically repeat the same circumstances in their lives over and over. I know someone who falls in and out of love regularly every two months and boasts of absolute success the first day of each affair and moans about being an absolute failure the last day. He isn't interested in learning how to love or make love; he wants once and for all at the age of twenty-five to succeed or fail at loving.

If learning is closed to many adults, it is the opposite with babies and young children. They are always learning, figuring things out, trying to understand their mistakes. I worried a lot about my first child. She fell a lot trying to walk, and made mistakes trying to talk. I tried to help her and picked her up too many times or corrected her words. I worried, pressed her, didn't give her enough time or space to learn. When Tonia was about one and a half, Judy told me to let Tonia learn for herself and stop hovering so much. I caught myself and began watching her. Tonia didn't mind making mistakes as long as I didn't respond to them with anxiety. She enjoys learning and doesn't need to be burdened with an adult sensibility that turns mistakes into failures and competencies into successes. Just the other day I was struck by the joy with which she was teaching herself to write. The mistakes were no problem as long as I didn't make them into a problem.

Understanding oneself as a learner and developing an anarchist sensibility involve knowing how to use one's own energy. It is important to expend no more energy than is necessary in political battling and to develop stamina. Many people involved in alternatives throw themselves into work or a group or a confrontation recklessly and with no regard for their own needs. They get burned out quickly and become apathetic.

I find myself frequently spending too much energy worrying about little things, and for a while was in a constant state of exhaustion. I became concerned about people misunderstanding my intentions; worried about the superintendent of schools or members of the school board not liking me when that issue was irrelevant. It took some time to understand how to use the least possible energy when dealing with the school board or the police, and how to keep my anger from corrupting my work with the students or my own personal life. After several years of struggling, I began to understand how much energy was available to me and how much I contributed to its dissipation. It still is hard to keep from overreacting to stupidity or cruelty. I have developed ways of checking myself and conserving energy. Frequently when I'm under tension, my fists clench unconsciously and I pace and drink too much wine. I've begun to pay more attention to my fists and have learned to catch them clenched and slowly open them and relax my hands, arms, shoulders, and mind; to catch myself pacing or drinking too much and think of energy flowing away. I force myself to relax and focus on the economy of energy in my life. Slowly I'm beginning to develop stamina and don't get so wiped out by opposition or confrontation.

Often, however, these resolves don't hold up and I regress in despair and pain. Tonia goes to our local public school now. She is in kindergarten—in a class that is fine for her and in a school that until recently was a horror for black children. I visit the school, have begun to imagine teaching there. I see so much when I visit the school and feel so much anger and powerlessness that I fantasize blowing the place up, punching people around, threatening teachers—anything to get people to see the kids' pain and prevent it or get out. With my eyes open, however, I plan small programs—teach games to six kids, work with another six on something loosely called reading, which is actually an attempt to help the kids feel strong enough to believe they can learn even on the school's terms. Occasionally it gets to me. I see five- and six- and seven-year-olds whom I know will fail and die and hate themselves if they continue in our schools and our society. And I know there is no magic or moral force that will change things for those children and for my children, who most certainly will find themselves unwittingly and unwillingly oppressors or victims of the violence that oppression and indifference breed. So instead of doing stupid things—yelling, trying to intimidate people, feeling guilty, getting drunk and hating myself I do the modest work and look for openings so that more can develop. I've learned enough about myself and taken enough distance from my ego to realize that self-destruction doesn't help the kids and that to indulge my pain is just another form of making light of theirs.

[5]

There are ways of coming into contact with oneself and not repeating mistakes endlessly in a neurotic way or accepting uncomfortable modes of being and feeling continually trapped. It is possible to learn how to change one's own life to be a learner as an adult.

Learning how to learn is not the same as learning to measure or compute. It involves a constant awareness of the self that is learning, a consciousness of style, and a continual critical look at action and thought. It also involves a sense of humor. There is a difference between a severe and paralyzing self-consciousness and an open self-critical consciousness that encourages rather than inhibits action. The former is self-hating, and strives to attain some idealized perfect self. The latter is more accepting and strives not for completion but for great understanding and generosity; it can laugh at itself for having been silly or foolish or wrong because it is constantly growing and because silly and foolish and mistaken actions are inevitable.

There are some humorless self-criticism groups that are devoted to discussion of personalities divorced from common work or action. For example, I know a group of Maoists who are constantly on one another's backs and who have devoted weeks to discussions of Mao's essay "On the Re-education of Intellectuals." The irony of this intellectualized self-criticism is that the point of Mao's text is that intellectuals need to work and become educated by the workers and farmers or else they will succumb to the dangers of abstract argument divorced from a direct involvement with people and work. The Maoist group, while agreeing ideologically with Mao, embodies in a grim and humorless way the errors it is studying.

An inability to laugh at oneself or one's group is self-destructive. All of us know people who though involved in liberating themselves and others cannot stand being wrong or looking silly. Anyone working with kids who has these problems will never survive. But, more important, the inability to laugh is symptomatic of an inability to deal with criticism and free oneself of past mistakes. The degree to which people have to defend everything they have done or believed is the degree to which they inhibit their own growth.

Laughter, however, should not be confused with scorn or mockery. Laughing at oneself is a way of integrating the past, acknowledging mistakes, and resolving neither to hate oneself for a nonreproducible past nor to repeat it. Scorn or mockery of one's past doesn't teach. It leaves one hating the past and the self that was part of it, and therefore colors the present and future with an unnecessary burden of bitterness.

One of my closest friends was Robert Jenkins, a black man whom I have known since high school. Bob and I were very close for a while, then disappeared from each other's lives, then came together again—Bob at that time was living with a white woman whom I had mixed feelings about. One evening I met Bob at a party with a black woman, and I blurted out: "Bob, it's so good to see you with a black woman." Bob and the woman were horrified at my obvious racist enthusiasm. I didn't say that it was good to see Bob with another woman; I put it on a purely racial level. Bob and I have seen each other since, but our relationship has not been close since that day.

I was racist although couldn't acknowledge it at the time. Now I can laugh at my own lack of self-knowledge. That laughter is not the same as a scornful guffaw or a putdown of myself. It is an acknowledgment of the degree to which I didn't know myself then and an acceptance of the challenge to change. I am not happy to have lost Bob as a close friend, but I am glad that moment happened, since it illuminated my racism.

[6]

C. G. Jung uses an interesting word: enantiodromia. It means the drama of the opposites, the battle of love and hate, pacifism and violence, sanity and madness, honesty and corruption, joy and misery, trust and suspicion, separateness and togetherness, individuality and community, creativity and destructiveness. For Jung, life develops through the interplay of these and many other oppositions and comes to its fullest integration when they all hold together about a center he calls the Self. There is no moment of completion in the development of the Self, but rather an open-ended process of continually integrating internal and external experience about the center. Neither one nor the other of the terms of the oppositions described above is denied; instead, they both serve other, humane purposes.

Love is necessary if any alternative is to remain together. Hate for the oppressor and of oppression itself is also necessary.

Pacifism is necessary within the family; defensive violence is sometimes necessary for survival.

Self-discipline creates a stable, regularized base for living; passion keeps life from stagnating.

Obsession with single terms of the pairs to the exclusion of their opposites leads to self-deception and intolerance. To fancy oneself as solely loving, pacific, sane, joyful, honest, and to attribute corruption to the world or the society or the culture is a dangerous way of avoiding responsibility for one's own weaknesses and inconsistencies. Many people involved in the so-called counterculture sound as if they believe that all children are good and pure (hence the belief in "complete" freedom), that love can be purified of all violent contamination, that people can be all trusting, totally honest, fully cooperative and unselfish, wholly creative. This ideology of purity (which once tempted me) leads to great expectations for alternatives and consequently to great disappointments. It tends to take people out of themselves in the search for a meaningful and humane life and leads to the belief that cultural, economic, and social revolutions can take place without personal revolutions. A corollary of this is the belief, frequently disappointed, that internal pain can be eliminated through social action.

These views represent a reaction against the psycho-analytic interpretation of personal pain as solely an internal matter to be mediated by the parts of one's own psyche and understood through a re-creation of one's family history. Health in analytic terms consists of adjusting oneself to the world as it is. During my own analysis the subject of the principal of my school kept coming up. Whenever I tried to speak to him, we ended up fighting. My analyst interpreted my response to him as a form of transference of my relationship with my father, which was ambiguous and often hostile. She felt our major concern was with my past and that once I understood the problems I had in coming to terms with authority in my family, I would be able to adjust to the situation at school and get along with the principal. After my analysis concluded and I had reasonably come to terms with my relationship with my father, I looked again at the principal and found him arbitrary, racist, indifferent to the students, and often positively damaging. To adjust to him meant complying with the oppressive social institution he represented and actively perpetuated. Confrontation was in order; it was not merely a family or personal matter.

However, the discovery that the society is as sick and oppressive as some of its members can lead to an extreme opposition to any psychological interpretation of behavior and cause people to blame abstractions such as society, culture, or the economy for all ills. There is a danger in looking solely outside of oneself for an understanding of our pathological society, just as there is a danger looking solely within. The internal and external worlds must change simultaneously if a reconstituted society is to develop. Any vision guiding action must be less than pure, it has to encompass the fact that people will always set traps for themselves, and that no final resolution of conflict is conceivable or even desirable. Growth requires conflict as well as love and understanding. The crucial process for me is defining a center, both social and personal, that can balance and integrate the opposites and lead to a humane, open, full life, and a decent and generous community. The center is what defines oneself as a learner. Understanding one's center is a form of the intimacy with oneself that I have been talking about.

Through the rest of this book I will describe some attempts at defining a center, as well as some of the battles I have been through or witnessed or heard about—some of the successes and many of the failures. I will also try to describe the ways in which people who have been involved in sustained radical activity have come to understand themselves and make use of criticism. Decontamination is a constant theme—the attempt to undo one's education and understand why one is constantly acting like the enemy and in opposition to one's own ideals. The main concern, of course, is change. People can change themselves, although the process isn't simple. It involves unlearning old forms of behavior as well as functioning naturally with new ones. And it involves conflict; a direct confrontation with what is cruel and oppressive in oneself as well as in the society.

The beliefs expressed in this introduction have developed over the past few years on the basis of my experience. They reflect a commitment to try to develop an alternative way of living without withdrawing from political confrontation with the existing institutions in our society. I have found that being nonpolitical and working solely on cultivating one's own alternative seduces one into feeling self-righteous and pure and therefore uncompassionate and closed. I have also found that being completely political seduces one into wanting power and enjoying the struggle for its own sake, and therefore also becoming uncompassionate and closed. The crucial question is whether it is possible to build and to destroy and to survive.

I can't answer this question—not for myself, certainly not for others. The only thing I can do is share some things —some obvious fuck-ups; some ways of dealing with pain, fear, anxiety, conflict; some forms of celebration; some ways of learning how not to quit, die, or regress too much; some images, exercises, stories, tales, fables; something of what it feels like to face an open-ended quest for a fuller way of being without retreating from direct conflict with what presently exists.

II

An Approach to the Center

Several years ago Nancy Johnson ran a small school for kids whom everyone else had given up on. During the morning she worked with neurologically damaged children. During the afternoon she worked with youngsters who had been declared "predelinquent" at the age of seven or eight.

Nancy's salary was paid by the Berkeley Unified School District, while rent for the building she used and books and supplies were paid out of pocket by Nancy herself and several psychologists who worked with her students.

At the end of that academic year the school district anticipated a budget deficit. Nancy's program was one of the first that was considered expendable since Nancy had neither tenure nor friends at the central administration building. Everyone acknowledged the value of her work, but, as one administrator put it to her, "We'll all have to tighten our belts and grit our teeth. Everyone will have to be cut somewhere."

It wasn't clear where that administrator would be cut, but there was no doubt that Nancy's program was scheduled for elimination. Nancy decided to fight for her kids and organized parent support. She went to one administrator after another. No one would take the responsibility for recommending her elimination, and no one would give her any assurance that the program would be able to continue. Conflict was avoided, commitments unmade.

A few weeks before the end of the school year Nancy went to see the superintendent. Her marriage had just broken up, she was moving into a new apartment, and she needed to know about work for the next year. The parents of some of her students (especially of the neurologically handicapped kids) were panicking, since no other school or teacher would bother with their children. Some even considered moving to another city that provided schooling for handicapped youngsters.

The superintendent welcomed Nancy, came out from behind his desk and sat down next to her. He put his arm around her and asked her about one of the students. They chatted pleasantly for a minute or two, then Nancy finally asked about next year. She explained about the students' needs, about the parents, and finally about her own situation. She had planned to demand action from the superintendent, but his coming out from behind his desk, his presence in the chair next to her, the arm around her shoulders threw her off. She didn't demand—on the contrary, she asked, almost begged for some definite resolution to the problem.

The superintendent, instead of making a commitment or explaining where the decision to eliminate her program came from, said to Nancy, "You seem very unhappy. This must be a bad day for you."

It was a bad day. She poured out her troubles, thanked the superintendent for being so kind and listening, and realized only when she was driving home that she was in the same situation she was in before she went to see him.

Nancy told me she felt turned around by the incident and was angry at herself for being so vulnerable. She knew the superintendent's techniques for avoiding conflict or decisions. She had seen other people charmed or seduced into forgetting the political issues; she saw other people's egos tripped by false sympathy, but she felt immune. She knew that the superintendent was her enemy in the sense that he was willing to eliminate her program, but she couldn't reconcile his manner with the role of an opponent. It would have been much easier if he had been hostile.

It is not only people in power who master the art of manipulation. About twelve years ago I taught in a school for severely disturbed children. I was unsure of myself and scared of the kids. Their bizarre behavior and apparent unpredictability had just the effect intended—it made me anxious and nervous and put the kids in an excellent position to manipulate me.

One day I was doing math with John Storm, a brilliant and resistant young man of nine. He knew how to read, write, add, subtract, multiply, divide, and avoid doing any of those. We sat together at his table looking at a workbook. I tried to induce him to do some multiplication. He refused to pick up a pencil.

I began challenging him, claiming he really couldn't do the work and suggesting he try a simpler book. He almost fell for my trick and in desperation turned to me and said, "You have bad breath. Please don't breathe on me."

I was crushed and couldn't even talk to him without smelling my foul mouth. For the rest of the day I spoke to people with my lips closed or my hand over my mouth. That evening at home I asked the woman I was living with a dozen times whether my breath was really so bad. After the fifth time of reassuring me, she said I was letting a crazy kid drive me mad on his own terms. I knew she was right, but that didn't prevent me from going out that night and buying a tube of sweet-smelling toothpaste and a bottle of mouthwash.

Both the schizophrenic boy and the political man need to manipulate others in order to survive with their world view and power intact. Because of that they are keenly attuned to the weaknesses of others and are masters of diverting conflict or criticism away from themselves. They are also masters of seduction, and there are very few people secure enough to put aside their easily bruised or caressed egos when necessary.

We are trained to be our own enemies, not merely in school and at home, but everywhere in the culture. At school we are taught to judge our worth by the grades we get, and in the media we are seduced into believing that our worth depends upon the goods we own or the chemicals we apply to our bodies. We depend upon so many outside props and crutches that it is not surprising that when someone goes to the core of our insecurities we fall apart.

While teaching at the school for disturbed kids I was struck by the uncanny way some of the youngsters had of making adults weak and nervous. The kids, being so defensive themselves, sensed and used the insecurity of supposedly sane people around them. They could tell when a person was uneasy about his or her body and would then tell the person he was too fat, for example. They knew whom to call stupid, whom to touch, and whom to cringe from. The pervasive sense so many Americans have that they are inferior and empty under the surface was a weapon the kids used to keep adults out of their already shattered young lives.

Another common trait of both the schizophrenic child and the powerful man is the disposability of most of the people they deal with. Nancy's life and her work were not concerns of the superintendent. He finally rehired her (although her program was discontinued) because there were people willing to fight for her. The decision was political and not personal.

Eight years ago I was seduced into becoming involved with a program sponsored by Robert Kennedy's office.

I had just met Fritz Ianni, who had been head of the Bureau of Research at the U.S. Office of Education under John Kennedy and was director of the Horace Mann Lincoln Institute at Teachers College, Columbia. Ianni flattered me with praise of my work with the kids and my knowledge of a certain segment of Harlem. This was before I had written on schools and before it was fashionable to use teaching as a way to maintain a socially responsible and radical way of living. I was lonely, discouraged, and therefore particularly vulnerable to praise.

Ianni told me that Robert Kennedy promised to "save" Benjamin Franklin High School, the only high school in Harlem, and that I could be the man to do it with his help and the occasional assistance of Kennedy's office and the Ford Foundation. He introduced me to members of Kennedy's New York entourage who confirmed what Ianni said.

Though flattered, I was very cautious at first. I tried to explain to Ianni and the Kennedy people that it was foolish and paternalistic for a white man to save black and Puerto Rican people for their own good. Furthermore, I believed and still believe that schools like Franklin will become meaningful places for the students and the rest of the community only when local people effectively control the money, hiring, and educational policies of the school. I told them that no preplanned program ought to be imposed upon the school. Rather, an opportunity had to be created for students and parents, with the aid of those teachers they respected, to plan their own school and control their own lives. I also said that my only role would have to be to bring people together, to get them resources and let them know what was in the minds of people like Kennedy and Ianni. This meant that everything had to be done openly, that I had to know what was going on in order to inform people. Finally, I had to get people I knew and trusted from the community to work with me and phase myself out when the community-governed school began to function.

Members of Kennedy's office as well as Ianni's office responded enthusiastically and encouraged me to go ahead. They swore up and down that there were no hidden agenda, no unrevealed plan that was to be imposed upon the community, no exploitation of the kids in the service of Kennedy's intended political ambitions. I needed to believe what they said and so convinced myself of their openness and honesty and went to work.

I enlisted the help of two teachers, Spencer Jameson and Nelly Jones. They knew many people from the community, kids and adults, and were incapable of playing deceitful and lying games at the expense of poor people. I also asked some friends to introduce me to a parent from the community, and Hattie came to work with me as well as Red, the husband of a former student.

We began to talk with parents and students. I talked with the principal and with groups of teachers. Spencer and Nelly set up an educational-resource/after-school learning center a few blocks away from the school. Slowly we hoped to bring people together to plan for running their own school.

Meanwhile, rumors started. The teachers heard that a plan excluding them was to be imposed on the school by Teachers College, Columbia. I swore this was false, but the rumors persisted.

Parents heard that a deal had been made between the principal, the district superintendent of schools, and Ianni. I denied that, but they persisted in believing the story.

Finally, a union delegate at the school discovered a copy of the program I swore didn't exist. He also had minutes of the meetings that supposedly never took place. Parents, teachers, even the people who worked with me turned angrily toward me. I was clearly the agent of betrayal in their eyes. It was crazy—I turned to Ianni, who assured me it was all a misunderstanding. There were a few details I didn't know about, but nothing of significance. In a few weeks more details of deals and plans and promises emerged. My role was untenable—I turned on Ianni and tried to expose as many of the lies as possible. I quit as director of the project and worked mostly with the kids. But because of my previous role many people in the community didn't trust my denials of complicity with Ianni. I was losing friends because of the role and because of that was becoming less useful to Kennedy and Ianni, who became increasingly inaccessible. I was angry, distraught, confused, confounded; I walked around like a madman in a constant state of rage and anxiety. It was like a dream—I was betrayed, the kids were betrayed once again, and I was the vehicle. I couldn't walk into a room without sensing distrust and feeling paranoid, couldn't sleep or make love. The events passed through my head over and over all night, refusing to cohere. On November 14, 1966, I walked across the street to my car in a trance. A car hit me. I glanced it coming and managed to jump a bit. My hip was broken, and I missed being killed by a few inches.

The next day I woke up in a hospital, where I remained for a month. During that time neither Ianni nor anyone from Kennedy's office bothered to so much as call to see if I was alive. I had become a liability to their plans, and my injury was an inconvenience and embarrassment. I had to be disposed of, treated as dead. I realized in the hospital that they had, as politicians say, "dumped" me. I was just another body on our human trash pile.

The disposability of goods and people seems to be a characteristic of the "American way of life." We all throw away old cars, clothes, television sets, and other appliances as well as tin cans, bottles, boxes, and paper bags. We also throw away people. There are numerous examples:

—Companies retire older employees because they are no longer "productive labor," and let them fend for themselves on subsistence pensions and social security;

—Families abandon or segregate the elderly in the same way;

—People accept "better" jobs although they may have made commitments to people they have worked with or served;

—Companies lay off people because profits aren't growing enough;

—People marry and get divorced, disposing of each other, sometimes with great ease;

—Magazines cut back on subscribers because they want to reach limited but more profitable audiences;

—People sell their businesses to corporate conglomerates, knowing that their public services will be corrupted by the corporate interests and that many of their employees will be eliminated. (Publishing is a great example of an industry that has sold out its public and its employees.)

It makes sense to look upon those people who affect your life and to whom you are disposable as potential enemies. This includes those people, perhaps very close to you, whose need for your presence serves solely their own purposes. Furthermore, it makes sense to consider that those people you deal with as if they are disposable will consider you a potential enemy. This might seem like a sweeping indictment of our communal lives, including, as it can, people we work for, politicians, salesmen and clerks we encounter casually, teachers, many allies, and possibly family and friends. However, it shouldn't be surprising that we are surrounded by potential enemies. Our culture, by making people into disposables, institutionalizes paranoia. Far from being a grave deviation from the normal state of mind, a healthy paranoia is necessary for survival in our society. People do treat objects and money as equal to or more important than other people, and therefore one must be wary of others. A small change in fortune or status can lead to a person's being trashed by friends, co-workers, bosses, teachers. Sudden reassessment of all one's personal relations is not unknown in our society although it would be inconceivable in other, more traditional cultures. For example, the revelation that a man is gay or a woman a lesbian can turn them into pariahs overnight. A college classmate of mine was driven to suicide by such disclosure and the rejection consequent upon it.

In a less dramatic way I experienced several re-evaluations of my life and work during my senior year at Harvard. My major was logic and philosophy, and I was headed, according to some professors, for a distinguished academic career. Several members of the philosophy department decided I was a clever enough student ("clever" was a higher word of academic approval then than either "intelligent" or "creative") to be taken up and groomed for a junior fellowship, a trip to Oxford, and eventually a professorship at a major university. My life and career were marked out by them, and I came to believe in their assessment of my worth.

Coming from the Bronx High School of Science, Harvard seemed overwhelming. I pretended not to be impressed and acted aggressively overconfident, although occasionally I would be attacked by anxious fears of my own emptiness and shallowness. For three years I performed well. Philosophy and logic excited me, but the academic world became increasingly repugnant. During my senior year I had to produce a thesis whose cleverness would confirm for everyone my value as a future academician.

I panicked and for a while either couldn't write anything or wrote down the first thing that occurred to me. I was so anxious about the success of the document, so afraid it would reveal me as a sham, that I couldn't think about the subject.

One of the papers I turned in was particularly careless and thoughtless. The professor who saw it decided that his estimate of me as a future academic superstar was mistaken and that I really wasn't so clever. The word went out to the teaching assistants, assistant professors, graduate students, and other precocious undergraduates like myself that I really didn't have it. People who were nice before became condescending. Other students who were competing with me were positively gleeful. Naturally I was crushed, convinced that I was nothing after all—that rejection extended not merely to my sense of intellectual ability, but also to my whole personality. I felt empty, anxious, doomed to failure, and scared of other people.

A few months after this incident I was involved in a seminar on logic with the same professor. We were trying to understand a particularly obscure though important logical proof that had just been published. The problem fascinated me, so for a while my anxiety subsided. During one session I was able to see something in the argument that the other members of the class had missed. The next day my academic stock rose once more—the word was that I was really clever after all. The experience sickened me, and this second reassessment convinced me of the need to learn enough about myself to be able to be free of such absurd dependence on others' judgments. I never recovered my initial false confidence in myself, but emerged resolved to deal with that part of me that was so easily crushed. Of course, I'm still dealing with it, although the fear of emptiness is no longer a problem. The need to be cared for, to be accepted, to be approved still keeps creeping into my life in unhealthy ways. I find myself wanting to be accepted by the superintendent of schools or by some critic or government authority when a part of me knows that I am just another disposable object to them. Like many of us I find it difficult to resist the smiles or embraces of my enemies.

Our culture creates overwhelming needs in many individuals to be loved, accepted, reassured, confirmed because it creates in them a sense of their own worthlessness and disposability. We deify mobility and profitability. People believe they can move freely about the country and through the social and economic hierarchy. They dream of being rich and popular and comfortable and at the same time fear that they are as likely to be disposed of as to succeed. And if they do succeed, the fear of being empty and of eventually being found out and discarded never disappears.

The overriding sense of loneliness, worthlessness, transience that envelopes many people in our culture leads them to a frantic search for confirmation and acceptance. Convinced that there is no core to their own being, no center they can define for themselves, they seek others to care for them, to reassure them of their own worth (and, by contrast, usually of the worthlessness of some others). This makes self-deception and blindness inevitable—anyone who offers confirmation will be believed if only for a little while. People who need confirmation will often deceive themselves into believing that they are being invested with value by someone who is, in fact, exploiting or even mocking them.

It is clear that people can be so confounded by their enemies as to embrace them, and so out of touch with themselves as to never understand why they are constantly deceived. When one feels disposable and looks upon others as disposable as well, life is lived under conditions of unreasonable tension.

Our culture imposes impossible demands on individuals —part of our cultural myth is that each individual must be measured in terms of profitability and is therefore potentially disposable.

Because of these demands, the growth of a personal center and the development of a healthy and continuous relationship to work and to others are nearly impossible. You can never trust others or throw yourself into an activity, because some small embarrassment might happen and you might end up thrown away. If you accept yourself as merely disposable, it becomes difficult to make the effort to learn and grow. If you are torn between a wavering sense of your own personal worth and a fear that you are nothing but a slickly packaged product, the energy necessary to develop a coherent and centered life is dissipated in unresolvable tension. There is a whole range of uncentered perverse forms of life perpetuated by our culture. It makes sense to examine a few of these life forms in order to understand the scope of unlearning that has to take place before many people can develop centered, un-cruel lives.

[2]

Dougie was one of the students at a school for severely disturbed children that I taught at. He was ten the year I knew him and was considered to have been autistic from birth. He hardy spoke, although his eyes indicated considerable understanding of what was happening around him. His anxiety was so great that he responded wildly to the slightest modification in the classroom environment. He would fall on the floor and scream, pound his head with his fist, and end up sobbing and exhausted if the slightest detail was changed.

After a while I began to understand what Dougie was screaming. Whenever a change in schedule took place (such as giving him a cookie before instead of after juice, or starting the morning with a story instead of a puzzle), his first words were, "The day is broken," and then as he got more upset he would scream such things as, "It's Dougie o'clock time/put the day together again"; "It's falling apart, it's time o'clock time"; "Fix the day." If someone then started the day all over again, by fixing the order of events, Dougie smiled contentedly, said, "The day is fixed," and fit into the set and rigid order of time he felt comfortable with.

Time was solid for Dougie, the order of events fixed from the moment he woke to the moment he fell into an exhausted sleep. Any variation in the order of events broke the solid day and panicked him, since he had never developed a self in time that could deal with the occasionally irregular flow of personal time. The rituals of the day were all that existed for him; that was his glue, so when they fell apart, he literally became unglued.

Dougie was the events that happened to him, there was no other Dougie. He had no center whatever, couldn't locate himself in space and time. If he tripped and fell down, he never knew whether to cry or not because he couldn't figure out whether he was hurt or not. I remember seeing him fall and take a serious bang. He looked up at me questioningly, as if he wanted me to tell him what the natural response should be in the situation.

I saw him every day for six months and never saw any desire on his part to change or vary the order of events. Occasionally I tried to expose him to a new game or puzzle, but he resisted violently and fell apart if I pushed the issue. The slightest change in his life threatened him with extinction, and he did everything his extremely limited repertoire of responses allowed to keep his world solid and unchanging.

Paul, another student at the school, was equally centerless, although he manifested it in almost the opposite way. He was unable to keep at anything for more than a second. He constantly forgot where he was and where he was going. He would ask the adults around, "Am I happy?" "Do I hurt?" "Should I cry?" "Should I laugh?"

Jokes puzzled him. He didn't know how to take them, whether they were meant literally or were to be laughed at (he knew how to imitate laughing but gave the impression that he didn't know why people made laughing sounds).

Anger was equally confounding. If an adult screamed at him, he would sometimes laugh, sometimes cry, but most frequently ask how he was supposed to respond.

He seemed constantly to be fleeing from rather than moving toward things. One got the impression that he was doing the opposite of growing. It seemed as if objects were always chasing him. He would start a single wooden puzzle and after a minute would begin to flee from the pieces, to accuse them of trying to confuse him.

He could never look at a person or even an object straight. His eyes always darted around, anxiously falling on one thing after another. During that same six months I never saw the anxiety level subside.

In the case of both Dougie and Paul I had the uncanny feeling that there was no person behind their actions, that what they did was all they were. They somehow were reduced to their behavior, which itself was always defensive. They were neither growing nor learning from experience, since there was no center to act as an integrative force.

These two severely disturbed boys manifest extremes of centerless being, and yet the characteristics they manifest can be found in less dramatic form all about us. Before examining the varieties of this peripatetic centerlessness,* however, I want to distinguish between Being without a center and the superficially similar state of Being I encountered in young people of thirteen or fourteen that represents an exploration of the possibilities of life and therefore is a stage in the development of a center rather than its denial. There are many adolescents who flit from subject to subject, who seem incapable of sustaining a relationship with anyone else or of completing a project. Their lives externally seem similar to Paul's with its constant activity. However, adolescent exploration is generally not a flight from the self, but rather an exploration of roles and masks and relationships that if not thwarted can lead to a centered existence.

Many of the young people at Other Ways were going through the process of learning their own interests, their sexual preferences, their political stances. There is little help for them in the family or in the society at large. Sexual exploration has to be carried out hidden from the adult world. Parents don't like their own work and encourage their children to be different without being able to provide actual work experiences for them. School, even the best of school, is centered on talk, when the youngsters want and need to act. Because of the inability

---

* So-called peripatetic schizophrenics are individuals who manifest many characteristics of the disease and yet have adjusted to society sufficiently to be walking about and occasionally to be quite successful citizens.

of adults to provide the auspices under which the young can work and love, youngsters make their own opportunities. The peer culture is extremely strong but, for many youngsters, too limited, since it too is remote from work and religion and politics. For people in quest of their own selves, necking, dancing, and doping provide only a small part of the range of experience they need.

Most adolescents are engaged in the process of centering their existence. Dougie and Paul, on the other hand, structured their lives so that the process of centering could be avoided. There are adults whose lives are as dead as those of Dougie and Paul. However, many of them have power in our society and are not considered disturbed according to the politics of madness in our culture, which equates abnormality with nonconforming defiance of legitimized authority (whether it be located in the family, the school, or the state). Listen, for example, to William Appleman Williams's analysis of Richard Nixon's personality that appeared in *The New York Review of Books* (February 24, 1972, pp. 7–12):

> We must therefore turn elsewhere for assistance in understanding Nixon. Specifically to the insight (first advanced by the Germans) about the middle-class individual who, denied any opportunity to realize himself as a consequential member of society (no sense of place or fulfillment), flees forward to escape destruction. To stop is to die because flight is identity. Life is a sequence of problems rather than a mix of difficulties, opportunities, and realization. And problems are solved either by fleeing past them or by resolving them into ever bigger problems.

> The most generous thing to say is that he had a secret hope that being President would give him the identity he had never been able to create. A frightening example of the man who thinks the role makes the man. To be sure, the Presidency *is* one of the two or three offices in world politics (at least since 1860) that have the psy-

chological power to bring out the best in a man. But it
cannot work miracles. Nor is it a loom on which to
weave finished cloth from raw fiber.

There is simply no sense of self, no putting it together
by Nixon himself.

There are advantages in being centerless and rigidly
conforming in our culture, and there are also advantages
in being constantly in flight.

For example, it is possible to imagine Dougie and Paul,
in slightly less severe conditions of Being, as corporate
functionaries.

Dougie is an efficiency expert. His own life is rigidly
ordered and his profession is to order the lives of others
according to criteria of economic efficiency and productivity. Every moment in his life is accounted for—he has
weekly and daily cycles. Even his weekends are planned
so that time is used efficiently and productively. He has a
family and sets up time to spend with his kids and make
love to his wife. He expects everyone else to be as efficient
as he is and has no tolerance for playfulness and no understanding of how people's lives can be troubled since he
feels no pain. The boss finds him a valuable and reliable
worker who also spies conscientiously on others and does
not hesitate to root out inefficiency. There is no way to
appeal to his feelings or to convince him that he has been
wrong about anything. His life was set once and for all
time some time in the past and time has stopped for him.
The only time he gets into trouble is when the demands
of his family life or work force him either to respond in
new ways or fail. Because of this, his life is beginning to fall
apart, but he can't understand why. His children don't
want to live structured weekends and are often too busy
to see him during the hours he has set aside for them. His
wife is tiring of making love efficiently and according to
schedule. And his boss is worried because the younger
employees are demanding that the corporation become

more flexible and let people choose their own work schedules and become involved in outside social service. Dougie can't respond to these workers, is becoming impatient and irritable. He is antagonizing many people whom the corporation considers valuable. His rigidity and emptiness might even lead to his downfall. Yet he is a good, upstanding, dependable citizen. He lives a mechanical and closed existence in which the rituals of his life have replaced the need for a soul. If change, in the form of losing his job or being forced to live a different style of life, ever confronts him, it is possible that there will be a total collapse and suicide. On the other hand, very few people are fully dead at the core, and he might begin to need his Self and change.

Let's look at Paul now: he is a young executive on the rise. He can never stick at anything for too long, doesn't trust anyone, and is always in flight. However, his flight from himself is leading up the corporate ladder, for his constant energy and ability to be ruthless and demanding toward others are very useful in the highly competitive industry he works in. Paul knows how to dispose of ideas and people with great ease. He has a reputation that is the opposite of Dougie's, for he is always looking around for new and different forms and once or twice has hit upon some profitable ideas.

Paul flees from woman after woman in the same way he flees from ideas and friends. He moves so fast that he never seems to know where he is. His life is lived in airports, motels, and hotels, and he doesn't care about food or drink or even possessions. He is involved in a race to the top of the business world he has committed himself to, and perhaps the only things that can stop him are a heart attack or possibly a young-comer more ruthless and moving more quickly than even he is capable of. There is no moment for Paul to slow down and consider what he cares about or whom he loves, no time to develop an understanding of himself or others. Even though he is rich, the money is little more than a vehicle to allow him to remain in constant, unconnected motion. Occasionally he feels sorry for himself and falls into monumental depressions, but those are so brief and so unconnected to the rest of his life that he brushes them aside as indications of a personal weakness that he must resist and eliminate. In that way he resents most those few experiences available to him that can lead to growth and understanding. He embraces his frenetic dance of death and unfortunately can carry many other lives along with him.

There are other manifestations of the Dougie and Paul syndromes throughout our society that are positively santioned rather than considered dangerous forms of spiritual death. For example, I can imagine Dougie and Paul as behavioral scientists, as politicians, and as members of the so-called counterculture.

As behavioral scientists :

Dougie, the quantifier, who believes in the objectivity and moral neutrality of his work, and who received his Ph.D. for a study of the tolerance of monkeys for pain induced by electric shock. He measures and calculates everything in his life and has been awarded a professorship to teach others to do the same.

Paul, the young scientist on the move, the entrepreneur of scientific ideas, the inveterate conference goer, the fund raiser and scientific manager who cares about more money and a larger lab though not particularly about the content or morality of the lab's work.

As politicians:

Dougie is dangerous to the lives of others, for he knows of only one way of responding to the world's problems. He authorizes the use of force and, when it fails, authorizes the use of more force. He does not understand anyone whose values might be different or whose life style isn't identical to his own. He is not interested in other people, feels awkward in intimate or informal situations, needs to have everything planned and scheduled, needs to work twenty hours a day and have each moment filled. Relaxation consist of playing golf with political advisors so that every moment becomes significant. Time to him must be filled completely, and he is hardly ever alone with nothing to do. He is most threatened and vicious when the orderly structure of his life and the manners of his world are disrupted in any way. He is capable of killing others in the service of the order he needs to protect him from himself.

Paul again complements Dougie. He is on the move, moving from state to state, wheeling and dealing, constantly acquiring power, developing alliances or dumping people. He is invaluable as a campaign manager and is often described, more accurately than most people realize, as being selfless in his devotion to the party.

Finally, there are countercultural forms of centerlessness:

Dougie is a philosopher of the counterculture. His life is devoted to extolling the virtues of being loving as well as having a hip life style. He feels that the straight world is beyond contempt. His life in its way is as tightly structured as the corporate executive's. Every minute of the day and evening is taken up with some form of meeting or encounter, but he never seems to change. The groups he attends have high turnover rates, but he is the senior citizen of his encounter group, food conspiracy, discussion group, extended family, and so forth. He feels that people are abandoning him all the time, and, since a few years ago he set his own position with regard to everything in life, he cannot respond to new issues or needs that have developed in the community. To the straight world he is the archetype hippy, very threatening. To some young radicals he is thought of as a"counterrevolutionary." It is not clear when he has the time and ease to think of himself.

Paul, once again, is very different. He teaches at a free school and is constantly getting into and out of things. He has run through macrame, tie dyeing, batik, leather,

demonstrations, trashing, free love, Eastern religion, and
is still running. It is a slightly bizarre experience to hear
him talk about macrame and political action as if they
were qualitatively the same in his life. He is equally
serious about everything he has been involved with; yet
for all of his enthusiasm and energy his actions seem empty
of substance.

At the school he is constantly bustling around, beginning projects and then forgetting about them. He seems
incapable of completing anything. He also tries to meet
all the demands of all the kids, and this leads to hopeless
confusion at the school. In the middle of a class, for example, three kids burst in demanding to be taken to a park.
He excuses himself, drives them a few blocks and returns
to school, having forgotten all about the class he was
teaching.

However, all the undirected energy has not led him
to be completely without success. He attends meetings of
free schools continuously, is rhetorically brilliant, and
makes his disaffection sound counterculturally proper (he
is helping the kids "do their own thing"). He is becoming
one of the leaders of the free school movement. Since he
can be as ruthless as his counterpart in corporate life, it
is possible he will be successful in the public life of the
so-called counterculture.

So far in this section I haven't said anything about
women. The discussion began with a portrait of two disturbed boys, and an analogy was developed between them
and supposedly normal adults who manifest similar ways
of being. There were no girls in my class and few girls
in the whole school for disturbed children. This is not
a special case, either. Most schools for disturbed children
have many fewer young females, although this inequality
in the distribution of madness in our society seems to even
out by adolescence. I think there are certain facets of our

culture that account for this fact. First of all, there is the question of who as a young child has to bear the pressure of being the focus of family expectations in our male-dominated society. It is quite possible that young boys are subject to greater scrutiny, are pushed harder, and are expected to indicate genius or talent sooner than young girls. Because of that parents are more sensitive to indications of pathology or disturbance in young boys than girls. It is possible that there are as many disturbed girls as boys, but the girls just aren't noticed. Certainly parents worry about a withdrawn and silent boy while considering that same behavior characteristic of "good" little girls. Furthermore, a wildly active girl can be laughed off as a "tomboy," while a boy behaving "like a girl" can be considered a threat to his parents' hope for social and economic mobility through the boy's efforts as a man.

It is interesting that in our culture so-called pathological females begin to be noticed during puberty and adolescence. When women become eligible to be considered sex and marriage objects, the male-dominated society begins to worry. A woman has to be a "good" wife, a docile though pretty object on the one hand, or a wild, inaccessible glamour girl on the other. Deviations from cultural expectations are frequently considered signs of madness. The line between revolutionary activity and insane behavior constantly shifts according to who is in power.

Because of the role of females in our culture it is not surprising that many women do not have the opportunity to grow, work, or develop fully. They are tied to homes, to husbands, to husbands' careers, to many things outside themselves. Because of this phenomenon, there are some variants of centerlessness that can be seen as forms of obsessions with revenge toward our male-dominated culture. For examples, hating the male-dominated culture and generalizing the hatred to males in general, a woman can come to use her role as sex object as a weapon to destroy and dominate men. She can find her identity wholly outside herself through using her body, her intelligence, and her charm totally in the service of conquest. Just as for some men, her life can become an uncentered, never-changing string of conquests. As soon as a person subjects her- or himself to domination the game is over. Another object has to be found so that the process of overcoming the will and possessing the soul of the other can begin again.

I know many young women in high school who fancy themselves witches and who quite specifically strive to dominate, possess, overwhelm, and control others. These young girls are not mad, nor are they entirely centerless. For most of them it is a stage, an experiment with exerting power and getting out from under male dominance. It is an experiment with health and personal liberation from the cultural definition of the woman's role. For a few of the girls, however, it is a substitute for living and seems to me like an obsession that will never leave them.

As a college student I went out with a witch, a young woman given to swallowing, dominating, possessing, and then getting bored when it was clear she had succeeded. It was a frightening experience for me. At the time I was obsessed with doubt about myself. Occasionally I had anxiety attacks and became convinced that I was empty. My life seemed a constant act to deceive people into believing I had a rich, deep, valuable, complex inner life although I was convinced that inside there was nothing. The young woman saw my anxiety and grabbed onto it. Her need to control and my need to be filled up and dominated meshed perfectly. I danced to whatever tune she cared to play.

After a few months she became bored with me. The contest for my will was over, and there was need for a new battle. For my part, the battle for repossession of my self was one of the most important experiences I had to go through at that time. I had to sort out what I wanted to preserve for myself, what I needed, wanted to do, felt.

There was a need to define and delimit my Self, to separate it from the other whom I was allowing to control my
behavior.

I suppose many men and women go through stages of
possessing and needing to be possessed (either role can be
assumed by men or women—there are male witches) as
they define their selves. The centerless beings, however,
are those for whom possessing others is the substance of
life and for whom possession is a constant and unfilling
activity resulting in boredom and the need to begin the
cycle again.

There are some characteristics that seem common to
centerless people in their relationships to others. Because
their lives are so bound up with the rituals and externals
of existence (whether through compulsive structure or in
flight), their relationships with people never grow or
change. People are pieced into their lives to cause a mini-
mum of disruption. These people, therefore, are assigned
unambiguous roles that do not change over a long period
of time. Some individuals, for example, might play sexual
roles in their lives, others might be assigned to be subor-
dinates or co-workers or golf partners or drinking com-
panions. Each role is defined as much as posible so that
the unexpected will not occur and the lack of a personal
center be discovered.

Relationships that do not change because the people do
not change themselves tend to become stale, formalized
affairs. The more ritualized one's relationships with others,
the more likely it is that one gets bored. If one person
changes and the other doesn't, things fall apart. The
changed one feels misunderstood, the changeless one betrayed. Relationships that fall apart leave gaping holes in
centerless lives that must be filled with relationships func-
tionally equivalent to those that existed in the past. A
lover who goes to bed at precisely ten thirty and comes

quickly must be replaced by another one that fills the same role. A friend who never asks questions about work or politics must be replaced if he or she oversteps these limits.

To centerless individuals, other people are talking and screwing objects, that must be pieced into the time of one's life. Centerless people seem shallow, uncomprehending, and unyielding. They seem soulless, damned, lost, and they make very dangerous enemies. If an unexpected problem arises, if someone tries to move them in a personal way and pierce their masks, they might panic and strike out—under extreme pressure, they feel their whole being threatened. They have no center to fall back on, they are not accustomed to self-criticism, do not know how to deal with being wrong. They are scared that they will be found out to be nothing. People who come too close have to be eliminated or, as Dougie said, their day will be broken, time will overwhelm them, and they will drift or even drown. There is nothing to hold onto, nothing to do but rebuild their lives and pretend that nothing happened.

There seems to be a particular way in which centerless beings occasionally decompose. Some become alternately violent and sniveling; they propound grandiose schemes, then a second later moan about the hopelessness of it all. The final stage of collapse sees them fall into a puddle. Their physical beings don't even seem to cohere. The wild swing of opposites, the incoherent substanceless void, the scattered eyes all resemble classical portraits of the damned, the people whose souls have been stolen, bartered, or sold. Centerless persons can at one moment be self-assured, in control, confident, handsome or beautiful, articulate. The next moment they become their opposites. If they are lucky, they have developed mechanisms for the construction of their masks and the repair of their rituals. If not, they can collapse into incoherence and undergo what is euphemistically called a nervous breakdown.

Recently there was an interesting illustration of the collapse of a centerless individual. Edwin Aldrin, "the second man to set foot on the moon," described his experiences following the space voyage. His life was rigidly structured during training and completely ordered and centered outside himself on the flight. His return to earth put him in contact with the public world. The orderliness he knew and needed (he was a son of a military man, his wife a military daughter) was swept away. He had not developed the inner resources and center needed to deal with public attention and the demands made on his time. In fact, he was chosen to go to the moon precisely because he was a well-functioning component of the space machine and manifested no inner idiosyncracies. Under pressure he collapsed and had, as he described it, "a good, old-fashioned American nervous breakdown" (*The New York Times,* February 29, 1972, p. 41).

[3]

Just as there are some people whose life is a flight from or compensation for the lack of a personal center, there are others, partially in contact with themselves and consequently with other people, who nevertheless act in ways that lead them to destroy or exploit people in the service of some complex and perverse combination of ideology and personal need. These people are not as prone to collapse as centerless individuals and are easier to like and harder to oppose.

Perversity is a complex, frequently confounding matter. I have a friend—or rather had a friend—who manifests the contradictory nature of what can be called a perverse center. He was the director of a multiracial alternative school.

Tod is self-educated, and about thirty-five years old. He has developed the most disciplined learning techniques for himself imaginable and during the last ten years has become in turn a first-rate professional flier, car builder, film maker, writer, and student of contemporary craft and technology.

Tod lives in a small house filled with books, cameras, tape recorders, and tools. He has made everything in the place including the lathe in the workshop. At present he is working on an electric car.

Tod is consumed by unmanageable love and unmanageable hate. He feels that the role of woman is to serve man and is violently anti-women's liberation. He is also consumed occasionally by a hatred for white people, which is general rather than specific. He has little problem relating to whites when he cares to, and equally little problem disposing of them.

Equal and opposite to his generalized though intense hatred of whites is his love of black people and his urgent desire to see the economic and social oppression in this society wiped out.

The love is combined with an anger and impatience that cause him to attempt to drive and even bully black students into learning how to function and survive in this society.

Tod describes himself paradoxically as a democratic dictator and means it. He wants black people to make decisions for themselves and tries to encourage the black students at the school to take control of their lives and specifically of the school's functioning. However, he refuses to allow them to make stupid decisions—i.e., decisions that he feels are wrong or damaging. In that he undoes his intent, since never allowing the kids to make mistakes makes them feel they have no real power. It seems to me that one has to risk being wrong and learn from mistakes in order to develop the ability to control one's life.

At Tod's instigation the white kids at the school have become second-class citizens and have been told that there will be a minimal attempt made to meet their learning needs. They will have to fit in with the black orientation of the school or get out and go back to the regular high school. He has even joked that what they need is a little oppression.

Tod is even more imperious with his staff. He has the power to hire and fire at will, constantly berates the teachers and tries to drive them to be as committed to saving the youngters as he is. He wants urgently to legislate commitment and compel learning. He wents to force the staff and students to have a sense of community and is intolerant of opposition.

His ardor and drive are sometimes overwhelming. He visits students' homes and rounds them up for school, deals politically to get money, checks up on his teachers, polices the building to prevent smoking, gambling, and so forth. Most of the time at school he is grim and joyless in pursuit of discipline. However, that is not his only face. After a class that he feels has gone well, he jokes with the students and occasionally plays the drums with some of them. All the students at the school respect Tod for what he knows and for the urgency of his desires to change the world. Very few of them love him and some hate his cruel and intolerant attitudes.

Tod is not at all uncentered. His work, his life, his vision, his physical being, his relationships with people cohere. There is something harsh yet beautiful about all of his work. His car is, as a friend once said, "overbuilt, loaded with the strongest metal, detailed, finished, polished, and at the same time rough-hewn." Tod is also physically tough, and tough on the people around him as well as on himself. His center has hardened—he will master many more skills but they will all be integrated to his driving central concern. He cannot let up, cannot afford to relax or be open to change or his center might fall apart and his goal be eluded. The perversity of his existence consists of the fact that his center excludes so much in order to achieve itself. This leads him to oppress and destroy others as well as to frequently negate his own intent.

At those moments when Tod's social program seems impossible, he retreats totally into himself. If he cannot achieve the liberation of black people, at least he can liberate himself. He dreams of packing up his tools, books, and cameras and flying off somewhere. It is between the liberation of all black people and the total indulgence of his own needs that Tod swings. There is no middle ground, no openness to new strategies or to the slow development of allies. He will not admit to failure that rests partially with his self. Either the world is or isn't ready.

Tod is driven but he functions. His situation is quite different from the fantasies of escape of a neurotic whose flight is not anchored in physical reality.

Tod embodies certain paradoxes of revolutionary consciousness. Che Guevara has said somewhere, "The true revolutionary is guided by great feelings of love." Tod is driven by a great and generalized love for liberated black people. But this generalized love makes him intolerant of specific individuals who do not embody his vision of liberated individuals. He has a scorn for weakness and confusion that can burn into bitter resentment and almost irrational anger. He is impatient, and that leads him to be cruel. He frequently becomes divorced from his most logical allies because he sees them as future free men rather than people involved in struggles both with themselves and the world, on a day-to-day basis. Tod's fervor, which also stems from an intolerance of any possible weaknesses in himself (and therefore probably from some deep-seated fear that even he, too, is empty and a failure), sometimes makes him ineffective as a revolutionary, since it alienates him from the people he is living for. Great feelings of love have to be tempered by little feelings of love, and that is the paradox—if one loves people for what they can become, it is very difficult to also love them as they are at present. The perversity of Tod's center is not due to its general orientation but to its closedness. Yet whether one can develop revolutionary fervor and stamina and still be open to change is an unresolved question which I will return to throughout the book.

Some of the conflicts and swings in Tod's life manifest

what I call the *tension of perversity*. A closed center strains to keep out threats, to maintain its preoccupations, and to ward off collapse. It is possible to be centered, to expend all of one's time, effort, energy in one direction that is also a natural one and consistent with one's own needs and talents. However, when the center becomes determined and delimited, anything new or unexpected can be threatening. A tension exists in closed lives, straining to make sure the center isn't pierced. This constant alertness to threat makes people like Tod particularly dangerous enemies. They are constantly attuned not merely to the threat of their total visions, but also to the weaknesses of others. The constant state of alarm makes closed, rigidly centered people develop a *perverse understanding* of the weaknesses of others that can always be used to eliminate, defuse, or confuse opposition. The superintendent's understanding of Nancy's vulnerability that I mentioned in the first part of this section is a good example of perverse understanding in operation. Tod's use of race is another one. He is particularly attuned to indications of racist attitudes in white people and to indications of what he calls white attitudes in blacks. Therefore, when attacked or caught being inconsistent, he shifts the level of conflict from a disagreement over fact or philosophy to an attack on self. White people disagree because they are racist; black people disagree because they are acting like white men. The understanding is perverse because although there is almost always truth in what Tod says during these attacks, the truth and his understanding of it are used to protect himself and not to foster the growth of others.

There are many different individuals who show symptoms of being perversely centered—i.e., centered in such a way as to exclude sensitivity to the lives and needs of others. There may even be even forms of *temporary perversity*. A quote from William Faulkner that appears in a *Paris Review* interview comes to mind. The interviewer asked Faulkner if the rumor that his mother scrubbed floors to support his writing was true, and he replied, "The lives of any number of old ladies aren't worth much compared to my books."

Artists frequently go through periods of intense perverse centrificity. They exclude others from their world and allow their lives to be given over totally to the work in progress. Anything that interferes with the work must be eliminated. The periods of intense and exclusive centeredness are often followed by periods of wild, amorphous dissipation once the work is delivered. It is well known that certain creative people can be dangerous people to become attached to. For them everything and everyone outside of the work is disposable during periods of intense creativity. However, the intensification and delimitation of the center all of us need at one time or other need not lead to perverse being. During periods of concentration some people who know themselves are able to warn others off and deal with their own perversity as a temporary and necessary phenomenon.

Jules Henry in *Pathways to Madness* quotes Picasso describing his relationship to creating (Random House, p. 290, 1971):

> Everyone has the same energy potential. The average person wastes his in a dozen little ways. I bring mine to bear on one thing only: my painting, and everything else is sacrificed to it—you and everyone else, myself included.

I have friends who are mathematicians and scientists, who go through periods totally absorbed in a problem and are irritated by the slightest intrusion of people or even noise or impressions into their consciousness. For the few hours a day that I write, a similar concentration of energy and effort takes place. If for some reason the work is interrupted or a new element (such as an unexpected noise) intrudes itself into my working environment, my head pounds and I go into a barely controllable rage. It is as bad as being interrupted in the midst of making love.

There are dangerous forms of the perverse center often manifested in politics and business. When the career takes the place of the work, one's whole life can become closed and perverse. The artist, at least, is periodically released from his or her obsession. If one's life is centered on a career (the equivalent of a society centering its existence on "progress"), there is no release, since a career binds all time. There is no final stopping point, no time to rest, deliver oneself of the work and begin again. One must climb higher and higher, attain more and more power. To rest or to leave the work and begin again is failure. The structure of a power-obsessed, perversely centered life is the same whether the nature of the power one struggles for is liberally, radically, or conservatively defined.

I have known people in the civil rights movement obsessed with their roles and with the issues they are battling. One particular person whose life has centered on the development of community-controlled alternatives acquired power to the point of making her increasingly ineffective at her job. She was exhausted by meetings, by the demands made upon her, which, of course, increased as she became more powerful. Late at night she talked about how much she needed to get out and rest, and occasionally even acknowledged her increasing ineffectiveness. But she once said that she feared that if she ever did step out, there would be no place for her when she came back. The whole thrust of her life, which was a movement toward the power to effect change, would be stopped short. Her career, which was also bound up with a genuine commitment to change this society, consumed her since it was all she had—it was her center. She was not in flight away from her self and the world. She was centered on the struggle for civil rights and brought her energy, intelligence, emotions, and her body to the effort. She consumed herself, lived with many unmet needs, occasionally acted intolerantly and insensitively to people outside the movement. But she never turned her back on her own self or center. I'm laboring this issue because it is crucial to distinguish this type of committed existence from the centerless being described before that can appear superficially similar. It is possible to throw oneself into a struggle to cover a void and find existence and the struggle identical. It is another thing, however, to commit oneself to a struggle not as an escape from emptiness but because of social need or belief. Centerless commitment is made to fill a personal need, while perverse commitment is a form of sacrifice. In the latter case the only reason I use the word "perverse" is that a commitment that overfocuses the self can lead to harsh, cruel, inconsistent, and inhuman behavior because its intensity closes part of the person down.

[4]

Moral inconsistency is a characteristic of many, if not most, individuals in our society. Different areas of life are separated from one another and different and contradictory codes of behavior are adopted in different settings. There is a code of business or professional behavior different from the code of family behavior, which is different from the code of behavior relevant to community involvement. Most cultures structure the lives of individuals differently according to kinship and work relationships. In this we are not special. However, what is a problem for us are the contradictory and confounding ways in which the various codes overlap.

In school I heard, on the one hand, that all men were equal, that others should be treated with respect. On the other hand, I heard that competition was the essence of success and even survival, and that it was the fault of the poor that they were hungry.

Love is supposed to bind the family together but is inappropriate in the business world. Competition is central to business and is supposed to be out of place in the family. But the worlds are not separated, and corruption is inevitable. Children and parents compete for love, which is used as a commodity in the family. And feelings invade the world of business so that guilt develops as one hurts a competitor or fires an employee who is no longer sufficiently productive.

Warmth and tenderness exist in all of us in this culture side by side with the murderous attitudes induced by the demands of a competitive society indifferent to the fate of individuals. We try to keep them apart, to remain blind to the contradictions of our daily existence in order to keep on going. If we started worrying about the people we hurt or exploit, if we took responsibility for the lives of others, we might be wiped out ourselves by some less considerate neighbor or competitor. Knowing our own schizophrenia and our own potential for cruelty, we know well enough to suspect everybody else of what we are capable of. We have to keep ourselves separated in order to keep functioning. We must stay insane and fragmented in order not to be destroyed. Sanity, the integration of the parts, is too dangerous for people who feel trapped, and our culture is built to trap individuals in unrewarding work and mortgaged lives.

I remember my father coming home from work and collapsing into a heap, exhausted and slightly hostile, looking beat. It was not from the nature of the physical work he was doing. My grandfather, his father, was a carpenter who worked incredibly hard. He came home from work physically tired, but his head was clear. He did not bear the burdens of other people's lives, did not have to battle for pennies to keep ahead of the competition, to fire a bumbling but warm and caring worker. He built walls and had time to play when he came home.

I saw the tension of maintaining a competitive edge and

at the same time being a loving man tearing my father apart, and I resolved never to be caught in that bind. Of course, there was no way to escape that competition and the insecurity it breeds. In the family love was the reward for competing successfully, just as money was the reward outside of the family. As hard as one tries to separate worlds and therefore parts of oneself, feelings, attitudes, and thoughts slip in to contaminate and confuse the self. For many people the only way to deal with this contamination is to keep busy all the time—to work long hours, play with the kids, watch television, sleep a lot but never think or rest, never face one's own fantasies or one's life as a totality. For people like this the center is a problem to be avoided.

There are many examples of the alienation from the center induced by our culture. We all experience major discontinuities in our lives and keep ourselves blind in order to keep functioning on a day-to-day basis. If we acted upon everything we saw that we knew needed to be done, we would have to give up our present comforts for an uncertain, potentially painful life whose only reward would be the process of living itself. In addition, we would have to bear the constant accusation of madness or irresponsibility. The American way of being charitable or committed is generally to make oneself comfortable first and then to assist others and remake the society during one's spare time. This requires the ability to remove oneself from the pain of other people's lives. As Jules Henry puts it in another context (*Pathways to Madness,* p. 438): "The secret of sanity is to exaggerate the good of the world."

There are subtle ways in which the culture contributes to keeping individuals separated and unable to figure out ways of understanding themselves and centering their lives. Recently I have noticed specific ways in which my child Antonia, who is four and a half, is becoming alienated from herself. She has begun to watch television and has just been exposed to advertising. She has been bombarded with images of pretty little boys and girls playing with hundreds of dolls and boats and airplanes and other toys. And she has somehow been convinced that she needs many of the things she sees on TV. Recently she told me with an urgent and pained look that she needed a twenty-dollar doll that talked, walked, cried, and wore mod clothes (at five dollars a change of dress). I asked her if she really needed the doll or just wanted it. She thought a bit and then said she didn't need it, but she did want it. Fortunately she has not yet been as damaged as many adults in our society who are unable to distinguish their needs from their wants.

One of the main functions of advertising in our culture is to confound needs and wants: people say that they need a new car, a color television set, an electric knife or can opener, a new refrigerator that makes its own ice cubes, and so forth. When pressed, some people admit that those objects represent indulgences rather than needs. Others are confused—the constant acquisition of objects is woven into the very fabric of their lives; is, in fact, at its center. For them there are felt needs for the acquisition of new objects, as well as an accompanying sense that without objects they are nothing. In our society possessions can be used to define the self and to present the illusion of coherence for separated being.

For a separated self the binding together of life is a problem—if one's being is too fragmented or one's life too full of contradictory action, one can either live in deliberate denial of the problem of developing a coherent center, or one can find a center wholly outside oneself. One can also rationalize a hypocritical unity of the self. Many people say that they are hard and cruel in business so that they can buy things to make a good and comfortable life for their family. Another version of this story is the claim some men make that they compete and use other people in order to enable, through what their money can buy, their children not to have to be so cruel or competitive.

Perhaps the most confounded need in our culture is the need to be part of a coherent and stable society of other men and women. This need is manifested on a personal level as the need to be wanted, connected, loved, approved. Because of the fluidity of our society and the institutionalized schizophrenia induced by its competitive culture this basic need of human community is transformed into insatiable wants and longings. People expect objects to redeem them or connect them or justify their existence. When people want to express affection, they give objects; when they want to end a quarrel, they come bearing expensive gifts.

I remember as a child my father soothing me in my greatest moments of unhappiness by taking me to a store and buying something I wanted. The experience was only partially satisfying—I needed sympathy and understanding and got an object. For many people this process can be further transformed, so that the wanted objects, which were used to substitute for the needed feelings, become so entangled with the feelings themselves that their acquisition is felt as the fulfillment of a need.

[5]

It is difficult for people in our culture to take a view of the whole of their lives and make coherent and moral sense out of it. Work, love; communal responsibility, personal indulgence; competitiveness, cooperation; mobility, stability—all of these tendencies exist within most people's lives in an unresolved state of tension that is comfortable to ignore. We are willingly blind to our lives because if we faced them we might have to remake them. The center is a problem in our culture and in our personal lives.

Often when people are forced through some major change in their life circumstances to confront the totality of their being, they collapse or, on the other hand, make great and unexpected changes. For example, there are many people who manage schizoid lives of harsh competitiveness outside the family and overindulgent smothering love within it until all the children grow and leave home; then the adults have to face themselves, as the young can no longer be used to justify the cruelty of the old. Many marriages fall apart at this time in life. The adults have to face their fragmented selves as well as the imminence of death, and some realize that it is probably the last opportunity they will have to develop as integral persons.

Other adults react so harshly to the confrontation with the totality of their lives that they close up and become cantankerous, intolerant, self-indulgent, unloving beings on the way to death. How else can one explain the phenomenon of a retirement community voting to exclude children? In our culture we frequently experience such madnesses as the young throwing out the old and the old willing to be totally separated from the young and being repelled by children. These situations are not accidental but natural consequences of the uncentered, schizoid lives that are defined as normal being in our culture.

The problem of developing a center and making one's whole life coherent and consistent can arise at most any age and in most any culture. It can never be fully resolved, although centering can be a cultural value in some societies and not in others.* In our culture, however, the rituals for centering are absent, and the adult guides who help people

* There are many rituals or teaching stories that focus on centering individual group experience. Here is a list of books where some of them are described:
1. *Centering*, M. C. Richards (Wesleyan University Press, Middletown, Conn., 1970)
2. *Technicians of the Sacred*, ed. Jerome Rothenberg (Doubleday, 1968)
3. *The Teachings of Don Juan; A Separate Reality; Journey to Ixtlan,* Carlos Castaneda (Simon & Schuster, 1969, 1971, 1973)
4. *The Sufis*, Idries Shah (Doubleday/Anchor, 1971)
5. *Muntu: The New African Culture*, Janheinz Jahn (Grove, 1961)
6. *Ways of Thinking of Eastern Peoples*, Hajime Nakamura (East-West Center Press, Honolulu, 1964)
7. *Symbols of Transformation*, vol. 5 (collected works), C. G. Jung (Bollingen Press, reissued 1973)

develop as wholes are replaced by teachers and bosses who criticize, judge, test, and generally tear down and wear out the self. Because people are seen as disposable, they are not valued for what they can become but are used for what they can do in the present and then discarded.

Because the culture does not aid the individual in growing, people must go through crises of centering by themselves or in the intimacy of psychiatrists' offices. Because centering and coherence go against cultural norms, people in process wonder about their sanity and normalcy. It is agonizing to live with the total truth of one's life and its coherence with the lives of others in our culture, and it is a lonely, difficult battle to pull the pieces together.

All of us periodically have to choose whether to bring our lives together or live fragmented. Making choices means giving up something, and many of us are so insecure that we are afraid of giving anything up.

A year before I began teaching, when I was twenty-four years old, I spent an hour a day five and sometimes six times a week talking at a psychoanalyst. I didn't go into analysis out of intellectual curiosity or because of social pressure. I ran to an analyst in panic and fear because my life seemed foolish and meaningless; because there was no center to my existence; and because I wanted to feel sick and be taken care of for a while. I needed a wise, older person to listen to my confusion, to give me guidance and comfort, and to tell me something new about myself, something that would provide me with an opportunity to begin all over again.

That was in 1960, two years after I graduated from Harvard. After a year in Oxford and a year as a graduate student in philosophy at Columbia University as well as a six-month flight from myself that whirled through Greece, Switzerland, and France, and ended up back in New York, I found myself empty and almost suicidal. There still seemed nothing worth doing. I lived out of a suitcase. My money was running out, I was drunk most of the time, I dreaded asking my parents for money or help (another defeat that seemed insufferable at the time). No one was interested in giving another academic dropout a job. I forgot who I was, what I liked. I didn't care for myself and therefore didn't care for anyone else either— in fact, I felt anyone who cared for me had to be worthless merely by virtue of their caring.

I was cut off from my old friends; weary of my parents' preaching, afraid to be fully independent of them yet hating all the childish dependencies I had; bored with philosophy and verbal showing off; scared of a woman whom I pretended to love. Most of all I was terrified of being empty inside, of being all mask and no substance. I didn't live anywhere at that time. For a while I moved from hotel to hotel, pretending to sell paintings. Occasionally I spent a week at my parents' home hearing myself torn down, seduced, tempted to return to professional school and pursue a career that repelled me.

My palms were clammy all the time, I had horrible fantasies, slept a lot during the day, partied and lied all night, made friends in bars and at gallery openings. Then one day I woke up in a room in the Great Northern Hotel on Fifty-seventh Street in Manhattan and made the mistake of looking in the mirror. The face I saw terrified me—it was the face of a panicked animal in mid-flight. I stared at what should have been a reflection of myself and cried for help. All my pretenses about being a gallery owner, a Harvard intellectual, a traveler, a hustler fell apart. I remembered the name of an analyst someone had given me a year before and called her up.

Being able to call myself sick was a blessing. I temporarily relinquished responsibility for my actions and was able to step away from many messy entanglements. My choice of analyst was fortunate. I am a Jew from New York. I know all the tricks of language and intricacies of analysis and argumentation that can be used to avoid confronting uncomfortable truths. I used to compete wildly with other males, especially Jews, and still have some problems containing my competitive instincts toward males who are my contemporaries. My analyst was female, Protestant, and from the Midwest. All my defenses against being honest with myself, of protecting myself from other people's insights about my behavior were of no use with her. Her style, manner, sensibilities, sexuality were sufficiently out of my familiar mode to be strange but not particularly threatening. She wasn't the kind of person I had grown up with and not even in my wildest paranoid projections could she become one of my personal demons. She appeared to me throughout analysis as the good, gentle, undemanding mother. I fancied her calm, wise, and self-assured, although meeting her after the analysis was terminated I discovered her to be an intense, nervous, brilliant, and somewhat tortured person.

I think had my analyst been male and Jewish instead of female and Protestant a highly competitive verbal game would have developed between us, engaging me interminably in the worst aspects of my defenses against becoming an autonomous adult. As it was, the analytic situation was a cultural and intellectual displacement from my usual modes of functioning. The personal context was not the same as I experienced at home, in college, or running away. If anything, analyst/teacher embodied the softer aspects of my grandmother—but that's not an accurate description, for my grandmother was a hard-driving, demanding, tough, and strong peasant woman who fought to insure that her children, my father included, would make it in America. The analyst, on the other hand, seemed to me confident, undemanding, calm, and noncompetitive. That was a fantasy arising out of my needs, as she later pointed out to me. Toward the end of the analysis, when we were dealing with my image of her, she told me that no woman in this culture gets to be a physician and a psychiatrist without being competitive, hard-driving, tough. Maybe she was a lot like my grandmother after all. I needed to be blind to those aspects of her person during the analysis and accept her in the role of wise healer. Her own problems were not my concern at the time.

When I entered analysis I initially experienced a great relief of tension and pressure. For the first time in years I felt safe to grow at my own pace, discover my center, and become re-engaged with the world on terms that I could live up to. I accepted the fact that my life was sick and I wanted very much to become well.

Initially the two of us talked face to face. A lot of my confusion poured out—I didn't know what I wanted to make of my life, was terrified of loving and not loving, wanted and didn't want to be fully free of my parents. I hadn't dreamed for at least six months. The last dreams I remembered were horrible water dreams I had had during my flight to Europe. The dreams had me drowned over and over in a world swept with storms and floods. By the time I returned to the United States I neither dreamed nor read. I experienced so much continual anxiety that it was even impossible for me to focus on newspaper headlines long enough to understand them.

After a few sessions I took to lying on the traditional analyst's couch facing away from the doctor. The room was semi-dark and I faced a bookcase filled with books on psychology. Behind me my teacher sat, notebook in hand, smoking, sipping iced tea, and occasionally asking me questions and encouraging me to say whatever flowed into my mind. After a while I began to concentrate on dreaming and kept a dream book, a habit I have continued for the last twelve years.

In order to concentrate on analysis I had to get my external life in order, find a place to stay, keep away from people, and begin to do small things I cared about. In retrospect my parents were wonderfully helpful at the time, although I couldn't admit it then. They paid for the analysis although they didn't believe I needed psychiatric help and were shamed by the idea. They provided me with enough money to take a small apartment and buy food. This increased my dependence on them while I was learning how to lessen it—but there was no way I knew of then to escape that paradox.

As far as I could gather from the interpretations the analyst made, she was a reasonably orthodox Freudian. Occasionally I found some of her phallicizing of everything a bit annoying and irrelevant but she provided me with a safe environment in which I could begin to unfold. In retrospect, it wasn't her interpretations or the ideology she adhered to that assisted me. It was the time and space that analysis provided for me to explore my dreams, fantasies, preferences, affinities. I had spent a lot of time training and tuning my intellect and this was the first opportunity I had to nurture feeling, sensibility, intuition, and fantasy. I feel that the pause in my frenetic flight from responsibility provided by analysis gave me a chance to center my life that no other experience had provided. It gave me a chance to become intimate with myself and act on the basis of self-knowledge.

One of my earliest wishes was to become a school teacher. One of my fantasies at Harvard was to go to the Midwest upon graduation and teach fifth or sixth grade in a rural school and write in my free time. Once I was careless enough to reveal this fantasy to some friends and professors at Harvard, and they laughed and mocked it until I too laughed and mocked myself. Teaching school was beneath the dignity of a Harvard man, working with kids was for ladies or men who couldn't do anything else. My parents agreed, and whenever I hinted at my dream my father quoted Shaw: "He who can, does. He who cannot, teaches." The society downgraded the role of teacher of the young and I was trained at Harvard to accept that elitist judgment. I wasn't sure enough of myself to dare to live the fantasy. In analysis I could consider this wish without fear of being mocked or rejected and take the time and make the necessary internal preparation to act upon it despite social and familial pressures.

Analysis was not satisfying in itself to me. I wanted to finish up with it and get on with the business of living. I didn't want to transfer dependence on my parents and professors to dependence on the analyst. What analysis did in my life was temporarily stop my unhappy present, and let me explore my past in order to make a meaningful commitment to a personal future. It was a learning experience I threw myself into as totally as I had thrown myself into learning philosophy in the past.

I became a hermit for a while. My apartment became the center of the world. I stopped flight and replaced it by ritual while working toward some definition of a center. I cooked dinner for myself, recorded dreams, began to build small models out of balsa wood and make woodcuts, read a bit, concentrated on dreams and fantasies, listened to a lot of music. I filled up the day for the first several months of analysis with small rituals, all concerned with lowering my anxiety enough so that I could attend to inner voices.

In retrospect, what happened to me during the hour a day I spent with the doctor was only a part of a whole series of transformations I was undergoing. During the time of analysis I began to speak freely to myself. The mere pronouncing of my fears, self-doubts, hatreds, and frustrations out loud reassured me that it was all right to change. Within that situation love was not used as a weapon to manipulate me. I was accustomed to experiencing rejection whenever I did something my parents, friends, or teachers opposed, and I had come, before analysis, to the point of being unable to function because I wanted to be loved and yet be free to follow my own needs. It wasn't possible, since love was used and is used in our culture as a commodity that is exchanged for obedi-

ence and conformity. In analysis that manipulation was
replaced by silence, acceptance, and support. I was given
time to look at myself and rebuild.

The analysis didn't revolve about a particular trauma
or horrible early experience. Rather it consisted of my
rethinking and to the degree possible of re-experiencing
my growing up—not just the actual events of my life but
also the fantasies, wishes, the choices I never made, the
possibilities that I dreamed of living.

There was no single event or series of events that led
me to despair. It was rather a complex and tangled web
of myself, my parents, teachers, and friends that was created by the way the social and economic demands of this
culture managed to put us in the position of acting against
each other. As I came to accept the fact that it was possible
to be wrong, mistaken, or foolish occasionally and still
be worthy of love and respect—that is, as I came to experience self-love and self-respect based on intimacy with myself rather than upon other people's judgments about
my performances—I began to reach out cautiously beyond
my apartment and the analysis itself.

I decided to fulfill my old wish to be a teacher and
pounded the pavement looking for a teaching job. I felt
it was safe to work with children even though I wasn't
ready to begin to relate to adults again. I was afraid of
reverting to my old intellectual boisterousness and my
self-destructive self-pity. As I came through analysis I
began to see how I undid myself in social situations and
began to catch myself and laugh. For example, I could
tell when I was forcing someone I cared about into the
position of rejecting or pitying me. I could see myself
rejecting someone I wanted to like first so that he
wouldn't reject me later. The social games that were the
strategies of my uncentered functioning became too trans-
parent for me to indulge them with any conviction. Analysis enabled me to see myself as responsible to a large
degree for my own problems, and at the same time it

helped me not want to have those problems. In the past there was no doubt that I got some pleasure out of controlling and being controlled, and I needed to play those games in order to avoid facing a terror I lived with for ten years—that I was empty, that there was nothing to me, no center; that all my academic and political success, my cleverness and verbal facility, were nothing but an elaborately wrought surface that concealed a void.

Dusk has always been the worst time of day for me. For several years before my analysis I had severe anxiety attacks every day as darkness came. A sense of meaninglessness, intimations of death, nothingness, a void, crept into my throat. My palms became clammy. It happened no matter what I was doing, no matter how excited or positive I felt. As night settled in the anxiety faded and I could continue with my performance. It was just that zone between day and night that terrified me.

As I emerged from analysis and began to put my life together, the terror subsided somewhat. At present it is only occasional and metaphysical—a periodic reminder that death, physical and spiritual, is real and possible. The feeling has almost become an old friend who keeps me from forgetting the past and reminds me to be patient with the present and future.

The freedom I felt in analysis and the rituals I built for the rest of the day gave me time and space to think and dream and indulge my fantasies. Things began to come from within me—thoughts, affinities, desires. I broke my bonds with roles I was expected to play and didn't find a void at all but a rich and initially chaotic outflowing of love and curiosity. I wanted to make things with my hands, to look at things all over again, to act outside of or despite the judgment of others. When I got a job at the Reece School for the Severely Disturbed I felt that other than going into analysis itself, that was the first free act of my life.

Teaching at the school was difficult—I worked with

Dougie, Paul, and one other, self-hating boy. My own self-indulgent problems seemed insignificant compared with those devastated children. Yet teaching—figuring out ways of bringing the kids out of their isolation and into their selves and the world—was the first unmitigated joy I had known. Being at a school, teaching, talking with the kids, exploring the world, playing games, and watching people as they learned—it was like coming home. When I was at school I was there and nowhere else. I learned all the time, became less and less self-conscious and more aware that my old longing to teach was right. Despite the problems and frustrations, the hopelessness of helping those youngsters piece themselves together and fit in some world, I knew I belonged. During all the traumas of my analysis, during the times when I wanted to be dependent and feel helpless or wanted to smash the analyst and run back to mamma, Paris, even Harvard, it was teaching that held everything together and became a centering principle for my life. As I settled into myself and realized that I was a teacher, it became clear that the Reece School was not for me. I wanted to work with so-called normal kids, to bring myself into the center of life rather than patch up the rejections of our culture. After six months at the Reece School I enrolled at Teachers College, Columbia, in order to get a New York City teacher's license and fulfill my dream of teaching the sixth grade and writing in my spare time.

I learned a great deal about myself during analysis. However, there were other ways in which analysis was a dangerous context in which to rebuild my life. My analyst was a Freudian, had an ideology that centered on family relationships and personal trauma. Everything was interpreted in terms of personal need rather than cultural pressure. Life within the family thoroughly overrode life within the culture, which was not at all questioned. Discontent and anguish that arose from family problems were not distinguished from discontent and anguish that arose from a sense of the injustice and hypocrisy of the larger culture. However, it is necessary to distinguish personal and collective pain and not confuse neurotic problems about the authority of one's own parents, which can be worked out on a personal level, with problems of oppression within the society, which can only be worked out through collective action.

During analysis I learned (i.e., admitted and came to act upon) certain simple things about myself. There were some other things I was supposed to learn in order to be a successful analysand that I rejected. The things I learned were:

—I wanted to be independent of my parents.

—I didn't want to be independent.

—I couldn't live with this contradiction and do any work or grow as a person and therefore had to make a conscious choice and live with the consequences of that choice.

Part of being dependent consisted of pretending to be weak, inept, and powerless in order to be taken care of. This pretense invaded all aspects of my life—sexual, physical, and intellectual—and functioned with respect to my parents, professors, friends. It inevitably led to resentment, since I also pretended to be strong and powerful in order to assert a bogus independence. I had no experience with collective activity, with people supporting one another and therefore integrating dependency and independence into a whole where each individual was valued despite his or her personal insecurities.

Wild swings from childlike dependence to aggressive independence and irresponsibility are common in our lives, since there is no center within our culture which serves as a principle for mediating between dependency and independence—a person has to be both victim and executioner when competition is the highest moral value.

What I learned in analysis was to recognize myself as self-willed victim and executioner while playing those roles. I remember moaning about how impossible it was to get a job without ever bothering to look for one. I caught myself one day in the middle of feeling victimized and in the safety of the analyst's room faced myself as self-willed victim. Understanding that I made myself into a victim with my parents, that I allowed my professors to judge me because it was easier than coming to judge myself, it became necessary for me to ask myself whether I wanted to continue to make myself such a passive victim. This self-questioning put me in an awkward position with respect to myself. Every time I tried to whine to my parents so that they would feel sorry for me or give me money, or try to convince a woman to go to bed with me because I was such an unhappy soul, I would catch myself in the middle of the act. There was one part of me acting in the old ways and another observing the act and assuming responsibility for it. By assuming responsibility the act itself became undone, since I could no longer pretend to myself to be a victim. Occasionally I allowed myself to be victimized, only it was different. I knew I was playing weak and allowing myself to be indulged, could talk about that indulgence and control it so that resentment toward others did not develop. I found myself involved in many fewer hypocritical relationships simply because I could tell people that I was pretending to be weak or needed some indulgence at that moment and let them know that my characteristic mode was not being passive or victimized.

I also caught myself being an executioner and took direct responsibility for that act. I caught myself putting down people, taking pleasure in witnessing other people's weaknesses and mistakes, collaborating with others in making gossip that tore people down and undermined their work. If I needed to hurt others, I had to assume full responsibility and therefore worked on checking myself.

The problem with learning compassion in an analytic situation is that you work alone on your psyche. The analyst helps but there is no community, no peers. I was an isolated atom working to perfect my isolated soul so that although I grew kinder and more compassionate in my daily life it took other experiences beyond analysis to understand how to connect myself with other people's struggles and function in a collective manner.

I also began to learn in analysis how to change my behavior and live with the anxiety and fear that accompany change. I feel that most of my development has taken place subsequent to analysis, which primarily helped me set myself free of past ties and behavior that was self-destructive and provided me with some strategies for changing my behavior. In that analysis was successful for me. It did not, however, solve all the problems in my life or in the culture, did not make me a good writer or teacher or lover. It performed a modest but essential function—that of releasing me from an unhappy personal history so that I could grow as a person. Many people I have known expect more of analysis and become bitter when it does not automatically make them competent to lead a new life. Those expectations are wrong and foolish—analysis at its best can randomize the past, develop some strength in the present to deal with fear and anxiety, and put people in a position to work on their own future.

Many of the things I learned through analysis have served me very well over the twelve years since my analysis. However, there were a number of attitudes that emerged as part of a healthy life as defined by psychoanalysis that are politically, socially, and personally dangerous and have led me to believe that alternatives to analysis and contemporary therapy in general have to and can be developed.

My analyst, whose orientation was Freudian, looked at events in my present life almost exclusively in terms of their relationship to my personal past and interpreted them as relating to family sexual competition. It was as if my family—mother, father, brother, sister, and occasionally grandparents—was an isolated cell separate from culture or the larger society. Influences on my development—friends, teachers, heroes, superheroes—were all interpreted as masks of my family members, when often they were representations of a world outside the family that I aspired to join. One of my recurrent fantasies as a child was that I was an orphan, that the people who claimed they were my parents were not my real parents. I wasn't the only person with those fantasies. My two closest friends, Bobby and Ronnie, believed in their own ways that they existed beyond the small definition of self imposed upon them within their immediate families. Together we put together a Spiritual League compounded partly of comicbook ideology and partly of our needs to experience more than the struggle of our parents to survive, become wealthy, and assimilate to American culture.

The League was a childhood utopia, a children's world that tried to be different from the surrounding and all-encompassing world of parents. It was a place where I could experiment with behavior that was not sanctioned by the adults as well as act free of adult judgment. It was a place where we could teach ourselves and one another and escape from the world of our parents. If we were supposed to be good, docile, academically successful young boys, in the League we were able to be slightly wicked and wild, and free of judgments about our intelligence. We were free to develop rituals, paint on our walls, experiment with chemicals—all without supervision or structures imposed by the adults. I feel that being able to live part of the day in that small world with just a few friends helped me resist worlds imposed upon me from without. However, my parents' world was powerful too, and the pull toward conformity with that world coexisted within me with the pull toward a freer, funnier, less grimly competitive world. This conflict manifested itself as neurotic paralysis in my early adult life.

During my analysis I struggled to come in contact with the secret world of the League and found myself led away from it into a world of sexual jealousies and competition, of battles for familial affection and power, which were certainly part of my past but not the whole of it.

It wasn't only that my past was interpreted exclusively in family terms, so that all of my relationships were looked at as variations on family affairs (i.e., as transference). My present was also interpreted in the same way, so that every event could be tied back to the past and looked at as controlled by past events.

I remember feeling terribly small and overwhelmed by Rockefeller Center one day. The hopelessness of being heard over the traffic and the buildings that scaled people down to the size of ants made me feel hopeless and depressed. It seemed at that moment that life in a city such as New York was insane. I tried to explain these feelings to my analyst and to look into whether it was indeed possible to change New York City or whether processes were at work that were beyond human control. I felt that I was trying to work out present problems and she felt I was resisting.

Resistance is a favorite and dangerous weapon therapists use to invalidate certain experiences of their patients. If a therapist believes he knows the origin and psychological significance of events in the life of his patient, and if the therapist's views of significance are not the same as the patient's, then the patient is considered to be using "defense mechanisms" and to be resisting the truths of therapy and the help of the therapist—there is no way in this context for the patient to speculate freely and come to terms with his or her own experience. In the case I mentioned above the doctor told me to relax and free associate to tall buildings, and to a feeling of smallness.

I resisted, wanted to remain in the present, but the more I refused to give in to free association, the more she built up the case for my resistance and implied that an important liberating truth was being covered up. I yielded after a while and gave her what I knew she wanted—an elaborate chain of associations leading to my feelings of sexual inadequacy, and to the notion somehow that Rockefeller Center represented my father's penis. Yet my father was victimized by New York City no less than I, and the building was his enemy as well as mine. I gave the doctor what she wanted and after that session played the game a lot as I was preparing to leave analysis. I no longer wanted to be sick—there was too much to be done.

One danger of analysis and therapy in general is that it can provide the mechanisms of and excuses for perpetual psychic sickness and dependence. If everything is referred back to past traumas, if people believe that their present dysfunctional behavior is explained somehow by past pathology it is easy for them to fall into the attitude of believing they can't do anything about their lives. They use therapeutic understanding as an excuse for not acting.

Just the other day a close friend of mine told me she was splitting up with her husband. She liked him, they got along well, there was no other person involved. But she explained to me that since she was an only child she never learned how to share and therefore couldn't enjoy living together with anyone else. She had a lot of experience being in therapy and had at least four different versions of the same excuse for not changing. She didn't believe that she could teach herself to share or learn to behave differently. Knowledge of the past did not liberate her; on the contrary, it seemed to have enchained her.

What happened to my friend is not uncommon. Many people who enter therapy believe that knowledge of the history of their problems will automatically liberate them. This, of course, never happens—except perhaps in the case of some hysterical paralysis caused by particular instances of severe psychological trauma. Because these expectations are disappointed, many people become resigned to living neurotic and unhappy lives and end up being resigned to discussing and making jokes about their inability to change. Others trip from therapist to therapist, still looking for liberation to come in a package.

Therapists encourage this, since they do not share the same lives and struggles as their patients. They usually define their territory as the individual psyche and its family history as if this can be separated from life in the present, from the culture, and from the fact that no healthy life is possible in a sick culture.

When the therapist deals with the individual in isolation and is not part of the patient's community in other ways, the goal of health becomes strictly an individual matter and therefore tends to lead the patient toward adapting himself or herself to the world as it presently exists. Another goal is to be able to relate to people on a personal level without abusing them or being threatened by them. Very few therapists see as a goal enabling people to be sane revolutionaries, able to sustain anger and a sense of justice without being consumed by them, and unwilling to tolerate this culture as it is presently constituted. The goal of most therapy is to produce people who are harmless to others and who see fulfillment in completely personal terms. I see this as disease, not health, as a form of separated existence. Unfortunately these days the sane maladapted revolutionary is as close to being healthy as is possible in an unhealthy world. Health is not a matter of individual happiness or contentment but a matter of the relationships between an individual and the immediate community he or she belongs to as well as involvement with the needs of humanity.

I did not find that psychoanalytic interpretations of my behavior added much to the bare facts of being dependent and wanting to be independent. Nor did they help me change my behavior. That was work I had to do in the present, with all the pain and uncertainty it involved. The fact that I was in analysis, that I could stop the past and randomize the present while coming in contact with myself through calling myself sick is what gave me the opportunity to change my life. I took that opportunity, accepted the pain, refused the excuse of being messed up in the past, and taught myself to behave differently.

The most significant moment in my analysis was probably the one time my analyst dropped her professional and theoretical principles and came directly to my aid. Analysts are not supposed to intervene in the lives of their patients. They confine their roles to the one-to-one analytic situation as the patient learns to act with others outside the analytic situation.

After a few months of analysis I began to re-enter the world. One day a woman who once terrified and possessed me showed up at my door and attempted to take over my life, or so I thought at the time. I had an impulse to give up everything and become absorbed in her world once again. I also had an impulse to kill her and make an end of my possession once and for all. During my time in analysis I talked about her, free associated, going back to my childhood, repeated a thousand times that the fear of leaving her and the inability to be with her could be explained by my past. I understood that all I had to do was tell her to go away and mean it, to close my door and my heart and I would be free. However, I was so terrified of her that I was paralyzed. Teaching became my only solace, as all my other resolves to change began to fall away. I saw her on one occasion and was devastated for days after, began to quarrel with my parents, to drink insanely, to let my apartment and my life in general fall apart. One day in desperation I asked the doctor to do for me what she had previously told me was alien to her role as analyst —that is, to act on my behalf and tell the woman who terrified me to get out of my life. She agreed, and they met. I never found out what happened between them but have always fantasized it as a battle for my soul that was somehow both within me and between two people outside of me at the same time. The woman left after that meeting, and I returned to the business of getting my life straight. When I saw her again several years later, the spell was no longer effective; she looked smaller, plainer, less powerful, and in greater pain than I remembered. We didn't have much to say to each other.

The fact that my doctor/teacher went beyond her theories and acted in my behalf gave me the strength to act as well. I felt safe and protected by her and strong myself at the same time. In a way, my going along with her psychoanalytic interpretations and not turning the situation into an intellectual battle about Freud's ideas was a gift to her in exchange for that crucial help she gave me. In mystical terms she showed me that her magic as a person was stronger than the other woman's and that the side of me which identified with her and strove to be independent could therefore also be stronger than the side that wanted to feel weak and dependent.

When my analysis terminated after a year and a half my life was quite different from what it had been before therapy. It's not that I was happy or that I knew all there was to know about myself, or that all my old neurotic conflicts were resolved and eliminated from my life. Rather, it was that I had become rooted in some meaningful work, had begun to care for myself, and was open to learn about myself and other people. I wasn't afraid to be wrong or concerned about being empty. I got a hold on myself, took responsibility for the way I acted, and believed that I could change. All my old problems with dependency and with doubts about my relations with other people persist, but they do not dominate my life, which now feels centered and consistent. I can be honest with people for the most part, although occasionally I lie under pressure; I know how to help others and do, although I still get some uneasy pleasure out of experiencing other people's failures. Analysis didn't purify me and I regress occasionally.

There were innumerable occasions at Other Ways for me to fall into confused, draining, exploitative relationships with others. Some of the people were willing to assume slave roles, others were willing to subjugate me or assume power over my voice. Others wanted to control and be controlled at the same time; to make love and fight; to stand together as comrades while trying to destroy the whole group. The criterion I have learned to use, and which functions automatically on a visceral level, has to do with the energy involved in a relationship with someone else. If I feel my energy being dissipated, exhausted, consumed—if there is no exchange of psychic energy or at least some equilibrium of energy established —I withdraw my feelings and direct my energy and attention another way. The draining of psychic energy (or its opposite, the bloating of oneself with someone else's energy) seems to me a sign of the presence of exploitation and oppression, which I want no part of. I usually act on this visceral response first, withdraw, and then analyze the situation afterwards. It is possible to be wrong about other people's intentions, but their emotional effect on one's own psyche is undeniable.

Another important insight I achieved during analysis was understanding that loving, caring for oneself and others, and becoming autonomous could be learned and that, equally, fears, anxieties, a sense of personal powerlessness and dependency could be unlearned, though with considerable effort. This meant that it was not possible for me to remain passive about my own behavior or think of myself as buffeted by fate or controlled by my parents. It didn't mean, however, that there is no coercion or oppression in the world—only that there was no reason for me to act in complicity with oppressors.

I think it is no accident that I met and fell in love with Judy, my wife, right after my analysis terminated. Before going through analysis she would not have attracted me, since she wanted neither to control me nor be controlled by me. My wild swings from dependency to outrageous flight made a stable and growing relationship impossible. By the time my analysis ended I had enough of a view of myself to know when I was being self-destructive or pushing someone away from me or making unreasonable demands. I could check myself, laugh a bit at my anxieties and occasional regressions, and live with someone who grew independent of me yet with me. I could translate my desire to love and be loved into small acts of kindness.

In addition to the many things I learned about myself, analysis provided me with the basis upon which I have built strategies for my own survival and development. The analysis was focused on my past, and since analysis I have had to refocus on the present, not by denying the power the past has over present action but by understanding that the past can be changed through action in the present. A technique I use for helping me act sensibly, which arose out of the habit of attending to dreams and fantasies developed during analysis, consists of articulating in a safe place and in as specific terms as possible what it is I fear/can't do/am doing but don't want to continue doing/is a source of unhappiness and anxiety/needs to be changed in my behavior. Having a safe place to face one's problems is crucial, since it often requires dreams, fantasies, free associations, imaginings, writing, painting, or drawing to make something painful and threatening explicit. It is important to let oneself go, to accept one's own weaknesses and failures as well as one's wildest hopes. It takes time and often silence. It also takes being as comfortable, secure, and un-self-conscious as possible. I have a special spot where I can lie down, face the wall, and let myself go undisturbed. I also have a study, which in many ways is an image of my soul. The room is a safe place for me, a place where I write and dream and listen to music. I retreat to the study to deal with anxiety, depression, fear, failure. Sometimes I talk to my wife about what is on my mind, but I have found it necessary to do most of my work on myself in private.

Once I have articulated a specific problem or focused on a particular action I want to do differently, I imagine performing that act, not once but a thousand times, imagine being defeated, rejected, attacked—all the worst possible consequences as well as the best ones. I encourage anxiety, try to experience the fear and nervousness the real act might produce, and in private force myself to live through it. At that point I find that it is necessary to emerge from myself and sneak a little action in, do something very specific that is different from what I would have done in the past. I initiate the change and wait for the consequences, which are usually less severe than my imagination made them out to be.

For me a great deal of anxiety accompanies change, as well as guilt and a desire to retreat or disappear. Even if the new act provokes no direct hostility toward oneself, the moments or hours after changing are usually difficult to bear. Let me give an example:

Every once in while I initiate a conference having to do with changing the schools. I end up playing a central role in planning and fund raising, often assuming too much responsibility. I promise people that things are all taken care of, that there is enough money to take care of expenses; usually the promises can be kept. However, occasionally problems arise—money can't be raised, facilities become unavailable, speakers who promised to show cancel out. At that point it is hard for me to tell the rest of the planning group that I cannot deliver on my promise. My impulse is either to pretend to be weak and powerless and tell the others the truth in a way that will make them feel sorry for me, or to become aggressive and tell the truth while accusing the others of not taking enough responsibility. Of course, the most sensible way of functioning is to tell the truth without trying to defend myself and then begin to work out the problem with the others. The fear of others' anger and rejection is paralyzing. These days, when I screw up I rehearse in imagination truth-telling, let the anxiety develop in private, practice the words I intend to use (although in actuality it usually comes out differently), and then force myself to act in the most sensible way. Usually no problem arises when I tell simple truths. However, after the event is over and everyone else has moved beyond my failure and begun to plan for other ways of dealing with the problem, guilt sets in. I fantasize other people's rejection of me, feel like doing something to prove myself inferior; that one minor instance of potential rejection generalizes itself so that other insecurities, remembrances of past experiences of rejection often flood back. In order to deal with this global anxiety I have developed ways of re-establishing contact with myself, with the center—I let the anxiety develop, welcome and expect the fears, and go to my safe place and sit with the pain.

The easiest way to deal with the pain on a temporary basis is to drown it by drinking or smoking dope. However, the only long-term way to deal with anxiety that results from insecurity is to live with it, accept it and learn to function despite it, and discover that one has not been destroyed. I like to sit in my study, turn on music, relive the event in fantasy, going over and over the fact that telling a simple truth is not a major problem. Occasionally I push matters further and imagine that rejection and hostility resulted (which occasionally happens). It is not necessary to be loved by everyone and not healthy to want to be. It is often more important that truth be told and rejection accepted than that people continue to pretend to care for each other and function in a deceitful manner.

After acting differently once and surviving, it is necessary to continue to act in a different manner while paying attention to the anxiety involved before, during, and after the act. Gradually the anxiety decreases as the act becomes habit, until finally there is not enough anxiety remaining to command attention. At this point it is probably important to focus on some other uncomfortable aspect of one's behavior and change that. After a while it becomes possible for a person to ritualize changing behavior so that as a matter of course one focuses on nonfunctional and cruel ways of behaving, changes them in fantasy, actually acts differently, deals with subsequent anxiety, acts again, and by virtue of the effort grows and assumes increasing responsibility for one's behavior. It seems crucial, however, that a person have a safe place to do the inner work in order to change behavior in the external world.

There are many reasons not to want to assume the burden of changing oneself, especially if life is somewhat rewarding and comfortable. It is easy to be obsessed with personal pleasure and growth and thereby ignore the world, avoiding social and political conflict whenever possible. Analysis in many ways encourages preoccupation with the self exclusive of its political and humane obligations to others not immediately involved in one's life.

The avoidance of conflict, especially when such charged issues as racism or oppression are involved, is an understandable stance. People in our society fall into the habit of retreating from problems and try to avoid pain even when the pain might lead to growth or elimination of oppression.

One evening several years ago, Jerry and Tom, two staff members at Other Ways, were arguing over whether open education made any sense for black kids. Jerry said that the open classroom was all hippy bullshit and that black kids needed tough discipline, that they got away with doing whatever they wanted in school anyway, that they needed to be forced to develop skills. He argued that someone has to whip the kids into shape instead of indulging them.

Tom countered by saying that black people in the United States had enough slavery, that they didn't have to treat their own kids like slaves, and that the kids would respond to a warm and open situation where they were given the opportunity to grow at their own rates.

Jerry countered that that was jive, that Tom was white at heart and that black kids have no respect for teachers who let them do whatever they want to do.

At that point Tom turned to me and asked me what I thought.

I went into a conciliatory speech on how kids need warmth and the opportunity to grow but also need to have demands made on them. I tried to put together the notion of choice and the notion of discipline, the need for free choice and the need for adults to make certain decisions. I short, I tried to make everyone right, because the arguing was getting to me. I was tired of conflict and screaming.

And Jerry and Tom were tired of my bullshit. Tom laughed and said, "There goes Herb splitting the zone again."

I asked him what he meant, and he explained that in professional football the defensive backs play zones. The best and slickest receivers try to run the line between zones and therefore confuse the coverage. There I was, he said, confusing the coverage and slipping out of the conflict like a liberal.

For a long time I split the zone whenever I could, avoiding conflict, taking a stand only when pushed against the wall, wanting everything to be adjudicated and worked out rationally. I pretended to listen to both sides of an argument, see the justice in the "other side's" viewpoints, claim that everyone was entitled to his own opinion—all of this, however, essentially to avoid acting to change some intolerable circumstances that are at the core of our society.

We are surrounded by injustice, racism, poverty, pollution; the liturgy of horrors has been repeated so often recently that it has little impact. There is another truth, however, for many middle-class individuals like me. We are equally surrounded by wealth, comfort, a measure of luxury. We can travel, play at times, feel all is well with the world if only we restrict our vision to the immediate surroundings and shut out the world. It is easier to limit our experience and close ourselves to the total world than to face the moral implications of the horrors we are perpetrating on others and on the physical world.

It is possible to close oneself down and reject or remain indifferent to the world. Many people in power are closed in that way, and many ordinary people struggle to remain closed, although they are constantly bombarded by the realities of war, racism, sexism, exploitation. They absolve themselves of all blame and angrily accuse hippies, militants, radicals, and others of stirring up trouble.

However, there are many people who are not fully closed, who have fine moral sensibilities, and a great capacity for guilt, who occasionally look at the world as a whole with pain and compassion, yet whose main characteristic is to use reason and argument to avoid the necessity of acting in bold and personally dangerous ways. "Liberals" is the condescending label attached to the timid though often cantankerous people who see the need to change the world but are too comfortable or too scared to assume the personal responsibility.

A while ago there was a meeting on standardized testing at the Berkeley Unified School District. During the meeting I advocated refusing to take the state-mandated tests and replacing them with more sensible and less biased measures of student competence. One of the high school administrators disagreed. He claimed that although the tests were racist, we ought to go along with them while giving our own tests as well. He felt that it made no sense to fight the test at present. Yet he sympathized with the black people in the room whose children would be subjected to the instrument. He held at one moment in his

life a distaste for racist tests and a rationalized unwilling-
ness to do battle to eliminate them.

My mother used to tell me in the midst of a heated argument that we weren't disagreeing, only discussing. She
wanted to believe that both of us were right, that we were
not actually engaged in conflict, and that if things were
just left alone, "everything would come out right in the
end." I have heard that phrase used thoughtlessly many
times by people as a justification for their inaction. A
phrase indicating the opposite, such as, "It's hopeless,"
or "There's nothing I can do about it anyway," or "I'm
only one person," is also used to justify disengagement.

Separated existence helps this culture perpetuate itself.
However, because the separation isn't total and moral sensibility sometimes invades the working environment, many
people live under constant and unresolvable tension. The
tension will only occasionally be relieved by inconspicuous
acts of generosity and kindness. Perhaps the occasional
release of tension needed by separated beings explains the
role of charity in our culture. The small donation to a
United Fund Drive, the support of a Vietnamese child
burned by our bombs, the donation to the NAACP or
CORE relieve the tension of paralyzed activity and substitute for the process of integrating the whole of one's life.

[6]

Liberality—the need for interminable talk, for infinite
consideration of all aspects of a situation—is a strategy for
delaying growth while avoiding on the one hand the
pain of becoming thoroughly closed, and on the other the
struggle of being whole. Most of us have liberal tendencies.
It is easier for people with moral pretensions to entertain
pangs of conscience and the nagging sense that one ought
to act while living in relative comfort than it is to live in
comfort and remain blind to the world. It satisfies a
need many people seem to have for being identified

with just rather than cynical action. However, it is difficult to remain paralyzed and comfortable for long. Sooner or later the world comes closer and closer, and people have to choose whether they will be oppressors or fight against them.

A timid life in the middle can be sustained if the world stays away and if one's inner energy somehow becomes diverted by games of the intellect. That is why in the protected, tenuring, and verbal environment of the university it has been, until recently, popular and fashionable to be liberal and inactive.

From the perspective of my central image, that of the process of centering, liberal being is a timid form of existence that tries to avoid integrating by the overdevelopment of verbal facility. For many people liberality is only a stage before they plunge into the battle for a saner world. It was for me. For others it is a stage before they angrily close themselves off and indulge their intolerance and hatred. And finally for some people a timid, slightly pained existence can be maintained until they die.

[7]

Timid existence, however, is a luxury not everyone can afford. In our culture there are some individuals who are torn apart, rendered hopeless in their very being by what is done to them. These people are driven to kill, either themselves or others, because they were not allowed to grow, because their centers were uprooted and smashed by threatened, closed, and sometimes even timid liberal "good" citizens. A particular instance of the process of devastation haunts me. Akmir was the friend of a former student of mine. He was seventeen when we met and had been out of school for a year. He had just become connected with the Blood Brothers, a black separatist group in New York City, and was beginning to take command of his life. That year he began to write, returned to school, and started to think about college, managed to get some work, and tutored a number of younger kids. Akmir was an extremely sensitive and perceptive young man. He was strong physically and looked strong. But his manner was quiet, gentle, and slightly ironic. His desire to become a psychologist made all the sense in the world.

I remember once asking Akmir to teach the son of a friend of mine karate. He met the young boy and after one lesson said that the boy needed something other than karate. The way he put it was, "Giving that kid karate is like putting a machine gun in the hands of a killer." He offered to help the boy in other ways.

By the end of the school year Akmir had enough credits to graduate from high school. He was admitted to Queens Community College and set up a job for the next year. Then came the first blow—the principal of his high school, a good liberal man, refused to give Akmir his diploma. The reason was his history of truancy two years before. According to the principal (I was present at the meeting), Akmir could only receive his diploma after proving he was a responsible citizen. This meant specifically that Akmir had to (1) take a class, any class, at a night high school and produce proof of his regular attendance, and (2) show proof that he held a job for six months. It was crazy—the same man who urged his students to get high school diplomas because they wouldn't find jobs without them was withholding the ticket to a job he was demanding as a qualification for the diploma.

There was nothing either Akmir or I could do to move the man. The same day Akmir heard he wouldn't graduate, he received a letter from Queens Community College asking for proof of high school graduation, which was necessary for enrollment. Three days later he received a draft notice. It was infuriating. Every way he turned he was prevented from growing. The self he worked so hard to build was crushed temporarily. He was in despair. The last time I saw him he seemed on the verge of tears or maybe ready to explode in violence—he wanted to cry or kill. He didn't know where to turn. Nothing his friends could do would move the institutions or their servants. Two days later he died of an overdose of heroin.

A number of times in my life I have been driven into a corner or had the feeling of being stalked. For example, there was a time a few years ago when Other Ways could find no place to function without being driven out by police, building inspectors, health inspectors, school bureaucrats. Our school wandered from place to place, and there was never time to develop a physical center. The staff became paranoid, and the students were at loose ends. As a group and as individuals as well, we were driven and reacted either by feeling ready to give up the whole battle or ready to turn violent and get revenge. I know some people who have been driven underground by F.B.I. and police harassment who have responded in the same way.

When you are not allowed to develop, are systematically deprived of space, time, food, rest, and love, life becomes consumed with frustration and anger. The damming up of a natural instinct to grow results in homicidal and suicidal feelings and actions.

There are many men and women in ghettos and barrios throughout this country who have systematically been prevented from developing. It is not merely crowded homes, hostile streets, poverty. The schools create stupidity, undermine the confidence of the young, and eventually drive the kids out into the streets, where they are harassed by the police. There are a number of teenagers who wander about New York City looking for a welcoming place to grow, to live without being harassed, to develop their skills and sensibilities. After a while being chased and deprived can break the soul. People can and do give up their selves, abandon their centers, and become the Living Dead. They dope or drink themselves into not having to grow any more, or they let rage and resentment consume their lives and become murderers. Vestiges of the center remain, however; people constantly at the most unexpected moments make efforts to "pull themselves to-gether," an apt image for repairing the damaged center.

Being devastated temporarily is a common experience. For many individuals there are moments of devastation when whole lives are wiped out or stopped up. A sudden economic disaster, a draft notice, a fire, the death of some-one depended upon, the discovery of betrayal, a major de-feat in love or work, the death of a child can all tempo-rarily devastate people and call a stop to their active lives for a while. We become the Living Dead, unable to work or make love or laugh. Mourning is a form of dying one-self because of the death of another or because of some other nonreplaceable loss. We mourn and then after a while begin to come alive again.

Under conditions of oppression and poverty it is dif-ficult ever to come alive. The state of mourning induced by oppression, involving as it does a mourning for the self that is hedged in and not allowed to develop, turns stale after a while and becomes compounded with frustration, resentment, hatred, and self-hatred. There is no end to oppression in the lives of many individuals and therefore no end to mourning. Only when oppression is opposed does the period of mourning end and the self begin to grow. This can happen to individuals without their chang-ing their material, spatial, or temporal circumstances. A new consciousness, an awareness of the possibility of engag-ing battle instead of being a passive victim, can awaken the vestiges of the self and push people into activity. Too often, however, a change of consciousness does not occur, and death in the form of suicide and murder is chosen.

There are many pathological forms of noncentered exist-ence—most of which we all manifest, if only temporarily, at one time or another throughout our lives. Just as Albert Camus described the acceptance of an all-encompassing ideology as philosophical suicide, one could call the abandonment of a coherent and focused commitment to personal and social change and growth the *suicide of the center*. Throughout this section I have described some ways in which we can destroy ourselves or withdraw from struggles that engage others. If centering can be thought of as the point of reference, then the following diagram is a convenient way of summarizing the forms of escape from responsible lives aspiring toward health that most of us assume at different times in our lives.

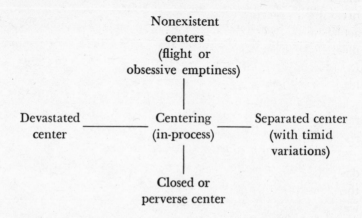

Nonexistent
centers
(flight or
obsessive emptiness)

Devastated   Centering   Separated center
center   (in-process)   (with timid
variations)

Closed or
perverse center

At the top is the nonexistent center, whose polar opposite can be seen as the totally closed center. A variant of the nonexistent center is the center totally outside of the self. On the horizontal plane is another opposition, that between the devastated or murderous center and the separated, timid, or liberal center.

[8]

So far I have been concerned with the pathology of the center and have only hinted at what a healthy existence would be like. Four words come to mind in characterizing healthy forms of being: wholeness, openness, specificness, and commitment. Let me elaborate on these concepts and piece together a picture of a balanced life in process. Then perhaps the pathological variants (many of which are considered normal in our culture) can be seen as deviations from or exaggerations of this form of existence.

To start with, *wholeness* means being conscious of the different components of one's existence; means keeping social and historical awareness present along with personal and psychological need and insight; means attempting to bind together the internal and external, physical and spiritual, conscious and unconscious, cultural and personal, communal and individual aspects of one's life no matter what pain or conflict is involved. This last means breaking away from the dichotomized life that is one characteristic of the "Western" way of living. Wholeness also means utilizing what one knows about the self and the world instead of filing away whatever knowledge might lead to conflict and change.

The contraries of wholeness are denial, schizoid separatedness, willful blindness, forgetfulness, evasive hypocrisy, compartmentalization of life.

There are many examples of what wholeness implies in daily life. For example, wholeness means keeping in mind the oppression others are experiencing and the subtle ways in which one's own acts are in complicity with the oppressor. Thus, consuming products produced by Dow, fruit grown on United Fruit Company plantations, wine produced by growers refusing to sign contracts with Farm Workers Unions puts one in complicity with corporate capitalism in the exploitation of the poor. Being whole means recognizing this fact and acting to undo the complicity by selective purchasing, following boycotts, examining the origins of the products used in daily life. This requires effort that many people find bothersome because of the picayune detail involved. It also makes some people seem silly in the eyes of others and often can be annoying and inconvenient. I remember going to wine store after wine store trying to find some cheap brand of table wine that wasn't being boycotted. Every once in a while I caught myself thinking "damned Chicanos," wishing the whole issue of the boycott would dissolve rather than inconvenience me. Racism and intolerance creep in everywhere, especially for anyone sensitive to the small ways in which our daily lives support the economic structure of the society. It is very easy to assume a pure stance on larger issues and fall into habits that contradict one's ideology in daily life.

Wholeness implies caring for the health of the world as an ecosystem. It means being aware of how one's garbage relates to the pollution of the world, how one's insatiable wants contribute to sanctioning overproduction and the accumulation of waste on the planet. It also means acting to take care of the earth household in every way possible, which again implies both the details of recycling one's own wastes whenever possible and the larger commitment to change the irresponsible aspects of our social systems that sanction and even encourage waste and overproduction. I am writing this of course on the same day I will drive to school, throw away uneaten food, use more electricity than necessary, smoke a pipe or cigar and perform many unhealthy and dangerous acts. Being right in all one's actions or doing what is healthy is a form of fanaticism in the context of an unhealthy society. I can imagine people so involved in not polluting, damaging, oppressing, or exploiting that their lives become completely impoverished and inactive. At present there is no way short of spiritual death to avoid conflict or live an unchanging life. Wholeness involves being aware of the interrrelationships of one's physical and spiritual, social and personal, cultural and individual aspects. It means developing consistency and striving to create a world where one's own growth and development does not necessitate the destruction of other people or of the earth itself.

Wholeness should not be mistaken for completedness, which implies that a person reaches a final fixed self. Completedness is a form of death—a putting an end to growth—whereas wholeness implies a continuing and evolving responsiveness to the totality of experience one is capable of encompassing.

This continuing responsiveness leads to *openness*, which accompanies and in some forms is just another way of describing the condition of wholeness. Openness means being able to face one's own inner contradictions and being able to change; it means learning from experience; it means being able to face new and unexpected experiences, on the one hand, and being able to respond in new ways to old conditions; it means being able to be wrong, acknowledge that fact and change; it means being aware of others without needing to fit them into one's own schema; it means being able to explore many different possibilities both within oneself and in the world and being sufficiently in contact with oneself to recognize *affinities* for ways of being and resonances with forms of activity so that centering, the discovery of vocation, sensibility, and style, can emerge. Finally, it means acknowledging on the level of one's being that life and flux are one and the same, that short of death there is no final form to one's being—it means being attuned to time and change, on the one hand, and to one's own centering of the process of living; it is a way of describing a cumulating process, a life of learning and giving, a social and personal form of evolving with a definition and a structure instead of a directionless wandering in a closed, fixed, unchanging being.

From the combination of openness and wholeness emerges the paradox of *commitment*. If we see the whole —the world in misery, on the one hand, and the infinite and gratifying possibilities for the development of self and community, on the other, and if we choose to remain whole and open, then we must be committed to personal growth and social and cultural change. We must come to some uneasy balance between personal growth and social commitment, a balance that is constantly reassessed according to inner needs and social demands.

This brings me to the fourth component of a healthy

life, which is *specificness*. It is not enough to be aware of
the whole or have an intellectual grasp of the problems of
growth and social change. One must also act upon what
one knows in many specific ways. One must act to change
oneself and not expect change to come through a book,
a sudden revelation, or a therapist. The earth will be preserved, oppression will be minimized, people will be liberated only through continuous, consistent, committed
actions on a very small scale as well as a large one. It is
in the specifics of one's life, the day-by-day acts, that the
self is revealed and the world either remade or destroyed.

There is a paradox involved in the question of commitment and specificness. Being open to the possibilities of
experience and being able to learn imply the possibility of
commitment to a skill, craft, art, or science that can be
fully absorbing and continually growing in depth and
intensity. Being whole means one sees the personal commitment in the light of others, of the society, the culture,
and the world. This might mean that some personal
growth demands modification in the light of the need to
confront oppression. There is only a finite amount of
time and energy available to each person, and what I
have called commitment makes the allocation of resources
an unending problem. Given the nature of the present
world, to remain open, whole, specific, and committed
means to accept conflict as an integral part of being. It
implies a continual re-examination of one's skills, talents,
and resources in the perhaps chimerical quest to develop
a full-centered self and a humane society and culture.

I have been successful enough in my career recently to
abandon old commitments and become a respected and
predictable education expert. Money is not a problem in
my life at the moment, nor is love or lack of roots or any
of the metaphysical problems of prolonged adolescence.
I could fly back to Spain or live in retreat in the country
—do most anything I cared to and yet I hang in and continue to battle with myself and with the society that

trained me as a child. Sometimes I feel like going back to the days when I taught in Harlem and could lock my classroom door and limit my world to what passed inside that room. However, I continue to be worried about the whole and willing to take risks to change things without being so obsessed by the wretchedness of much of human existence as to be unable to function well in small ways every day. The tension of such a marginal life often gets me down. Without the rewards I receive from teaching and writing there would be no way to sustain the other larger battles I have joined.

It is extremely difficult to sustain a whole, committed, open, and active life in our culture—that is, to be healthy. There are too many rewards for oppressing others or merely remaining blind to the circumstances of one's own comfort as well as too many risks consequent upon defiance for many people to choose to remake the culture and their selves. Overriding the rewards for conformity and the punishment for opposition is the fear of one's own disposability. People are thrown away so relentlessly that all of us live with constant fears of rejection and do the craziest things to try to create situations where we belong or at least feel only minimally threatened. It is not insane to think of everyone in this culture as a potential enemy, and for many people it is an absolutely realistic wariness that will protect them from being devastated by the decisions of others.

I find myself, almost as an involuntary response, looking suspiciously at people who have managed to secure and maintain legitimized power. My fantasies are full of plots and betrayals, some of which actually occur. People turn on each other all the time, feed on each other's failures and weaknesses. It is not sick but merely sensible to maintain a moderately paranoid suspicion of anyone one has not known for a long time and under conditions of crisis.

Because of the small value put on our lives in the overall functioning of this society it is necessary to develop ways of protecting ourselves. Logically we should choose to get to the roots of our insecurities and change the oppressive and unhappy circumstances of our lives. However, because we have all grown up in the culture, have gone to school, have learned our sexual and social roles, have developed our eating habits and table manners as well as attitudes toward work and social responsibility here, whenever we try to change things, we behave in the culturally dominant ways despite ourselves. Most people are not conscious of the ways the culture pervades their lives and conditions their behavior and therefore don't know how to change themselves. Cultural conditioning is literally drunk in with one's mother's milk (or in the case of our culture, with bottled, homogenized, and pasteurized milk). Not only do we have enemies but we also behave like them, because we have been trained to be each other's enemies and accept those roles even when going about so-called revolutionary or countercultural activity. We are intolerant, competitive, murderous while mouthing the opposite ideas.

Recently I witnessed a particular hostile and futile debate among a group of free school people. They were arguing about which of the schools were the best and came close to fighting. However, they were all in need of money and needed one another's support and some collective action in order to survive. The need for mutual support was the reason they came together, and yet they didn't know how not to compete. At the end of the meeting these people were as isolated from one another as before, and their prospects for survival were very slim.

I have seen the same thing happen when groups of men and women get together to take collective action. The men compete with each other to impress the women— they make sexual invitations and act angry or surprised if they are accepted; the couples eye each other jealously —and nothing politically necessary happens. Once again the ingrained culture defeats the will of those who would change it.

[9]

When worrying about enemies it is always a good idea to start with yourself. If you can understand the culturally encouraged though distorted ways in which you behave, you can learn to work with other people as well as know your external enemy and prevent him or her from using your distortions to destroy you.

I know that I am often an enemy of myself and therefore of my friends and people I love. My analysis of the center and its distortions has helped me understand more about myself and provided insight and perspective that are crucial to survival if one functions under pressure and without much hope of immediate success. I use the schema discussed earlier to provide a framework for understanding myself in the present at the very moment I have to decide how to act. A trip around the edges of the center has often been of major value:

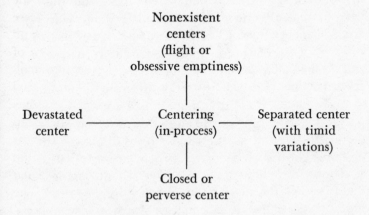

I ask myself: When am I closed and perverse? What threatens me so much that I refuse to allow myself to see it? How do I deal with new people and new experiences?

Ten years ago I was teaching the sixth grade in an all-black school in Harlem. There were two black male teachers at the school, both of them extremely gifted musicians and aware of their own blackness. Black awareness was not common at the school in those days. The greatest insult one kid could throw at another was the epithet "black." The darkest-skinned kids in the school were mocked and considered themselves inferior. To feel black and beautiful was unknown to most of the students and most of the black staff as well.

Harry and Fred set out to raise the consciousness of the kids. They wanted to introduce James Weldon Johnson's "Black National Anthem" to the students and have them sing it at assemblies. They wanted to emphasize black poetry, literature, achievements at the school. I opposed them partially because I felt that the students needed exposure to the Western tradition that I had been exposed to at Harvard, and partially because like most liberals I was ignorant and afraid of the tradition of blackness.

My students were reading and writing, were involved in Greek and Latin mythology, in opera and theater—what more could one want, I argued. Fred and Harry got angry at me, claimed I had no idea what it was like to be black or what the needs of black kids were. I disagreed and claimed all kids had the same needs. I attributed their anger to some personal frustration or missed opportunity. The more we argued, the more closed I got, so that the only thing left for them to do was to call me down for the insensitive and racist attitudes I was displaying. In my obsession with making *my* classroom beautiful, with interesting *my* students in what I liked, I didn't understand their pain or the needs they had that were not also my needs. Because I was not black, blackness was not my problem and therefore I was blind to what Harry and Fred were saying.

I was wrong, and they were right—the best I was doing was to help the students become competent, sometimes skillful imitators of me or of my teachers. The kids were not dealing with the experience of being oppressed or with the question of obtaining power; they were not dealing with the reality of self-hatred and racism. It took me a year away from teaching to see how wrong I was—it took listening to the students articulate their feelings about blackness two years later, and seeing the way "black" became a proud, rather than a hated, word. While in the school I had too much stake in my own success to step back and feel free to admit I was wrong. My singleminded, closed commitment to working with the students in my way made me have too much stake in being right. With temporal distance I could loosen up, reflect upon my actions, and change. I could also respond to the recent flowering of black culture rather than be threatened by it. If I had stayed in the school, continuing to defend my way, it is possible that I would have ended up as one of the liberal, though blind, Jewish professional teachers chased out of the Harlem schools for misunderstanding and opposing the demands of the community.

It is certainly easier to admit you were closed and wrong years after. The problem is how to catch oneself in process, to perceive how being closed leads one to become a stupid, sometimes brutal oppressor while one is actually doing it. Perhaps the clue lies in not needing to be right all the time, and therefore not being so serious and defensive when criticized. I know that for a long time when anyone kidded me about my work, I bristled with anger. My defensiveness didn't distinguish between someone who was kidding me or mocking my superseriousness and someone who was genuinely angry and critical. The defensive stance prevented me from looking at myself—being closed was a substitute for being strong in myself, for having an ease with other people and an affectionate regard for myself that was independent of what I was doing.

These days I am much more capable of checking myself, of perceiving closedness while actually living through it.

I have come to know the sound of my voice and feel the set of my muscles when I am about to embark on a perverse tirade and can catch myself, step back, relax, open up a bit, and begin again in midstream.

This doesn't mean there are never times when one must close down. For example, I have to consciously close part of myself whenever I am working seriously on a book. I refuse to see people or to talk about my work, build walls about myself and am quite conscious of it, can even laugh at the lengths I go to avoid people and make exceptions. That conscious, temporary closedness is quite different, however, from the closedness I discovered in myself toward black self-consciousness. I did not consciously choose to be closed to those needs of my students. It was rather that my self-involvement, my stake in teaching, closed me to any fundamental opposition to what I was doing. In defending myself so hard, there never was a moment to change perspective.

Other questions I ask are: What devastates me? What are the circumstances that reduce me to a state of feeling (however temporarily) that the only possibilities are murder or suicide? How do I deal with those states short of destroying myself? How do I devastate others? How can one tell when a person is devastated and what are the ways of bringing oneself and others back to life? What sorts of things do people hold on to when they are in despair? Is everyone periodically devastated?

People under constant pressure come apart at times, especially when they get boxed in and feel that all their alternatives for productive action, on the one hand, or escape, on the other, have been removed. Under those circumstances they begin to act crazy, drink too much, take a lot of dope, sleep a great deal during the day, and wandering around aimlessly and hostilely at night.

Obsessed, self-hating people are vulnerable to devastation. The more delineated and obsessive a person's commitments and visions are, the easier it is to box that person in and devastate him. The broader, more complex, and flexible, the more wide-ranging a person's conception of the role, the more he can avoid trapping himself in a losing and killing battle. It is crucial for people who wish to destroy or change the culture to develop the ability to shift perception—to see situations (and, more crucially, their own role in situations) from many perspectives. One has to know when to fight, but also when to move away before trapping oneself into destroying pointlessly or being destroyed to no end.

So far I have escaped and these days am trying to find ways of catching myself before hopelessness and despair lead to homicidal or suicidal fantasies and actions, or of grounding myself and putting myself under strict personal discipline when I feel like going crazy.

The most powerful and common weapon of murder and suicide in our culture is the automobile. I mentioned my accident at Teachers College, Columbia, before; there have been other times in my life when I nearly killed myself or others behind the wheel of a car. I have also known more people killed in or by cars than by any other means. A fine, Berkeley alternative school director died in a car crash two summers ago while all of us were under great pressure. Other people have been killed or injured when they let themselves drive when they were troubled or obsessed. The culture provides, encourages us to take our lives in our own hands and provides us with the weapons. To counter this we have to acknowledge the possibility of our own devastation during conflict and slow down, hide ourselves, and decline the temptations of speed and power provided by cars, and the loosening of self-control provided by alcohol.

Anyone battling to change this society in fundamental ways is bound to experience devastation occasionally. The battle will last our lifetimes and there will always be many temptations to withdraw, die, or kill—especially as one is first beginning to learn to live with conflict and struggle.

That makes it all the more important to understand what devastates us, how we trap ourselves into believing there are no alternatives to dying, and how we can build strategies for survival. We must develop means of coming in contact with our centers and sort our temporary despair from more abiding and nurturing modes of being. One way is through dreams.

[10]

Over the last few years my dreams have been occupied with the spiritual and political voyage that engages my waking hours. They teach me about myself, warn of crises, and provide access to parts of myself that have not been articulated into consciousness. They sometimes appear with a particular strength and stay in my mind until I can write them down and think about them. Some dreams flit in and out of my mind and seem insignificant—more like casual conversations than prophecies or messages of life and death. I let those dreams go and record the strong ones although perhaps I shouldn't, since important messages are sometimes whispered instead of shouted. It is a matter of the amount of energy that can be put into understanding dreams at this particular stage of my life. During analysis I recorded all of my dreams every day. For six or seven years before analysis my life was so out of tune with itself that I hardly dreamed at all.

When I began dreaming again and recording the dreams for analysis I initially accepted the terms under which my analyst dealt with dreams. The dream was supposed to conceal an unfulfilled wish (usually sexual) of mine and could be used as a stimulus for free association that led back to my childhood. For the first few months of analysis this was an extremely fruitful way of bringing me out of a present state of anxiety and getting me to focus on the past and the way I allowed it to control my behavior. It is even possible that I dreamed the kind of dreams that my doctor wanted in order to please her as much as to refocus my consciousness. In any case, after a while the traditional Freudian way of dealing with dreams seemed inadequate. The dreams contained messages themselves and I felt that free association, which took me away from the dreams and into memories of my childhood, was a denial of the dreams themselves. As I began to live again in the present, to teach, and make friends, to deal with my parents in new ways, to write, and to develop an awareness of this culture and society beyond my limited childhood world, the dreams began to refer to the present and the future and to tell important things about myself and the world. When I dreamed that my school was on fire and that I had to choose between rescuing the students at great risk to myself or escaping with the other adults, an interpretation that referred to my childhood was out of place. The school I was teaching in at the time was destroying the children, and anyone who taught there had to choose between taking the risk of changing the school or abandoning the children and joining the other adults. This particular dream occurred after my principal offered me an administrative role at the school, which I refused because I wanted to remain in the classroom. My analyst wanted me to free associate with the dream and turn the principal into my father and the school into my childhood home. I complied half-heartedly, but the fact was that the principal was the boss of that school in the present and that the children were burning. The dream forced upon me a reality I had not yet fully articulated to myself—the need to make a choice that involved risks. The dream also indicated how I had to make that choice, since it ended with me hesitating and then rushing toward the school.

In other dreams about that time I found myself faced with superheroes, with terrifying black people, with friends and enemies. I found myself acting cruelly at times, at other times being gentle and compassionate beyond anything I could actually do. My dreams were full of contraries and contradictory behavior—people transformed into each other, good/evil behavior, kindness leading to death, destruction leading to bliss, things turning into their opposites, people behaving uncharacteristically. Throughout this period the dreams seemed to be indicating things about my center and presenting me with a portrait of myself in the world that was free of the constraints of logic and yet represented truths about behavior. Usually it took me a while to understand what the dreams represented. After my analysis was terminated I kept on recording dreams and still do. I let a dream sit for a while after recording it and then reread it as a map of my soul or an insight into my world or as a hint about resolving a particularly distressing problem or as an indication that I am about to enter a new stage in my life.

Dreams can bring a person into closer contact with his or her affinities and with the particular ways in which that person integrates the contrary demands made on the individual within a sick culture.

On January 19, 1969, seven years after my analysis and during the first year of Other Ways, I wrote the following in my dream book:

> A dream of spiritual quest—I have a role to play, a journey to make. There are many enemies about including older (and straight) men and young boys. I also have allies—Jim Hinton, the first of whom appears in the dream (this evening we were talking about the role each of us can sanely play in the revolution). Jim helps me escape from a nightclub type piece where I witness two acts and performances and yet am the target of the ownership and the people involved in the club. I escape and must fulfill my mission though it constantly involves attuning myself to the enemy, knowing who he is and how to deal with him.
>
> At one point I meet with my allies, with members of the quest (perhaps Hesse's League on the Journey to the East). They identify me as one of them and give me talismans made of jade. They are two sets of animals, four animals whose power and nature I can assume

when needed. One set of the animals is large (about 6″–8″). The other is pocket-sized and I can and do carry them with me on the journey (it is not clear if it is a journey to bring something precious to its rightful place, or a quest to find the precious and valuable, though elements of chase in the dream imply I have something of value others are seeking to possess or destroy). There is one scene where I escape narrowly into a beautiful woman's car on the way from an airport to a city (New York?).

My animals—powers—talismans are:

tiger	whale
elephant	prehistoric bird
	(large, vicious, meat-eating,
	catching her prey)

These are my powers and at one time in the dream I run away from the enemy with the strength, speed, and gait of a tiger. I am a tiger at the moment I need to be.

The appearance of these animals is not incidental. I can lie as quiet as a tiger or be as bellowing as an elephant, can crouch predatorily or lie around blubbery. Often my virtues and defects derive from the same characteristics:

—My tiger makes me silent, observant, ready to pounce. It also makes me furtive, suspicious, constantly sniffing, never fully relaxed until I'm in my den.

—The elephant is strong too—the stomping and bellowing tendency and at the same time the possibility of being stampeded by a mouse.

I love the water like a whale, yet cannot breathe it. It is necessary for me to relate to desires, wishes, knowledge that are not immediately accessible to consciousness. On the other hand, I can't live with the tension of the unconscious, can neither be mad nor a great artist. I need the fresh air, need to verbalize, trivialize, temporize, minimize, and stay in the present.

I also can fly in my mind or with words and can use this skill to tell the truth or seduce people into believing the most absurd nonsense.

The dream represented powers and forces that operate in my everyday life. It is possible that the same four animals could be understood in totally different ways by another person to describe different characteristics. That doesn't deny the amazing fit they have to essential aspects of my personality that I couldn't have come to terms with without symbolic intervention. The animals, the symbols, provided me with images to use when taking a hard critical look at myself. It was easier to hang on to them than to try to dissect my every action and come to a general and reasonably honest view of myself.

Dreams can also sometimes lead away from the individual and provide insight into the present and possibly the future that is not available to logical consciousness. I have a metal plate in my left hip, which was broken in the automobile accident. Several days before a storm my hip starts aching, since either the broken bone or the plate picks up signals from the atmosphere that I don't receive otherwise. It is possible that a part of the self understands currents within society and the self that can't be perceived quickly through logical analysis, and that sometimes dreams are a first articulation of this information, serving as internal teachers.

In the dream told at the beginning of this section I was able to transform myself into several animals, whose powers I could assume. I was also warned about enemies within the system: older ones (administrators) and younger ones (students who were capable of destroying Other Ways by selling dope at school or refusing to be part of our work). It was made clear that allies existed and that we could help one another if we could only find the proper roles for ourselves. It was also clear that danger was present, that there was no end to the struggle (which I did not want to believe, being exhausted at the time and hoping for some sort of final victory), and that unless all the strange, contrary powers available to oneself are used it is possible to be caught and destroyed by the enemy.

Sometimes dreams indicate very painful and unpleasant truths. They reveal hidden hatreds, fears, secret longings, self-destructive wishes. They also reveal strengths, affinities, joys. There is no single way to interpret dreams, just as there is no single function of dreams in the life of the individual.

It is practically impossible to understand the present as it is lived or to command enough information about the future to make an intelligent prediction. Therefore, logic and reason function best with respect to the past. It is in dreams and fantasies, which are able to embody many of the contrary tendencies that function simultaneously and from which action emerges, that one can come in contact with knowledge about the self and the culture not available elsewhere. However, dreams are of little use in and of themselves. For many people the dream is a safety valve, an unintegrated part of life where wild, forbidden, or threatening truths can emerge and then be forgotten. For other people dreams are legislated out of psychic existence because any expression of psychic truth is a threat to the whole coherence of the self. However, it is possible to read dreams, to accept them as teachers, and develop means of understanding their meanings, if only partially.

First, it is important to record the dream, since memory is not as strong and reliable in our culture as it is in cultures where there is no writing. In recording the dream, put everything down that comes to mind, including comments, interpretations, and new fantasies, since often the recording of a dream serves as a first attempt to understand it. It is also useful to record the date and a few words about the context in which the dream occurred—e.g., at night after making love; in the morning before getting up; after a battle; on the day you heard bad or good news; at a time you had to make a decision or were about to take a trip, and so forth. Of course, not every dream need be recorded. It is an individual matter how many dreams seem to be of significance. It probably is best to start by recording everything and then sorting out the dreams that retain significance. After a while it is possible to develop a personal way of recognizing dreams that need to be recorded. For me the sign is that they are not easy to put out of my mind until they are recorded.

Next it is important to get away from the dream for a while—perhaps a few hours or a few days, even longer, depending upon the sense of urgency you have about the dream or the level of anxiety you have in your life. If you feel particularly distressed, it probably makes sense to force yourself to look at the dream within a few days at most.

There are certain questions I have found useful in helping me understand what my dreams are trying to tell me. They provide a series of coordinates for developing interpretations of dreams that relate to the present and the future rather than past pathology. These questions are:

—What is the dream trying to teach me about myself or the world? Am I in a position to learn or do I feel closed and tired every time the prospect of rereading dreams occurs?

—How is the dream situated in time? Does it occur in past, present, future, or mythological time? How does the dream time relate to my way of living in time? Am I bogged down in the past? Obsessed with the future? Wrapped up in the present? Looking for a new time and a different way of dealing with time? Does the dream indicate opposition to or confirmation of my present temporal life?

—How is the dream situated in space? Is the space indoors or outdoors, is it open or closed, friendly or hostile? How do the characters fit in the space? Do they move with ease or jump around or just lie in a lump?

How does the space of the dream relate to the space of waking life?

—Who are the characters in the dream? Am I, the dreamer, present within my own dream? Do the other characters or presences resemble actual individuals or do they embody heroes or demons?

—Who acts and who is acted upon? How is behavior initiated and motivated within the dream? How does this active/passive dimension relate to my present ability to initiate action or feel acted upon?

—What is the structure of the dream? Is there a beginning, a middle, an end? Or is the dream cyclic, so that the same thing occurs over and over? Or is it just amusing, a series of seemingly unrelated events and happenings? How does this structure relate to the structure of my waking life?

—How does the dream relate to the centering process of my life? If the dream were to be considered a portrait of the present and possible future state of my center, what is implied? Are there danger signals, warnings of any kind? Are there indications of strengths that can be mobilized, confirmations of decisions that were made recently? Feelings about right and wrong action? Indications about the need to change or about roles that I am playing or that need to be adopted?

These questions do not generate an authoritative single interpretation for every dream. Sometimes, in fact, dreams remain a mystery for a long while and their significance can only be grasped in retrospect, when the information they were trying to provide for the dreamer is no longer of use. The questions at most can help an individual come in contact with parts of the self that are not readily available to consciousness. I find that dreams are both mysterious and not mysterious at all. People exist on so many levels other than the conscious one, and it is magical and yet not surprising that indications about the totality of life, about what I have called the center, arise within the course of life and beyond the ordinary processes of consciousness. Dreams, not being bound by logic and often compounded of contraries and impossibilities, can represent the center, which emerges from a personal and collective past, unfolds in the present, often determines the future, and is itself compounded of contraries and seeming impossibilities.

On June 15, 1970, after Other Ways was evicted from its building and we moved the school to 1414 Walnut Street, which is the location of the central administration offices of the Berkeley Unified School District, I recorded the following dream:

> Dream of Other Ways at 1414 Walnut Street where everything is business as usual except for Other Ways People. I running around completely naked (though occasionally there was time to put on my red bathrobe, the one I put on when cop came to arrest me for hit and run last week). Nobody at the administration building responded to my nakedness overtly yet I knew that at least eyebrows were raised and feelings were offended.

Let me use the questions listed above in analyzing the dream:

The dream is teaching me about my nakedness at that time, the wild, slightly hysterical way I was confronting the school administration out of anger and outrage and with too little regard for our future or survival. Judy suggested that my nakedness might be a sign of fear that my role at Other Ways might be analogous to that of the Emperor in *The Emperor's New Clothes.* Certainly I feared that all the battle over Other Ways might be worthless, and I often had doubts (which I pushed out of my mind) about the value of our work.

The dream is clearly in the present and in its outrageous presentness was just like the life I was living. Just the week before I got drunk after a particularly hostile staff meeting and rammed my car into a neighbor's parked car on my way home. A policeman woke me up at three that morning to ask me about the accident. The dream reminded me of how dangerously I was living. That red bathrobe was one I got in New York City to wear in the hospital after I had been run down by a car and broke my hip.

The dream took place exclusively at 1414 Walnut Street and time and space were completely bound up in that austere, ungenerous place where all of us from Other Ways must have seemed like naked savages to the well-dressed and polite administrators. We did not fit the space and perhaps the dream was implying that we should have disengaged ourselves from the confrontation and sought new options for a location.

The characters in the dream other than my naked self were real people, the actual administrators of the district, the polite but clear enemies of our work who were looking for confirmation of their worst ideas about our existence, which was considered violent, chaotic, and promiscuous. I guess we gave them the show they wanted and probably shouldn't have.

We acted—the Other Ways gang, as some of the kids called it—we acted and the administrators pretended to be passive and polite. However, I knew something about their real responses, which were hostile. They intended to destroy us and eventually succeeded.

The dream gave the impression of a formless repetitive running activity. Its structure accurately pointed out the formlessness of our existence after being put out of our fourth location in six months. There seemed no end in sight.

The dream warned of "offended" administrators and I didn't pay enough attention to that warning. A few years later those same people rejoiced when I finally quit out of fatigue. They felt free to fabricate rumors based on their contact with us at 1414 Walnut Street (for none of them had ever bothered to visit the school in stable times) in order to justify the demise of the school and, indeed, in their minds we were running around naked offending the good and responsible people of the world.

I deliberately chose this dream to share because it is fairly easy to interpret. Other dreams are harder to penetrate, although often upon rereading after a long period of time they seem clear.

There are several ways to reread one's dreams. One way is to do it a dream at a time, asking these or some other set of questions. Another way is to read a whole series of dreams as if they made up a continuing though quite limited spiritual autobiography of oneself. I do both —usually reading and thinking about each dream I record some time during the next day. I also reread dreams recorded over two or three years in sequence about two times a year. Occasionally when I experience despair and feel nothing is worth doing, when I feel out of touch with my center, I reread the dreams as a way of catching up on myself. They have become one source of perspective and provide me with a sense of continuity and the possibility of change.

[11]

Dreams are only one form of personal access to the center and the process of centering, however. Active fantasy, the calling forth of imaginary beings and worlds, is another way to learn about oneself and test out possible solutions to social and personal problems. Children are very facile and usually at ease with the world of fantasy, but somewhere in the passage to adulthood in our culture people lose intimacy with their own fantasies and become frightened of active imagining and fantasizing. My children spend a lot of time play acting and projecting themselves into imaginary worlds they create both individually and collectively. Not only do they create a fantasy; they also sustain it and live in it for hours at a time. In addition, every once in a while I come upon them talking to what adults condescendingly call "imaginary playmates." However, they are beginning to be afraid to communicate with their fantasy friends with adults around. Probably people have ridiculed them, put down the fantasy beings they have called forth and managed to communicate with, and despite all of Judy's efforts and mine and their own resistance, the kids are learning to kill their fantasies, become literal-headed, and consequently impoverish their own lives because that is how grown-ups are supposed to be in our society.

I remember when I was about eight or nine the most important time of the day was when my parents said goodnight and left my bedroom. At that point, which I had often waited for all day, I closed my eyes and summoned the Maskedrider, my hero, friend, and teacher. He would appear before me, beckon, and all of a sudden we were traveling together in another dimension of space and time. My voyages with the Maskedrider were quite different from dreams, which came to me unexpected or without any sense of their being under my control. With the Rider it was different—I summoned him, could engage in conversation with him, ask questions, reveal my anxieties. Most of the time I followed along as a witness to his adventures. Sometimes I played the sidekick role and was his Tonto or Sancho Panza or Kato or Robin. At other times my mind controlled the adventure. This is what I remember about him. He was found as a child wandering across a vast plain wearing a dark mask, and he had never seen his own face.

The Rider lived on the dark edge of the world. He had no companion and lived alone except for a secret bundle of sacred objects. He had stones that resembled faces, a root that looked like a clenched fist, four beautiful steel knives, a few empty jars, and a vial of black sand. His most sacred object was a small clay head worn featureless by time, that he had found when he was a child.

The Rider also had a horse, a sword, and a rope. The horse was black and featureless like his master and was only present when necessary—they were often one, horse-and-rider.

I used to try out all kinds of things with the Rider: I would ask him to help me plan running away from home, to teach me how to fight, or be by myself and take control over certain areas of my life. The Rider appears in retrospect as the voice of my emerging self, as an internal teacher or shaman.

Jung talks about summoning voices and presences through the active use of fantasy or what he calls the transcendent function. It is a matter of clearing one's conscious mind as much as possible and welcoming whatever comes into consciousness instead of chasing things away. The mind can learn to focus, to call up internal visions and voices if it can relax.

I have a friend, Hal Bennett, who has written a people's guide to medicine.* One of the main themes of the book is that people can have access to considerably more knowledge about their bodies and their state of health than is available through so-called rational analysis. Hal suggests that people relax, close their eyes, and concentrate upon hearing from an inner healer whom they can talk with about their own personal health. He suggests that, once relaxed, one should imagine a box with two large doors, then approach the box and concentrate on healing and being healed, and then in imagination open the box and welcome and enter into dialogue with the healer that emerges. I know of many people who think this is a silly and fruitless exercise. Others think it is dangerous to give oneself over to fantasy, especially if one's hold on a personal center is tenuous. There is always the fear that one might get so deep into the world of fantasy that return to normal waking life will be impossible. This is probably a real danger for some people and if they allow themselves to

* *The Well-Body Book*. (Random House, 1973).

go into a world of fantasy, they should do it in an extremely structured way and with a trusted person who is willing to play guide and teacher.*

I suggest for most people coming into contact with their fantasy worlds for the first time (since childhood, anyway) the following procedure:

First, it is important to find a place where you feel safe and relaxed and so can deal with some difficult encounters. The place could be in a corner or in the middle of a room, in a chair, on a cot, under a table. For me the spot is on the couch in the middle of our living room. I feel at home there, as if that particular end of the couch was made to receive my body.

Next, it is important to find the right physical position so that you can relax, withdraw your attention from the immediate surroundings, and receive the fantasies. I lie down facing the back of the couch; other people sit or lie on the floor or crouch or take some yoga position. It is a question of how your body rests easiest so that the physical world can recede from consciousness.

Next, one has to become relaxed, cleared of the sights and sounds of the everyday environment. There are a number of techniques of relaxation, ranging all the way from massage to breathing exercises to meditation. I find that lifting weights or tensing and releasing my muscles puts my body in a relaxed condition. Clearing my mind is harder, and I have sometimes to chase the world away or exhaust all the sights and sounds that remain with me after I close my eyes. One way I have learned to deal with the ordinary world is to concentrate on whatever remains in my consciousness and try to go right into the heart of the sounds/people/objects that refuse to disappear. I come closer and closer to them in fantasy until I break right through them into the world of my fantasies or until they

---

* There is no need to use drugs to gain access to the center, although for some people the process of developing active fantasies can be facilitated by some drugs.

fade away. Sometimes, of course, the ordinary world refuses to fade and I can't get access to my fantasies. In cases like that it is because I am trying to use fantasy as an escape from an obvious though painful action I am trying to avoid in the present. My fantasies do not allow themselves to be used in the sense of retreat from necessary action. They function not as a withdrawal from the world so much as a nonordinary way of illuminating my role within the world.

If the world does "disappear," at this point it is possible to begin to call forth fantasies. Hal's box method has a lot of other equivalents. You can imagine a door and then slowly approach the door in your mind, then grasp the doorknob and feel it, then open the door and allow yourself to observe whatever is on the other side. Another method is to imagine yourself sealed in a box flying through space and time, then slowing down and stopping. Open the box within your mind, step out, and observe where you are. Greet anyone you meet.

It is possible to think on the kind of fantasy you want to enter—whether it involves health, sex, political battling, decision making—whatever world you want to explore. Sometimes I put myself in a fantasy position, relax, and let myself go altogether. It is a strange feeling, quite different from being asleep. I am peripherally aware of everything around me and can usually move out of the fantasy at will. I am also active within the fantasy—ask questions, move myself around. There is a great deal of personal volition involved in active fantasy, so that sometimes it seems as if the world summoned from within is quite as real as any other one lived in. One has an active role within that world and, in addition, can test questions and behavior that could not be tried in waking life. It is as if the mind has created an experimental theater for the self, where roles and masks and actions can be played out with intensity before risking action in the world of other people. What is curious to me is that characters within the fantasy respond—it is as if parts of the self play out a drama to teach the waking person how to behave.

Let me give a specific example. I hate public confrontations, although I am willing to go through with them when necessary. However, I need all the internal strength I can muster. Talking to other people, no matter how close they are to me, doesn't really help. I have to come in contact with my self/center and draw strength from it, so I take to the couch. I relax, close my eyes, and concentrate on the enemy, go up and begin to examine the enemy in fantasy, act out many possible ways of dealing with the confrontation, then let myself walk away from that situation and respond to whatever is produced by the fantasy world. Usually after the first encounter I begin to meet people and visit places that are particular sources of joy for me. It is as if I check in with these sources of strength and joy within myself before taking a risk in the external world. I do not have regular beings I converse with in my fantasy world, but a whole range of beings that have had historical, fictional, or in some cases purely a mythic and imaginary existence. My fantasies are kaleidoscopic. People I know have much more orderly and regularized relationships within their world of active fantasy. The structure of one's fantasy seems to be dependent on the nature of the self/center, of that complex, often contrary combination of powers and qualities that makes up the person and that is only partially accessible to ordinary conscious functioning.

[12]

It is possible to come into intimate contact with the workings of one's own body and senses in much the same way that one can learn to understand and be guided by fantasies and dreams. The body and the senses respond directly to social situations, to other people, to thoughts and feelings and fantasies, to ideas and visions, to natural phenomena and animals. Often these responses, which are not mediated or controlled by consciousness, are ignored or negated by conscious behavior, leading to tension within the self. For example—a person in power talks to you, agrees, says everything you need to hear. The person is pleasant, open, funny. On a conscious level you accept the person as he or she defines himself or herself. However, you have some vague visceral repulsion. Something unsaid and not immediately apparent gives you a sense of physical unease. It is easy to overcome or deny that feeling or put it down as unimportant where you would do well to heed the warning.

At Other Ways almost everyone who walked through the door had the rhetoric of open education down. They could charm, convince—they knew how to talk about young people, learning environments, radicalizing consciousness. However, the great majority of people were seeking something for themselves and were not interested in the school, the students, or me except as we served their personal needs. In some cases people wanted interviews, information for theses or articles. In other cases they wanted to work out sexual and political problems, using our students as dolls and experimental animals. Some people, though, were merely curious or cared to offer what they knew in exchange for what we could teach them. It was crucial to sort out people's intentions. We were always under such pressure that we couldn't afford the burden of working out other people's problems. It was generally left to me to become the gatekeeper and sort out people. I made many mistakes and during one year almost allowed Other Ways to be consumed by the number of troubled adults who were always around.

As I reflected on the mistakes I made, it emerged that somehow I wasn't surprised that specific individuals screwed up. A part of me knew from the beginning that they would. I felt it, sensed it—yet conscious and verbal analysis seemed to disconfirm my uneasiness. My body as a whole—senses/feelings/breathing (it is hard to put a word to the physical-physiological-psychic complex that responds outside of consciousness, although sometimes it is called intuition)—knew that something was wrong although I was not able to assimilate that knowledge into my consciousness. I was unaccustomed to stepping back from an encounter with another and forgetting about myself and the impression I was making. I never let my self observe the other, take in all the impressions, tonalities, modalities that the senses and body can pick up without analysis. I was too uncentered to let myself go. I still had to (and sometimes do now) let people know who I was when I should have been finding out who they were.

However, after having been burned a few times I began paying more attention to my viscera. I have consciously begun to let my body and senses respond to people and situations and push my ego out of the way. I believe that the response of my body/senses comes from the center and is capable of responding to small direct indications from within and without the self that the ego in its vanity misses. That doesn't mean that the body and the senses are always right and that conscious intellectual perception is always mistaken. What it means is that one's total response to a situation has to be valued when deciding who to trust and how to act.

Recently I was involved with a few friends in trying to develop a teacher training program affiliated with the University of the Pacific in Stockton. Everyone at U.O.P. seemed enthusiastic and it only remained for us to talk to the academic vice-president of the university. Three of us saw him. He was extremely stiff, yet friendly and enthusiastic. He praised us, talked about innovation and forward-looking ideas, and showed genuine interest in our work. During our conversation I took a step back from Herb Kohl talking about education and while part of me functioned automatically in the conversation, the rest opened itself up to the man. My eyes responded to the tense hands, my ears to the tone and not the meaning of his words.

My muscles responded to the tension of his muscles, my breathing to his breathing. There was something wrong— the man had no rhythm, was tense and angry, was clearly masking many things. My body/sense impression was that the man was totally untrustworthy and quite dangerous. After a while I returned to the conversation. When we left, one of us was sure everything would be fine. Another remained quiet, and I expressed my delight in the vice-president's words while warning that something about him made me sure he was not to be trusted. I was willing to be proved wrong (and hoped to be, for I wanted the program to develop), but I prevailed on people to begin to develop plans for functioning if our relationship with the U.O.P. didn't materialize. In the past I would have allowed my desire to see the program created blind me to the deceitful nature of the man and would have left the meeting fully enthusiastic. However, when the university withdrew I was not surprised, disarmed, or unready. Because I allowed myself to understand the man in the beginning and not worry so much about what he thought about me, there was no need to even waste time despising him later. We got on with the alternative plan.

I still make mistakes and trust my intellect and ego when I should be listening to my body and senses. Recently a school asked me to help choose a new director. I was on an interviewing panel. We listened to all the candidates, asked questions. One of the candidates zeroed in on me— we exchanged glances, he made flattering, intelligent, though somewhat oblique references to my writings and work. He told Jewish-type jokes, and put on a little New York style—all of which flatter me. I vaguely sensed, however, that the man was sly and weak, a sham. While I formed an intellectually favorable opinion of him, my whole body went cold and tense. I ignored the uneasy feelings he gave me and approved his candidacy anyhow. A few months later he was fired for lying and being unable to deal with the students in a responsible way. I was not the only person responsible for choosing him but much of the blame is mine, since it was within my power to have rejected him.

It is important to attend to the sensibility of one's body and feel comfortable and intimate with the way it responds within the world. For many people in our society this is impossible because the body is considered an object, a machine to be regulated and controlled through dieting, exercise divorced from art or work, and occasional indulgence. Separating the body from its functions, from the mind and heart and center of the person, does produce a machine that allows itself to be shaped and controlled and eventually considered a burden by the consciousness attached to it. It produces a fragmented being, one that embodies the classical mind/body dualism. I remember throughout my youth all the crazy things my parents and relatives did to their bodies and those of their children. My family is Jewish, mostly short and broad, dark and curly-haired. They aspired to be "Americans" and have their children be "Americans"—i.e., in their minds tall, skinny, and blond. It wasn't their fault in the sense that the culture taught them that they weren't beautiful and that you had to be beautiful in order to succeed and be happy in America. They bought the myth—straightened and dyed their hair, dieted like crazy—then, feeling hungry and deprived, they bloated themselves, then dieted again.

My parents liked me when I was skinny—even gaunt and emaciated. In an unarticulated visceral way they didn't care for me when I was chubby and somewhat content. As a teenager my body was a problem—whether it was strong and skinny or flabby. It was an object to be maintained and serviced, not a growing, changing part of an integrated living being. The year after I graduated from college my mother persuaded me to get thin once and for all and our doctor gave me diet pills, which I popped like lifesavers. I lost weight, ran around like crazy, experienced nausea merely walking down the street, talked incessantly and frenetically, and was a socially sanctioned speed freak in the service of making my body something it isn't. Those days I was running too fast to know what was happening to me, but there were warnings. I blacked out a lot, found myself shaking and chattering to myself. In disgust and despair one day I threw the pills away and decided to let myself grow fat. I don't know what caused me to change, but the decision was as absurd as the condition I was escaping. There were no alternatives at that point in my life to manic abstinence or overindulgence, since there was no center to my existence in which my physical life could be rooted. The ability to be at ease with my body and therefore have it develop in consonance with the rest of my self, as well as the capacity to relate to the world directly through my body and senses, did not seem to be possibilities. It was not a matter of exercise or yoga or diet—all these techniques are artificial forms of trying to control a body turned object if the whole life is uncentered. They try to force upon the body what is lacking in the soul and produce patched-up parody versions of spiritual and physical self-discipline and growth. It is not difficult to perceive the fragile relation of bodies and souls in our culture—just listen carefully to people's words and watch their bodies; take them in as wholes and feel the contradictions and hypocrisies:

—I am liberated; my mind and body are free so it is up to you to satisfy me.

—I am into yoga and see the world in a new way. Too bad you aren't so liberated.

—I can now touch you, so you must subject yourself to my touch or you're not together.

—You've gotten fat. You should do yoga and exercise like me.

There are people, of course, who are not alienated from their bodies and do not hate them or use them as instruments of power. To be in contact with one's body does not mean to appear beautiful to the world or to be stronger or faster or whiter or darker than anyone else. It is more a matter of ease, intimacy, knowledge, and affection. It is a form of knowing who you are and who you can become. In this culture a healthy body, just like a healthy life, is probably not a possibility. To live in a city and breathe its air is a slow form of suicide. That is true no matter how much yoga or exercise you force upon your body. To retreat to the country and live a pure life on the land can mean abusive physical labor. To live a "gentleman's" life of leisure and planned activity is a form of atrophy. Being healthy is not a matter of being physically strong or fully exercised. It is a matter of the body and senses and mind and the unconscious being attuned to one another. It means constancy, consistency, understanding.

There are a number of ways of dealing with not looking like the person you're expected to be. One is to feel guilty and try to change. I tried at times in my life, felt all the requisite guilt when I was at Harvard for not looking beautiful, pinched at my body, tried to cut myself and occasionally succeeded. At that time I felt something of the hatred of my own physical appearance that I encountered in a much more bitter form in my black students when I taught in Harlem in 1962, a few years before the kids began to understand that black is beautiful.

It was strange to see people disappointed with the way I looked and pull away from me unconsciously. Sometimes I would deliberately go for those individuals, attack their ideas, try to make them as uncomfortable as they made me feel. Other times I tried to seduce them into being attracted to me despite the way I looked. These days both those responses seem variations on the same fundamental insecurity. It's now possible for me to laugh at how cultural stereotypes pervade people's imaginations and to respond to others without worrying overmuch how they respond to my physical presence. It is not a matter of becoming resigned to how one looks, on the one hand, or falling in love with one's mirror image, on the other.

Rather, it is a matter of caring for the totality of one's being, of being intimate with the center and all of its manifestations and, because of this, living beyond cultural judgments of beauty and goodness. Engaging the process of centering, welcoming the process of growth, developing all the strengths and powers of one's being in the service of creating a healthy world all imply full engagement of the body and senses as well as the mind. This means attending to the body, listening to its warnings as well as following many of its inclinations. It implies developing the body and senses within the context of work and learning to use it to express aspects of one's being. It means dancing and moving instead of "exercising," and building and inventing instead of buying all the time. This sounds romantic, yet it is really quite simple—the body and senses are intimate parts of one's being and should function as such rather than as servants of the mind.

Often the combination of body and senses is aware of danger before the conscious mind. The body has different ways of displaying its awareness and it is important to learn how to understand these signals and use them rather than be victimized by them. For example, anxiety is often manifested by clammy palms. Sometimes when I feel completely unanxious my palms all of a sudden become cold and clammy. When that first started happening to me I used to wipe off my palms and often kept a handkerchief in my hands at all times. I avoided shaking people's hands or holding hands with women I was going with. I turned away from the anxiety that my body was calling attention to and pretended that everything was all right. These days I have learned to pay attention to the anxiety, to take gratefully the signal that I am anxious and try to get to its source. Anxiety does not paralyze action—it often tempers it with sensible fear. When I am anxious it is usually because I am afraid of doing something or having something done to me. The more specific I can become about my fears, the more I can prepare myself to act.

Fear and anxiety are not causes for shame or excuses for inaction. They temper foolish action, warn of risks, and call attention to the need for adequate preparation of the self.

I feel that almost all bodily manifestations called in our culture "psychosomatic symptoms" are messages from one's senses and body about one's present state rather than indicators of fundamental underlying neuroses. The language of these physical manifestations has to be learned, and then they can be used as a source of strength. I have been an asthmatic all of my life, although the attacks have pretty much receded these days. My first attack came when I was six months old, so there is probably some physiological predisposition for my body to relate to the world through my lungs. I know breathing freely and avoiding smothering situations have been themes throughout my life. My lungs respond to threat from within and without like an extremely sensitive barometer. According to my breathing, I can tell when I feel pressed or caged or smothered—and, conversely, when I feel free and at ease with myself and the world. It is not pleasant being asthmatic, nor is it crippling. I have found that the more I accept the way in which my lungs respond to the environment the less urgent the asthma is. It is almost as if by paying attention to the message I have made it possible for the body to talk to me in a softer voice.

As my asthma has receded, I have found that my eyelids puff up when there is a high level of pollution in the air combined with a high level of tension in my life. Sometimes the pollution alone or the tension alone causes the lids to swell, but most of the time it is a combination. It is almost as if I no longer fear being smothered but have developed a visceral desire not to see certain things, and the swelling, by making it physically difficult for me to see, calls my attention to aspects of my life I am trying to avoid facing. Several years ago I was in the position of having to confront the superintendent of schools in Berkeley. I walked around bragging about how I was going to do him in and allowed myself to say many irresponsible, undocumented things that would discredit me and give the superintendent the weapons he needed to win that particular battle. The day before the public school board meeting my eyelids started to swell, as I vaguely knew they would. All my fears came pouring out—I really didn't want to make a scene, hoped the man would like me, was afraid of what he could do to me, afraid I would get too violent and blow the whole thing, afraid, really, to show up. The eyes gave me an excuse not to show, since my face was not pretty to look at. They also told me that I didn't want to see the real issues and warned that I had better prepare what I was going to say quite carefully. The fact that my eyelids were swollen, however, did not keep me from the meeting. I wore sunglasses. However, I did prepare in fact and fantasy for the presentation and managed to do and say what I had to.

These days I can sense when my eyes are about to inform me that I am turning away from something that has to be faced if I am to grow and remain open and honest. The swelling occurs quite infrequently and isn't particularly serious. Again, through attending to it rather than being shamed by it, the impulse to blind myself seems to have become less dramatic and insistent.

I wrote these paragraphs about my eyes this morning. Just an hour ago the lid above my right eye began to swell, almost in response to this articulation of the function in my life of swelling eyelids. I knew what it was about. I am involved in a small reading center at my oldest daughter's elementary school. We have four students who have been identified by their teacher as "problem learners." I am working with a small teacher training program that was put together after our attempt to develop a larger program through the U.O.P. was killed. Three of the students are working with me in the reading center, presumably in order to learn how to work with "difficult" students and use success with the school's rejects as a way of confronting teachers and administrators with their own failures. Although I haven't cared to face it, things have not been going well. The kids are overwhelmed by having to deal with four adults in the small closet we work in. The adults are of good will but are extremely busy and the hour a week we work with the kids is just a small and noncentral part of their programs. The central problem is different, however—I know how to help those four kids teach themselves to read and learn how to function without being wiped out by the school system. I also could help the students in our training function. The problem I did not want to see is that I'm really not interested, am not involved in the lives of those kids and adults, and am involved in the program only as a way of paying my social dues and trying to keep involved in school battles while licking my wounds from old battles and trying to store up enough energy to begin again. That half-hearted involvement is the death of any program, and I am very hard on people who hold themselves back from their work. My eyes were telling me today to be hard on myself, too, and they were saying even more strongly that if I dared to write about my body no excuse was left to ignore the fact that I was slipping into the same irresponsibility characteristic of people who use the lives of the young as a way of developing their careers or solving their own personal problems.

I mentioned this interpretation to Judy and she said she saw it another way. Everything about me tells her that I want and need to teach again and that I am nervous that I have forgotten how to be effective. And she's right. Nothing is more frightening to me than the possibility that I won't write another book I am proud of or that I will fail as a teacher. These are vestiges of the old fears of being empty and a sham that I guess will always remain with me.

I don't always understand what my body is saying, but

I am blessed by being unashamed of all my crazy ways. There are friends, as well as Judy and my children, who can help me read myself. I don't need to hide from them the ugliness, anxiety, and pain I seem unable to shake and can listen because I know I am loved. That is a feeling that transcends any need I have for self-deception and enables me to deal with misunderstanding of myself.

The body has signs that must be attended to if one is to survive, however difficult they are to decipher. Most people I know who have committed themselves to battling this culture are fighting almost all the time; there is so much to be done and so few people willing to take risks. These people push themselves hard and are pushed by their enemies, who consciously try to exhaust them. There are many forms this harassment assumes: arrests on misdemeanor charges that are then not pressed; the withholding of money or the giving of less money than was promised; rumors; the denial of space to meet or function; the refusal to honor agreements; the loss of crucial documents; and so forth. No victories are permanent, so that people find themselves always returning to the same battles, since members of established institutions do not feel obliged to honor agreements made with radicals under duress.

During these battles people become tired—not merely mentally fatigued but physically exhausted. There are days and weeks and months when there is no time to rest, when every meeting seems to involve survival and every encounter seems hostile. Struggling and running from place to place, meeting to meeting, person to person become a way of life, which can only be borne by ignoring the body's insistence on rest and leisurely artful indulgence. People develop all sorts of symptoms of fatigue—headaches, aching joints, sinus trouble, pulled muscles, coughs. Under pressure the easiest way out is to deny the messages of the body and silence them by drinking or smoking dope or popping tranquillizers.

Many people who ignore the messages of the body do

not survive. Sometimes it is necessary to attend to physical pain and withdraw from confrontation when the body is screaming for rest. This is hardest for people who are fighting isolated individual battles or for people who allow themselves to become so central as leaders that the group will fall apart without their continual presence. A caring group is necessary for sustained struggle. Otherwise all the individual members will be burned out, exhausted, consumed, spiritually emptied. Despite fighting for righteous causes, despite battling with other people and taking risks with them, if techniques of mutual support and renewal are not developed, there is always the possibility that the struggle will fall apart altogether.

At Other Ways, despite great pressure and fatigue I was unable to withdraw or rest. I made myself too indispensable. Other people made it clear that if I stopped battling they would too. At some point it would have been healthy for me to test these statements and by withholding myself force alternative leadership to develop. However, I was too tied into my leadership role and too fatigued to reflect on what was happening. The struggle was taking too much out of me and the staff at Other Ways never learned how to support one another. My hip hurt and I doped that away with wine. The others saw me drinking too much and never told me—they were embarrassed perhaps, afraid I would deny what they were saying and attack them or quit in a huff. I needed support and rest—I had to sleep more, walk, run, move around outside of meeting rooms and classrooms. We all had that need, yet at that point didn't know how to meet it. So one day I quit and several months after that the school fell apart.

Since then I have taken the signs of my body much more seriously and rest when necessary. In a battle I am sure will last well beyond my lifetime I have to develop stamina rather than be consumed or drained, and the body is honest about fatigue. It indicates to consciousness certain facts about the condition of the center—about the processes of growth (or retardation and dissolution) one is undergoing. Like dreams, fantasies, and psychosomatic symptoms, some bodily pain bears messages about the state of the self that can be assimilated and acted upon.

The ability to understand and integrate these messages, however, depends upon global understanding of oneself in the present.

However, no one can struggle alone with as much energy as is required to sustain something of value in this culture. To survive and make a different, saner world possible we have to work collectively, nurture one another, provide mutual support and meaning as we change our lives and try to remake this culture. To have the strength to dare to lead committed active lives that aspire toward wholeness and openness—that is, to dare to become healthy—we have to work together or we will be devastated one by one. This is not a time for prophets but a time for action initiated and sustained by small groups of people. However, to put together a small loving group that can stand, fight, persist, and cohere is even more difficult than maintaining an honest and centered personal life.

III

The Group
and the Problems
of the Center

Most groups in our culture make cruel and unreasonable demands upon their members. In certain neighborhoods one must be a racist in order to fit; in most businesses one must be cut-throat and value profit over people. Public institutions such as schools, hospitals, or prisons value order and power (over the student or patient or prisoner) above caring humane values. Individuals are expected to fit themselves to the cultural and social forms of pre-existing groups in order to become predictable group members who perpetuate the group.

Many people in our culture are no longer interested in joining groups that embody the competitive, racist, and fascists strains in our culture. Rather they want to remake the nature of group life within this culture, extend the bonds of intimacy, create new rituals to bind groups together, and embody and encourage a diversity of styles and modes of being.

There are aspects of life within this society that make the formation of new groups possible. People are mobile and usually do not live in the same places or with the same people they knew as children. The drive many adults feel to "better themselves" or make a better life for their children leads parents to encourage children to leave home for college or work.

People are constantly exposed to new social worlds where they have opportunities to experiment with a variety of roles and values. This makes change easier than in many traditional societies where young people's lives are defined by the family. Although the family can oppress the young, it also can provide collective security and emotional sustenance. People alone in large cities or at universities want and need more than casual acquaintances. It is not enough merely to know people at school, in the bar, at work—that provides no protection or sustenance. Many people dream about turning informal and casual relationships into sustaining social bonds that provide some of the strength that a family can offer its members. Sometimes people try to go beyond informality and try to develop mutual responsibility and concern. Sometimes all it takes is a few people in a group to suggest that they act as a family or collective to move people from thinking of themselves as casual friends to posing the problem of creating collective identity.

When the question of commitment to the group emerges some people will leave. For others the suggestion will be an exciting, romantic challenge.

However there are dangers. Whenever one gets together with people one hasn't known very long it is difficult to know who to trust or how to distinguish style from substance. Often one is charmed or seduced by an idea or a promise of love. It is easier for people to claim they love and trust each other than to love or trust, even with the most serious intentions. For most of us the desire to change runs ahead of our ability to change.

Very few of us realize the extent of our miseducation, understand how we are taught to be dishonest to ourselves and to exploit others. Any time a new group comes together the old culture emerges in unexpected ways, undermining trust and creating for many adults the impression that it is impossible to change their lives.

At Other Ways we certainly learned how difficult it is for adults to change their behavior no matter how humane their sentiments. In addition to myself there were a half dozen central people during our first year. First there was Betsy Barker. In a usual institutional manner she was assigned to me as a secretary during the six months I taught in the Education Department of the University of California, Berkeley.

As a secretary Betsy was treated by most of the professors as a typing, transcribing, and telephone-answering mammal. She was also treated as a beautiful young woman, admired, eyed, ogled, put down. However, she knew and cared more about schools and learning and children than most of the faculty. Betsy is short and thin and it is sometimes hard to believe that so much energy can be contained in such a slight frame. We talked a lot during my six months at Cal, and when Allan Kaprow and I got the grant from the Carnegie Corporation of New York to do a teacher training program, I asked Betsy to work with us as administrator/secretary. She accepted, since she was fed up with working for the university.

There were two problems, however. I didn't really want to do teacher training and didn't want to have a secretary. Allan Kaprow was committed to doing happenings with teachers and was quite easy about considering Betsy as a secretary. This led us to some trouble later as our group developed, but seemed fine at the beginning when Allan, Betsy, and I set up in an empty storefront on Grove Street in Berkeley. We were assigned the storefront by the Berkeley Unified School District with which we were loosely affiliated.

Kaprow and I set up open houses for teachers on Monday afternoons.

At the beginning of Other Ways a fourth person, in many ways the craziest, bitterest, and most brilliant of us, joined the teacher sessions as a consultant on folktales and fables. Collingwood August is a Southern African, a Bantu (this is a misnomer, he constantly told me, since Bantu simply means people). Collingwood was short and thin, sharp almost. "Herb," he would tell me, "you are a racist and don't know that you are a Jew." Collingwood knew that every white person in this culture is a racist and after a few glasses of wine would let others know his feelings. For twelve years he had taught in a Protestant high school in Capetown. Then he came to understand that Christ's passivity was destroying his people and he became involved in revolutionary and anticlerical activity. He had to leave the country, his wife, and daughter, or be imprisoned for incitement to violence. Colly was very good at incitement. He was also an elder for us, slightly indulged though revered. It was strange; Betsy, Colly, myself—and later the other people—eliminated the usual cultural roles of boss, expert, secretary, consultant, and found ourselves filling the void with more archetypal forms—with elders, fathers, mothers, clowns, priests, jesters.

Our Monday sessions were fun. We bought a few gallons of wine, several six packs of beer, some soda, coffee, potato chips, and pretzels for the teachers and ourselves. Then after school we welcomed whomever showed up. A lot of kids began dropping around steadily. We put up posters in the public schools and got between twenty and fifty teachers each Monday afternoon. Each week we began with a different event, happening, writing session, poetry reading. Then we just talked and talked about schools, kids, racism, revolution, hopelessness, hope.

The storefront got pretty messy on Mondays, so Betsy suggested we hire Darryle, her boyfriend, as janitor, and we did. Darryle had been a member of the Black Panther Party and before that an Air Force technician. He told me that when he got out of the Air Force he worked at the Alameda Air Force base as a jet mechanic at about three hundred dollars a week. One morning he woke up and decided he couldn't go back to servicing planes made to kill. He quit.

When he started with Other Ways he had just left the party, although I never found out why.

In a way Darryle was more of a kid than most of the kids we ended up working with. He loved to play basketball, hinted he never slept in the same bed twice. Darryle hung around with the kids at the storefront a lot and took to teaching them to write poetry and play ball.

There were several contradictory, often infuriating aspects to Darryle. He is one of the most perceptive people I know. He can sit back and watch people, listen to them, and understand them very quickly. But he doesn't act on what he knows. He withdraws from conflict, disappears when things get tight unless pushed to be responsible. He also functions on his own internal time and comes when he comes. Darryle's role as a janitor at the storefront was silly and embarrassing. He was around most of the time, worked with the kids, played and drank with the teachers, and was paid to sweep the floor. Even though our rhetoric was egalitarian, the situation was hierarchical until we all took the responsibility of cleaning (except Colly, of course, who gave a disquisition on cleaning while we swept up on Monday evenings or Tuesday mornings). Collective cleaning didn't work and later on in the year we decided to take in another janitor, Dave Conley, who in turn also became a teacher.

Dave is a man of temper. He is perpetually red in the face, wild-haired, excited, full of fire and energy; sometimes it is directed. Some of the kids called Dave White Jesus and there is something messianic about his temper. I first met Dave during a talk I gave to an English class at Cabrillo Junior College. He graduated from Cabrillo, enrolled at U.C., Berkeley, took a fling at street politics, confrontations, and demonstrations, and, still angry and hungry to get involved, he showed up at the storefront and asked if he could help. So Dave came on as our second janitor with the understanding he could work with kids who dropped in and join the teachers' sessions as long as he cleaned up. Of course, as Dave became part of the group, we returned to collective though inadequate cleaning.

There were a lot of people around that first year, but only two others, who became part of the group, determined its character. One was Mike Spino, the other Frederick Douglass Perry.

Mike was a teacher at Richmond High who began coming to the Monday sessions. He is a long-distance runner, and running toward and away from things is the central metaphor in his life. Mike had visions of integrating running with music and poetry, of developing noncompetitive athletic programs. With a little prodding he wrote a moving account of his own spiritual experiences of running and training. During one of the Monday sessions Mike took all the teachers out running around the block. Later that year he set up a basketball game that was accompanied by a jazz band and a movement festival where people meditated, ran, jumped, played music, wrote poetry, ate, and drank.

Mike had trouble at Richmond High. He was accused of being too familiar with the students, of being uncooperative, radical, and bothersome. After he led a student strike against the school administration and published with his students an underground paper called *Pigassus* he was fired. He became one of the storefront regulars.

Fred is last of the central people. He was a senior at Berkeley High School who started out as a student in a guerrilla theater class I taught in the costume and prop room of the Berkeley Community Theater. Fred is big and so it was hard to remember all the time that he was only sixteen. He became the son to Collingwood's grandfather in the structure of the group that emerged.

Fred's father was black, an articulate, radical man who died a number of years ago. His mother, also a political radical, is Italian-American. Fred was a young man with elements of an old man, a cherubic, kind, and gentle person with a fierce and violent component, a good poet who aspired in romantic or drunken moments to be a poet-warrior. His craziness fit well with the rest of ours and he was the only student who became intimately involved in our growth as a group that year.

It is hard to understand what the affinities were that bound us together with such emotion and energy. There must have been at least five hundred people who came through the storefront that year. Many people came often. However, only seven of us came together with such intensity (Kaprow was not part of the group and he left after the first year of Other Ways). Allan Kaprow once described us as a bunch of failures and in a sense he was right—we were all marginal in revolt, groping for new ways of living and working, in the midst of the painful process of remaking our selves and our social world at the same time. But that's certainly not the whole explanation, for many other people who passed through were in the same situation in their lives. I don't have a full explanation of why the seven of us—one woman and six men, one Jew from New York, one Irishman from California, an Italian from New Jersey, a WASP from New England, a black man from Berkeley, another black man from New York, and a black African—came together. There are several partial explanations, however. None of us was or wanted to be a dropout, although all of us in one way or another had been kicked out of the main culture. But none of us wanted to take a rest or mark time. There was a need in each of our individual lives at that moment to become involved in something of importance. This involvement meant something different to each one of us, and this fact led to lots of conflicts later on. We did not have a common vision as much as a common need to have a vision, direction, focus, center, and to have an arena in which the vision could be worked into existence.

We also had lots of time, and a small amount of money from Carnegie. No one who needed or wanted lots of money could afford to join us.

Then there was the Herbkohl phenomenon, which played a part in our coming together, although it is impossible for me to know how significant it was. Herbkohl is the person who wrote my books as he is constituted in

the minds of the people who read them. Often he bears
only a minimal resemblance to me. He is a romantic,
centrifugal figure who attracts people and then repels
them because of his lack of resemblance to my flesh and
blood. He is the person who many people feel has the
answer to unanswerable questions, as well as a whole bag
of tricks to make growth and learning easy. I'm sure that
a lot of people were disappointed to discover that the message, the only message, was to act to learn to love oneself,
and try to love, and maybe something better would
emerge. I was as unsure about the future, as undeveloped
in myself as many people who came to consult and question me. Fortunately I have a Yiddish sense of humor
about knowledge and folly. Otherwise I might have ended
up being Herbkohl.

Anyway, I'm not sure how much my public role initially
caused the people who became part of Other Ways to get
involved. I harshly rejected anyone who seemed as though
they were making love to an image, no matter how flattering their attention seemed initially. People who resisted
the image and fought its authority attracted me and that
made it possible for them to stay.

It was also impossible for all of us to get close to people
who didn't drink or smoke dope, who couldn't laugh, who
didn't try to make love to the world in their own way.
Dour people, superserious people, earnest people never
felt at ease at Other Ways. Life was always moving too fast,
there was too much noise, stumbling, groping, joking,
screaming, touching, too much madness and silliness, too
many blunders, too much ecstasy or pretend-ecstasy. Half
the time we took ourselves seriously when we were only
foolish. In thinking about the first year of Other Ways I
feel affectionate toward that time, slightly awed that we
were able to survive without tragedy or tragic folly, and
yet I know that there is no way I would go through that
experience a second time.

We were a group of individuals who negated very well

—redistributed the money from Carnegie, avoided hierarchy, attempted to deal with racism and later sexism. We also tried to reach out and affect others—the Berkeley Unified School District in particular, as well as people throughout the county concerned with schools. We strove to create a whole, open, committed group dedicated to working with young people. In the process we passed through many stages of internal perversity, fought external battles with hostile public authorities, and occasionally got a taste of health. After three years we ceased to exist. However the original negations of our group gave rise to positive though unexpected roles and identities that are not unique to our experience. In the beginning of Other Ways, family bonds formed out of the remnant of people who remained at the storefront on Monday evening after the session with the teachers was over. Usually one of us went out to buy some more wine or beer, some bread and cheese and sausage. Everyone was a bit high and we usually felt good with ourselves, special. People had come to our storefront, we were invited into different classes in the school district. I worked with some kindergarten and first-grade students and taught a guerrilla theater class at the high school; Mike had set up a running class at the high school; Darryle was working with some junior-high kids, although no one was sure what specifically he was doing. Colly told kindergarteners folktales and taught a class on racism and black studies at the high school. Fred was one of the central figures in the guerrilla theater and taught in a kindergarten too. Betsy, although she didn't teach formally, spent time talking with many of the kids who were regulars at the storefront as well as making contacts with school administrators and learning how to exploit the weaknesses of the school system. We all felt like fugitives infiltrating a system we dreamed of overthrowing. We felt big and powerful Monday evenings in the storefront. Tuesday mornings, when we went to face the kids in the context of the large cold builidngs in which they were confined five hours a day, we experienced our own smallness and insignificance. I think those Monday evenings gave us the courage to do small things on a day-by-day basis in the service of a large vision.

As we sat around Monday evenings eating, drinking, and bullshitting, feeling close, comfortable, and quite crazy, like little kids who feel they have gotten away with something, we romanticized one another's strengths and abilities, projected our needs and fantasies upon one other, and turned ourselves, in a fantasy we tried to live, into a healthy and vibrant clan or tribe or extended family. We saw in Colly the elder, the wise man who needed to be cared for, but who had knowledge to gift us with. Colly needed to see himself this way too, and our fantasies and his fantasies came together to define a role for him. We did need a wise man, a navigator, since we groped and floundered so much. From Tuesday to Sunday Colly was the least likely navigator in Berkeley, stumbling from brilliance to inanity, losing his way more often than finding a new way. But on Monday nights he was the wise man, the tribal elder, and it felt good to sit and listen to his wise bullshit.

If Colly was the elder, Mike and Fred were the young men about to be initiated into the mysteries of tribal life and test their worthiness to be full members of the group. They listened, drank to keep up with the elders, kept on pushing for more and more stories. It was as if we were sitting about a fire under the stars and swapping stories that had hidden meanings.

I am afraid that the role of stern and responsible father fell to me. It was flattering—part of me needed to be confirmed as a rock of stability. I was just learning how to father my own children and the fantasy of already being competent was useful in working toward that goal. Of course, I told my share of growing up in the Bronx stories and chided Colly as was expected of me. But I couldn't be as mad or seem as wise as he. My role was sterner; I had to bring the food in and make sure we didn't starve. The role of father provider and manager was more comfortable to me at the time than that of project director or boss. Externally I was the project director, the responsible party, the highest paid citizen, the accountable one, the boss. I was not comfortable with that role, yet had to embody at least the appearances for the sake of the B.U.S.D. and the Carnegie Corporation of New York. It was easier to take that burden as a family member than as a project director. I did not want the responsibility of being the sole and ultimate source of decisions, since I was floundering as much as anyone else. After all, how do you change this incredibly resilient and resistant culture?

Because I shared my salary with other people, it was easier to share the responsibility of defining the direction of the group and assume a role within a collective rather than a controlling role above everyone else. However, the stern father has to confront the growing sons, whose role in life is to take over his role themselves. I assumed my role easily and with relief, not suspecting or understanding that the role once assumed has a logic within the group that is not fully controllable by the actor. I now see that it was inevitable that I confront Colly, my elder, and that Mike and Fred confront me. I also understand that wise cultures are prepared for these archetypal confrontations and that we are not a wise culture. But at that time, on those Monday evenings, I was high on the romance of being part of a new group.

Betsy was the only woman in the group and had to assume more roles than any one person can bear. She was Motherways to the kids; was sister, lover, daughter. I am not sure why no other women were part of the original group. Many women came to the teacher sessions on a regular basis, and some women joined us when we gave conferences. Karen Jacobs, a dancer, worked with some of the kids. Judy and I live together. Collingwood was not celibate. Mike had innumerable lovers. However, for the first year none of the women came into the group and relieved Betsy of some of her functions. Part of the explanation might be that Betsy kept other women out. A more likely explanation is that the men at Other Ways kept women away because we believed that changing the schools was primarily men's work. Many groups fall into the sexist attitude of believing that even in revolution it is the women's role to support the men and not direct or participate in the struggle. Other Ways almost fell apart every time a strong woman came into the group and tried to break the male dominance of the organization.

Betsy had a voice in decisions, could assume what responsibility she cared to. Yet in the family structure she assumed a feminine role—not feminine in the sense of playing at being inferior, exploited, second-class, passive, soft, compliant, but in a more archetypal sense. She was the earth, the ground, the foundation out of which the whole group sprang. She was always there, harried, pulled apart by people who needed comfort or wanted a listener. We all ran around and she sat at her desk smoking, talking to people, protecting the more irresponsible of us, trying to meet everyone's needs and demands, which was of course impossible.

If Colly was the grandfather to my father, and Fred and Mike the sons, Darryle was the irresponsible though playful and charming favorite uncle. He was the one whose role it was to indulge the children, to be slightly removed from everything yet a part of family. His irresponsibility along with his charm were integrated into a role because he was part of the group. Any traits can be integrated in a seemingly positive way if a group needs to bind itself together. Irresponsibility, irascibility, silliness, foolishness can all become characteristics of roles and therefore accepted as part of a whole as long as they are held in tension by their opposites. If someone is expected to be irresponsible, his more positive aspects can be built upon as long as someone else is expected to be responsible. If we were all fools or all irresponsible, the group wouldn't cohere. If we were all grimly responsible and wise, the group probably would not have had that tension and energy, that willingness to do crazy and different things that characterized the best and worst of our functioning.

As the roles we chose became more explicit, so that Colly was referred to among us as grandfather (though usually not in his presence), and Betsy was jokingly called Motherways, our rationalizations of the family or tribal structure became more elaborate. We talked about new cultures, re-formation of relations, about remaking the world through creating small tribal/family cultures. We convinced ourselves that the roles we had fallen into had greater importance than our lives. We liked to think of the group as a new archetype, as I am sure every new group does. We needed to think on and celebrate our uniqueness and newness and often ignored the fact that our new roles were ancient and represented if anything a groping, painful, uncertain reconstruction of a caring human group, of a group without exploitation or insane competition but with diversity and compassion. We also overlooked the harsher fact that our roles were diluted not a little by what we brought to the group, by our training in competition and cruelty as well as our just not knowing how to support one another. We all had our own demons and we didn't know how to help one another deal with them. We manifested a very common American malady—the tendency to reject anyone who shows too much pain or acts too crazily. We struggled to keep from rejecting one another and in the end didn't succeed. But at times it seems as if we came close to understanding how to care.

Collingwood introduced us to Bantu ritual that bound the group together more than any of our rationalizations and explanations. He explained to us that in his Nation (for the Bantu, the people, number in the millions) it is customary for people to drink together in a particular order, from youngest to oldest, with the understanding that no matter how often the drink goes around the circle, the last drop must be preserved for the oldest person present. It was a ritual institutionalizing respect. The first drink was to be poured into the earth to give the ancestors, both dead and unborn, their share. The second drink went to the youngest member of the group.

After a while we always shared wine according to the ritual of Collingwood on Monday evenings or later on when we traveled together. I remember pouring the wine on the rug, thinking at first it was silly but eventually coming to believe that the ancestors should be given their share. I remember Fred taking his first sip and Colly killing the bottle.

One time we even had all fifty teachers at a Monday session rank themselves according to age and share in the ritual. Some of the teachers were ashamed to reveal their ages and Collingwood chided the older ones for not demanding respect and turned on the younger people for identifying age with obsolescence. He played the elder at that moment and enabled some people to take a new prouder look at themselves growing old.

[2]

At Other Ways there were always problems that had to be dealt with that our so-called family allegiances didn't resolve. There would be times when people didn't live up to their commitments—when Mike would miss a class when he was tired or I would act in negotiating with the school district without informing anyone else. Darryle often didn't show up at crucial times, Betsy delayed doing some of the endless paperwork There were more serious crises to deal with—shortage of money, students getting busted or harassed by the police, the neighbors attempting to evict us from the storefront, staff members battling with one another over power. We had to develop new ways of dealing with conflict and avoiding lying to one another.

Problems arose when people failed to abide by collective

decisions or acted in the name of the group without telling others what they were doing. We talked behind one another's backs, and often took joy in seeing a member of the group fail or flounder. These conditions, which are quite normal in the established culture, are not supposed to exist in the new one, and in celebrating our newness we remained blind to the old competitive and hostile forms our behavior actually assumed.

In our culture it is hard for one member of a group to tell another directly that he is messing up or lying or acting in a way destructive to the group. There are no limits to the ways in which such truths can be denied or turned back on the person who tries to tell what he or she sees. The rhetoric is that people should always be open and honest with one another. The reality is that people have never learned how to be open or honest, are so unsure of their centers and identities, are so fundamentally tender and fragile that they will go to amazing and often bizarre lengths to avoid or deny something that confronts them with their own inbred nastiness and dishonesty. Everyone, especially in new groups, needs to feel good and pure, wants to have reached the new world without struggling to create it, wants to be in the future already. Truth directly told in most new groups like Other Ways cannot be easily integrated into the ongoing process as a matter of collective responsibility. People, though pretending to new familial bonds, are unsure of one another and afraid to trust. I discovered that if dishonesty is not to tear the group apart, the truth must be told indirectly, in a nonthreatening manner.

There are traditional, indirect, truth-telling roles, the most common throughout history being those of the jester and the clown. The jester tells the truth indirectly though cleverly and helps a person see himself or his situation while laughing at it. The jester is a storyteller, a confidante, a parody of the people he is enlightening. This distinguishes him from the clown, who makes people laugh through his own silliness. If the jester is a teacher, the clown is a reliever of tension.

In most small groups a clown is often needed to take the edge off the tension and let people relax and feel unthreatened. The clown's role, among other things, is to help insecure people feel secure. In humorless groups, where no one is capable of being a clown, things tend to repeat themselves endlessly and never get resolved. In the midst of a serious discussion about whether someone has lied or not, there comes a point where all the information has been brought out, where all the affirmations and denials have been made, and where the tension is almost unbearable. At that time the group has no option if it continues in the same grim way but to repeat the information and arguments or break apart. A vicious, uncomfortable, circular, interminable argument can develop, or a member of the group can temporarily become a clown, break everyone up in laughter through a joke or fart or facial expression, and give the group a moment of ease to reformulate the whole problem. Not only does the laughter break the tension, but it also temporarily unites the people who are laughing, it makes it possible for them to look at one another again with a minimum of hostility and suspicion.

I remember a significant incident at Other Ways: I had acted out of turn by promising some money to an artist for teaching a class in painting without consulting the others, who in theory shared responsibility for dealing with the money. Mike discovered this in a casual talk with the artist and was outraged. A meeting was called, we drank with the ancestors, and then got down to dealing with my noncollective action. Mike related his conversation. I lied and said that a promise hadn't really been made—I had told the artist that if the group approved, then I would promise him the money. Dave and Fred brought up several other instances where they felt I had acted in the same unilateral way. Betsy defended me and lied a bit to do it. As the accusations turned into general hostility and frustration, I both became more defensive and developed accusations of my own. After at least an hour, Mike returned to the original point and I followed with the same defensive lie, only this time I was angrier and more self-righteous. Colly at that moment got up as if he were about to speak, silenced us all, waited a bit, looked as serious as he'd ever looked, and then did some weird, wild, beautiful flip-flop. He tripped himself or turned around with comic elegance. It started so solemnly and ended so absurdly that we all cracked up.

When we quieted down, I felt that we really did and could like one another; I admitted my lie and tried to explain how much the others threatened me, and how much my own actions infuriated me. I was used to being project director, boss, despite my protestations and desires to the contrary, and got some confirmation from the role. At that moment I found it possible to ask the others for help and understanding rather than to turn my guilt into hostility. Without the clown, however, there would have been nothing but unresolvable conflict and a legacy of lies within the group.

The clown role, the reliever of tension, is an ambiguous one. It can work for the group in the service of unity and it can also work against the group by minimizing or joking irresponsibility away. A general rule seems to be that the unifying clown is not a party to the conflict being dealt with while the defensive clown is usually a person on the spot or another member of his or her faction.

If the clown can sometimes help the group deal with its own problems, the jester is a continual teacher who enables individuals to see the worst in themselves in a manner that makes it possible for them to change. Indirect teaching, story and folktale telling, which have all but disappeared in schools in the scientized Western tradition, are some of the commonest and most effective ways of conveying painful knowledge that human groups have devised.

Colly was a natural master of telling the truth through story. I learned how to do it a lot through my grandparents.

Many times when I am pressed to say something I know
will upset someone else or make him angry with me, I find
that using a story or tale or illustration makes the point
without mobilizing hostility or creating so much hurt.
People will get the point and yet the tale serves as an inter-
mediary; it becomes a vehicle for self-analysis that can be
held at a distance, examined, related to the self, thought
about in privacy. It does not hurt unnecessarily and is the
opposite of the raw and direct confrontation that many
advocates of encounter group techniques use. I find direct
confrontation often useful but equally often unnecessary.
I would rather gentle people I care about into facing a
difficult truth about himself than assault his center,
and I feel the same way about being taught unpleasant
truths about myself.

The need to use indirection is especially true for children, who devour stories and thrust themselves into the
lives of all the characters, and do not need to be torn apart
even in the service of some fanticized honesty and purity.
I see my children acting out the stories Judy and I read to
them or make up. They start out by assuming the hero or
heroine roles—the princesses and fairies and princes and
angels. Then they get to the demons and pirates and bosses
and dictators. They try all the roles on and it is often easier
and more effective to refer to a story in explaining to them
how they have messed up than to confront them directly
and harshly with their failures. The indirection gives them
time to think things through themselves and doesn't put
them in a defensive and anxious position.

Telling stories can also be a way of pointing out to people some truths you believe are too difficult for them to
acknowledge in your presence. Since I am not connected
with an old and established tradition of teaching stories I
use stories about my personal past as a way of trying to help
people understand me or come in contact with themselves.
I have found that tales of my own possession, my failure,
my analysis, of the struggles I go through to make a book

or prepare a class, of the problems I have with my own children make it possible to say things to friends that they wouldn't accept if I confronted them directly with my perceptions.

In our culture most people have forgotten how to tell and understand tales. That is part of the cruelty that characterizes many of our acts. We either tell painful truths directly and heartlessly, pretending to be tough, or we avoid telling the truth at all, or we lie. These three modes are as common in new groups as in the main culture. People do not know how to help one another change, how to jest and cajole and tell a good tale that is to the point. They don't know how to tell others painful facts about themselves while insuring there is no loss of face or respect.

I tend to get carried away by a situation and become impatient with people. I want things to happen now and sometimes ruin an opportunity to move someone in power by losing my temper and accusing that person of not caring or of being a hypocrite. My anger in many cases is righteous, but it can be harmful to the group. And my impatience can get on people's nerves. I used to have a pocket watch on my belt and would keep on pulling the watch out every few minutes. Sometimes, almost unconsciously, I would look at the watch five times a minute, pacing all the while, wanting things to happen right away. Some of the people at Other Ways decided to break me of the habit, to slow me down. For three days they asked me the time every time they saw me. Sometimes I would be asked the time ten times in a half hour. I got the point and threw the watch away. If someone had told me directly that I was too impatient and that I was bugging people, my immediate and defensive response would have been to accuse the others of being irresponsible and not impatient enough. The way it was done I could laugh at myself and change without feeling done in by my friends.

This does not mean that people should never tell one another hard truths directly. It is a matter of developing

trust within the group and strength in the individual so
that direct truth telling can be accepted in the spirit of
growth. Until such strength and trust develop indirection
is an effective and kind way for people to push one another
to change while offering support in the process. Furthermore, good stories are a pleasure.

I think it makes sense for people embarking on living
and working closely and intensely with others to study as
much as they can of oral and fablic teaching, to read African, native American, Yiddish, Appalachian, Asian tales
and stories; to become acquainted with the oral tradition
and the ways in which stories teach. It is important to learn
how to be indirect as well as to learn how to be direct. One
is not being dishonest or deceitful by being indirect. If a
story is not understood or an action misinterpreted, one
can try to communicate in another manner. If a person is
strong enough and a group trusting enough, then there
may never be a need to be indirect. However, I don't know
of any such human groups.

[3]

New groups have to develop ways of handling personal
crisis and neurotic group behavior. Sometimes individuals
need others to share their burden and support them. At
other times the group itself will act in a self-destructive and
repetitious manner and will need help to assist it in changing before it blows apart. For these reasons, Other Ways
and many other groups who reject any appeal to the socially sanctioned soul-healers, the psychiatrists and psychologists and group therapists, have to reinvent the role of
shaman within the group.

Personal crises—death, separation, loneliness, defeat, loss
—and their attendant emotions—depression, mania, misery,
terror, uncontrollable anxiety, hysteria—often lead to rejection. In our culture people avoid others who seem distraught, suicidal, or homicidal. Within a small group the
luxury of rejection cannot be afforded. People must learn

how to share one another's pain as well as celebrate together. And it is not merely enough for everyone in the group to agree that this sharing is necessary. Structures must be evolved and rituals established so that people in pain are actually supported. It is hopeless to depend upon a spontaneous flow of generosity and love, which is as unpredictable as it is often smothering and inconsiderate. One person or a few have to assume the responsibility of calling attention to personal misery and dealing with the group's tendency to reject the sufferer.

One of the shaman's functions in non-Western cultures is to bring an individual or group from a state of crisis back to normal functioning. One characteristic of most shamans, as Lévi-Strauss points out in *Structural Anthropology,* is that they have at one time in their lives experienced some severe personal crisis that they succeeded in overcoming. A central resource available to the shaman is his or her own disease and cure, which are looked upon as structurally similar to the crisis of the person who needs assistance. The shaman relives his or her disease for the sufferer and takes the sufferer through all the stages of the cure. This is usually done in dramatic form, through ritualized recitation, song, and dance, with the shaman telling the sufferer and the other witnesses when and how to join in. The effective shaman respects the suffering of others, and does not degrade the sufferer by pretending superiority. Rather, the shaman is a living example of the cured sufferer. He or she shares some of the burden and suffers with the person in pain. This surrogate suffering on the part of the shaman may be real or may be a dramatic performance. To be effective, however, it must convince the person in pain and direct attention away from the pain and the sense of inferiority and vulnerability it produces; it must focus attention on the passage through and beyond the pain. And, of course, to every sufferer the shaman also holds out the possibility, beyond a mere restoration of health, that the sufferer too can become a shaman by overcoming the pain.

Not everyone becomes a shaman, but an awareness of that possibility is often enough to change a painful and potentially degrading experience into one that provides a strengthened sense of self and a greater belief in the possibility of human community.

There is at least one example in our culture at this time of what could be called shamanistic healing. A number of former herion addicts in many different organizations work with addicts to help them kick the habit. There is a great deal of preliminary work that goes on, but the shamanistic moment is the time the addict decides to go cold turkey. Addicts are usually terrified of the process of withdrawal. The shames, former addicts talk of their own experiences, shout and scream, take the burden of bearing the pain alone away from the addict, and suffer for and with him. The passage through the pain is shared and, because the ex-addicts have genuinely suffered the same experience in the past, the present suffering of the addict assumes a ritual and nonpersonal aspect. The possibility of movement from pain and despair to some greater strength is embodied by the former addicts and conveyed by them. And the person released from heroin has not merely been freed of pain, but through that release becomes qualified to be a shaman for someone else should the need arise.

The shaman affirms what many people in pain cannot believe—that it is possible to change. In this function the analyst and the shaman are often opposites. The analyst says I am the doctor and I will cure you with my knowledge. The shaman says I too was sick and in pain, and learned to overcome my problem—let me help you, since becoming cured provides strength that can be shared.

[4]

Young people in our culture, in which families tend to be unhappy and generations war with each other, greet the death of a parent with an ambiguous mixture of sorrow and joy. In addition, the dominant culture hides death, disapproves of overt displays of grief, and finds the joy a young person might experience on being released from an oppressive parent repugnant.

The mourner can take the death of a parent as a private affair and let the ambiguity turn into unacknowledged and unassimilable guilt. To the degree to which this happens the guilt can permeate all of the person's relationships and the death never be overcome. The dead parent can control the living child through the unresolved guilt.

The parent's death can also be hidden away, deritualized, and sanitized. The parent can die quietly somewhere in a retirement community, unnoticed, living his or her death the last years of life. The child can note the death, which had already been accepted when the parent was exiled to live surrounded by other old people, as he or she notes all the death announcements in the daily newspapers. Doing that, however, is also to admit the possibility that one might die equally unnoticed and unmourned and that is a terrifying thought to live with.

When an individual lives isolated from family and community, it becomes increasingly difficult to deal with death in a collective way, and to integrate the dying of one person into the living of others. In our culture there really are no ancestors who gift the living and watch out for them. There are only dead bodies who served a function for a time but are of no present value to anyone other than visiting guilt and terror upon their children's lives.

There can be new ways to celebrate and mourn, however; to acknowledge the fact that hate as well as love has colored the lives of families in our culture, and that people die bearing the sins of the culture. It is difficult, yet essential, for people to acknowledge that the hatred between parent and child is not a personal, but a cultural, event. My battles with my parents were over jobs, future security, hair length, dress, sexual habits. My parents' insecurity was real and not imagined. If people do not battle and slave at work, if they are not willing to hurt others and turn their backs on poor and unsuccessful relatives and friends, they might be wiped out themselves. If they do not make their children competitive, the children might not survive. A culture based on fear and insecurity such as ours probably has to develop hatred between young and old. The old have to be cruel and harsh toward the young in order to prepare them for a world that is cruel and harsh. It is, of course, worse when the young realize that the world they are being prepared for is not worth living in, and that modest desires can lead to richer living than competition and consumption. Then the rewards of being cruel are not worth the effort, and the parents are resented for teaching their children to survive using the same methods they knew. Most parents cannot be expected to prepare their children for living in a world totally different from their own.

Mourning for the death of a parent in this culture must also be a mourning for their lives. Very few individuals have not succumbed to the madness of the culture. Most lives are lived out in pain, guilt, or despair. A person can afford to hate his or her parents only insofar as he or she understands the parents as victims and therefore martyrs.

In mourning the death of one's parents within the context of a new group the hate and the love, the sorrow and the joy, the awareness of the evil of the old culture and the potential of the new one can be bound together. Mourning the loss, acknowledging the love and the hatred as well, living through the pain without needing to forget the dead ancestor and his or her struggles are all possible.

At Other Ways death was present only twice. Betsy's mother died of cancer and Buddy Jackson, the director of Black House, one of the other alternative schools within the Berkeley Public School System, was killed in a car crash. Betsy's grief was essentially individual. We did not know what to do about her pain and were quiet and awkward about the dying. Buddy's death at twenty-four was tragic and immediate to all of us, as we were involved in battling the same enemies. A number of Buddy's friends and colleagues at Black House decided to mourn Buddy in a way that would reaffirm his life. A funeral ceremony was created, blending drums, poetry, words of hope for young black people; the loss of Buddy's presence and strength, though accepted, was transformed into future strength—he had become one of the ancestors whose spirit would guard and guide the school. The ceremony itself was a binding together of the community—the loss of a brother was cement to hold the other members of the group closer.

I can imagine a number of ways in which people can learn how to mourn and deal with death rather than hide it. These all assume that the individual is connected with other people and not ashamed to appear weak or cry or break down. They also require that someone step forth as shaman and bring people together to mourn.

The shaman can put together a story-telling session of mourning, asking the bereaved person to tell of the dead parent, to relate tales and anecdotes, to think on the best and worst of the person, to think of their struggles to survive in this culture. Welcome the love and the hate, let it all come out, with everyone else in the group sharing, applauding, crying, toasting to the dead and to the future. The mourning can be part wake—eating, drinking, singing, a renewal of life as well as a pause to respect death. The death of one person can be turned into a collective loss—people can go through the pain together, not forgetting the dead but committing themselves to rebuilding the world for the sake of the person the dead one could have been.

Another possibility is that a funeral procession with music and masks can be created, with a coffin or urn or some other symbolic equivalent of the dead parent, and a communal returning of the dead to the earth can be re-enacted. Included in the burial service can be confessions of love and hate for the dead, crying and rending of the self, dirges and dances, followed by a feast celebrating life.

There are many variations on the way in which the

finality and irrationality of death can be celebrated. I remember my student Akmir's funeral. His parents provided a moving Christian funeral. His friends respected his parent's wishes and waited until the end of the service. Then they placed a star and crescent around his neck and filled the coffin with apples and other fresh fruit—Akmir's favorite food. They acted out of love and respect for Akmir and for his parents, and buried him with a symbol of the world he was trying to attain.

However, the creation of new communal mourning rituals must respect that element of loss and grief that is completely private and personal. Not all mourning or celebration should be communal.

There are other occasions for collective and ritual celebration or mourning:

—The end of a love relationship
—Depression resulting from a sense of inferiority caused by personal failure
—Marriage
—The birth of a child
—Divorce
—Triumph
—The giving of adult responsibilities to a young person as well as other rites of passage from one stage of life to another

Childhood memories are often painful and many people's relations to their parents remain ambivalent and unclarified for their whole lives. Psychoanalysis is one way to deal with the personal past. However, analysis is part of this dominant culture and therefore accepts behavior that members of groups such as Other Ways are trying to change. It is possible to develop forms of support and celebration that can within small groups provide a member with help overcoming nonfunctional neurotic behavior developed in childhood while at the same time avoiding the dangers of traditional psychotherapy.

Suppose that within the group the childhood of each member is dealt with in the same way I suggested the death of a parent could be ritualized. Time could be set aside for each person to tell the story of his or her life—the earliest memories, the most delightful, the most painful experiences. People could be encouraged by others taking turns playing shaman or guide, to try to explain their present behavior in the light of their personal past, to make excuses for all the worst things they do, to elaborate on feeling

> rejected or
> denied or
> deprived or
> nurtured or
> loved or
> smothered,

to tell tales about what people did to them and what they did to people to lead them to their present position in life.

Sitting around the storefront on Monday evenings, we fell into telling stories of our childhood. Mike talked about growing up in an Italian community in New Jersey. He talked of his parents, his relatives, wove stories that made him out hero and victim. We answered his stories with stories of our own—about growing up in Boston and Berkeley and the Bronx and Capetown. It was a way of educating one another about our strengths and weaknesses, a form of developing trust among a group of strangers that was trying to become a new kind of family. It was also a way of trying to explain and come to terms with our own infuriating imperfections—the irresponsibility, competitiveness, and paranoia we all manifested despite our intentions or rhetoric. It helped, too—I came to understand the strengths and weaknesses of the others and I think they began to understand me. Because of our shared personal information, it was possible after a while to avoid having people do what they were least responsible about and to support them when they messed up.

I am convinced that within the group the past not only can be dealt with on a personal level but it also can be rethought in broader, more social terms, so that statements like "My father was too busy with work and rejected me" can be rethought and turned to "My father was forced to work in order to survive and suffered from having to reject me, but I was too young and too protected to understand." In this way hatred and rejection can be transformed into compassion. It is possible to bring out all the pain as well as the joy of growing up in our culture and rethink them in terms of forces operating on the family from the larger dominant culture. Love and hate for the self and family are natural consequences of a social life like ours that promises so much and yet demands such a price in terms of conformity, competition, and violence to others outside the family.

From the rethinking of the personal past it might be possible for people within the group to rephrase their usual excuses for inaction or powerlessness so that statements like "I can't share because I was an only child" are publicly acknowledged as meaning "I am not used to sharing and use the only-child bit as an excuse not to try."

It is a short step from this admission to trying to learn new, more generous forms of behavior and to ask others for help when changing seems too difficult a thing to do alone.

It is essential that individuals trying to remake their lives believe there is no force in their past preventing them from changing. On the other hand, the fear generated by past experiences can grip a person's soul and it is through the support of a group (instead of a therapist) that change can become actual. The change can be in the service of health of the individual and the group, which from my perspective involves social and political commitment as well as personal enrichment, and it is true that such change might not lead to happiness. Freeing oneself of dependency, of the need to acquire objects or control people in order to feel powerful oneself, might lead to the opposite of contentment. It might point a person toward increased struggle, a consequence of which might be a feeling of fulfillment and self-love. But there can be very little joy. The more one learns of the lives of most people in this world the more pain one has to integrate.

If each individual's past history can be told and known, if excuses can be eliminated, then a group of people might be in a position to ask one another for help.

Sometimes it makes it easier for everyone to ask for and offer help and criticism publicly. For example, if a person asks everyone for help to become less selfish, then it becomes socially expected to tell that person when he or she is behaving selfishly, to joke about it and periodically examine whether things have changed. Of course, egos will be bruised as people begin to attempt to change or help one another. In a group of people who care for one another there will be enough trust for slight bruises to be healed without pain or recrimination.

The group, acknowledging that the culture is sick, can also acknowledge that its members are sick and in need of safety and support while they learn to change themselves. It can provide its own therapeutic environment. This won't come easily, however, since it takes a long time to establish trust within a group.

The person who assumes the responsibility of being a temporary shaman for the group has to be a bit of a performer; has to be honest about his or her own imperfections and suffering; has to be able to cry, scream, shout, celebrate. The shaman has to be aggressive, too, because the moment for ritual mourning or celebration is not set by tradition.

Some rituals will fall apart, seem empty, ineffectual, even silly. It is painful to begin a mourning ritual and have it end in an awkward ceremony that embarrasses everyone. The attempt might even increase the pain of the bereaved. That is a risk people engaged in creating

new forms have to take. Ease of association and familiarity
with the nature of ritual and the positive effects of communal mourning and celebrating have to be achieved.
They are not part of the education of many people in our
culture.

[5]

The shaman can have a group as well as a personal role.
There are times of group crisis—e.g., political defeat, economic disaster—when there is a tendency for members of
the group to panic. Someone must take the responsibility
of bringing the group back together and celebrating its
mission. Panicked people lose their memory and self-confi-
dence, overreact, and can destroy years of work in an hour.

Often you just have to force yourself to act to bring
things together—shyness, a sense of embarrassment, self-
doubt have to be dealt with harshly if a group is to survive.
People have to come out and act when they might want to
hide. One of the great problems groups face is the defeat
of their leaders. If someone is generally expected to support or prod or inspire others during crises, his or her
defeats can create a void that shy and scared members of
the group have to step into. Everyone is periodically devastated, and the more groups depend on individual leaders
the more vulnerable they become. The groups that have
the greatest chance of survival are probably those that have
overcome the destruction of their leadership.

I remember a moment of panic during the second year
of Other Ways. We had decided to become a school at the
end of the first year and by January of the second year
had sixty-five young people and ten adults involved. On
January sixth, after spending all Christmas vacation painting and fixing our building, we were evicted by the Berkeley Fire, Building, and Health Departments. Not only
were we evicted; we were given one hour to vacate and
lock the building. Near panic resulted. The kids, who had
an enormous emotional stake in the school, felt crushed,

punished, oppressed. Some of the staff talked as if our mad adventure were all over and others sulked quietly or sat around on the verge of tears. We had worked so hard, put so much into school; it all seemed over.

Mike, Darryle, Dave, and I—the old hands—decided to play a shaman's trick upon everyone in order to give us some time to reformulate our plans and find a new way to survive. At a time when we should have been mourning we decided to celebrate.

Instead of retreating to our separate homes that afternoon all seventy-five of us—staff and students—went to an Italian restaurant and ate and drank together for hours. We came together instead of falling apart, celebrated our life rather than mourned the loss of our building. The next day we decentralized the school, and for a while met in people's homes, in the parks, in restaurants—wherever we could get together and go about our business.

There are other problems that might be untangled by the art of the shaman. For example, one of the shaman's traditional roles is to randomize expectations and set a group out on a new path when usual behavior leads to failure. In small hunting cultures during years when game is scarce and hunger becomes a problem, a shaman is usually called upon to bring back the game. The hunters themselves have exhausted all their resources. They have visited every traditional hunting ground, stalked prey in all the ways known to the culture and have come up empty-handed. The shaman is called and usually performs a ritual that opens up new and unexpected routes for the hunters to seek game. In Siberian Lap culture, for example, the shaman holds an antelope skin over a fire and waits for it to crack. The cracks produced by the heat are then interpreted as a map of new routes to seek game. Frequently, the shaman's strategy of randomization works. The hunters have been so conditioned to traditional methods of searching for game that they panic when these are exhausted. It takes a madman, a shaman, to randomize their experience, undo some of their old cultural responses, and set them on new roads.

Often we are in the same circumstances with respect to our own culture and our attempts to develop stable and durable alternative institutions and ways of living. We fail because we have been so well conditioned in traditional ways of behaving that we repeat the same futile actions over and over.

For example:

—We repeat the same patterns of confrontation over and over again (e.g., antiwar marches) even after they have lost their effectiveness. Many people, instead of creating alternative means of facing the enemy, give up when they realize this ineffectiveness.

—We look to packages or simple answers to complex questions. We also seek painless ways to resolve painful conflicts.

—We run away from friends in trouble, get seduced by our own success, and forget the goals of the battle.

—We find ourselves as unable to trust our friends and allies as our enemies and therefore are susceptible to doubts that can be planted by enemies. As are most people in this culture, we are strangers to one another and have no confidence in our relationships with others.

A role of the shaman could be to systematically rephrase and redirect thinking about seemingly insoluble problems. For example, many alternative school people have difficulties obtaining buildings that will pass the school codes. They spend months looking for a suitable building, worrying about raising money to bring a place up to code. Sometimes it might be profitable to stop and rephrase the whole issue—Why a building at all? Why a school? What other possibilities are there?

There is a tendency for group thinking to get stuck in grooves—change the schools by offering the same kind of education; change welfare by giving more money; change medical care by producing more of the same kind of doctors. Alternative groups have the same problems with getting stuck in one way of thinking that most people in this culture have. Consequently there is an occasional need to turn all the questions upside down, to bring in seemingly irrelevant associations, to drive the group mad with speculation and fantasy, which pulls people away from old and unsatisfactory patterns of thought. A person assuming the shaman's role could be given the right to call special councils occasionally whose function would be to rethink a problem with the prior agreement being that people should be prohibited, for the time of the council, from taking positions they have taken before. The council would be a deliberate group exercise in fantasy and imagination with the shaman as provocateur and resident madman.

Consider a specific case. Last year in Berkeley one of the alternative schools got stuck with the problem of what to do with a thirteen-year-old girl who sat around the lounge all day and refused to attend classes. One faction of the staff insisted she be kicked out of the school for doing nothing. Another said she wasn't causing any trouble and had a right to do nothing if she wanted. The arguments went on for weeks. Finally one faction forced the issue and the girl was kicked out. The disagreement was never resolved, and the issue of "doing nothing" factionalized the staff for the rest of the year.

A shaman *might* have been able to turn the situation around and facilitate some collective rethinking of the problem. Suppose: The shaman calls a meeting of the staff. Everyone sits around the table and the shaman says the first five minutes of the session will be devoted to doing nothing. Everyone has to concentrate on doing nothing until the bell rings. Five minutes pass, the shaman watches the eyes, breathing, nervous movements of the people. When the time is up, the shaman says the next five minutes will be devoted to doing something. A second bell and the shaman asks everyone in turn to describe nothing or to free associate with the word "nothing." Then the shaman proposes that everyone describe something the young woman was doing when she was hanging around the lounge—breathing, keeping her eyes open, smiling, moving about the room, occasionally reading, chatting.

Then the suggestion is made that the situation be described by both factions with the condition that the word "nothing" not be used.

At the end of the session, which need not last more than a half hour, no decision is made. A day is allowed before reconsideration in a more direct way is given to the problem.*

At the second meeting people could return to the problem of what the young woman was doing—and what other people at the school were doing with or to her. It's possible that the same conclusions might be reached, but it is also possible that some of the teachers might decide to change their own behavioral expectations instead of exiling the girl. With time to change and new ways of looking at the problem everyone is given time to reconsider, to be their own shamans, to develop ways of giving up old ideas and not feeling guilty or vindictive about having been wrong or stupid.

On a personal level it is possible to practice randomizing experience through systematic negation. One can practice doing the opposite of what one has done in the past, or negate treasured ideas and consider these negations. If you have been obsessed with free schools, think of nonfree schools or nonschools. If you are obsessed with forcing change, think about the consequences of forcing something not to change. Try to be left-handed, take your glasses off for a day, put your clothes on backwards, eat dinner first and breakfast last, cut your meat with scissors instead of a fork—let yourself be a clown or jester. Invert your world for a while, and perhaps when you return to

---

* Some techniques for shamanistic thinking are described in Edward de Bono's book *Lateral Thinking* (Harper & Row, 1971).

your customary life you will be able to change more easily.

The shaman is not only a problem solver and healer. He or she often is a master of the techniques of ecstasy who conducts celebrations intended to heighten the group's experience of itself as unity. There are many times when groups seem on the verge of dissolution—when goals are not realized, when people are fed up with one another, when the whole reason for coming together is forgotten. At those times there is a need for rededication and revitalization if the group is to survive. With most people tired and depressed, someone has to be able to overcome personal despair and assume the responsibility for trying to bring the group together. At Other Ways for as long as he was there Collingwood was the Master of Ceremonies, the shaman who got us to laugh and sing and feel proud of ourselves as a group when we were all ready to quit. Later on Mike and I shared that role—taking the entire school out for pizza, having parties during times of crisis, encouraging the students to sing and dance and chant poetry. During its second year Other Ways was always alive with music—the black students drumming all day, reciting strident militant poetry, the white kids playing guitars and flutes and recorders, also reciting and chanting. There were times when the drums battled the flutes and times when they sang together. During our most difficult times—when we were evicted from buildings or caught in the middle of the horror of People's Park and the ROTC riots and the Kent State demonstrations—there were always music, poetry, and dance.

Collingwood left after the first year or rather was forced out by the rest of us because he was finally too crazy and bitter for us. He said one too many "racist motherfuckers," insulted too many school administrators, and scared too many of the students with his love and hatred all mixed with despair for his people in South Africa. We really didn't know how to deal with him, how to support him when he was suicidal and make use of his enormous talent and understanding of people. He threatened the existence of the group and our response was to push him out.

With Colly gone, Mike and I were bad substitutes and the students themselves conducted most of the ceremonies. They were more musical, less inhibited, and at least as much committed to group survival as the adults. So they developed techniques of celebration on their own.

Dave was the only adult who really celebrated with the students instead of getting strength and pleasure out of watching them celebrate, as I did. He was always in the middle of things, partying with the students, kidding them, reminding them always of how fine Other Ways was or at least could be.

Those days the shamanistic function was spread throughout our group rather than concentrated on a single person. There was no officially designated or even covertly acknowledged shaman and anyone could assume the responsibility of bringing the group together, convening a meeting or initiating a celebration. There were so many crises we faced and so many celebrations and meetings that when pressure let up we collapsed of fatigue and the group finally began to disintegrate.

The shaman's role, however essential it was in helping our group deal with pressure, also involves great dangers. Since it is so powerful, it can be used to establish personal power rather than to heal. A group can come to depend upon a certain individual during crises and become paralyzed without him or her. The shamen can also subtly control a group rather than facilitate self-discovery. I occasionally caught myself subtly leading our group to a position I had already decided upon, trying to convince them that a decision I had already made was arrived at collectively. I led people to my solutions of their problems instead of helping them solve their own problems. Perhaps they saw through this but never told me. I know a number of times people who realized I schemed this way took a paranoid view of my behavior and believed I always had hidden agenda and wanted to control everything. There was even a time when Mike and Fred and a few other students came to my house to rough me up because they fancied I was making money off Other Ways and dealing with the superintendent secretly and selling out the school.

Small abuses of the shaman's role can lead to major distrust in a group and the role has to be assumed cautiously, temporarily, and self-critically. There is always the temptation to take power, to manipulate lives, which even the most open and honest person can unwittingly find him or herself doing.

The shaman was not the only nonfamily role that was assumed as Other Ways tried to achieve cohesion and develop trust within the group. At different times we became hermits, midwives, seers, prophets, teachers, spiritual guides, generals, warriors, inventors. Those roles merged with the family roles we assumed and often existed because of temporary needs. For example, in making a presentation before the school board and bringing out our partisans the group had to organize itself. Someone had to organize the presentation, other people had to make phone calls, set up car pools, make signs, and so forth. We had to become a small disciplined army with clearly allocated responsibility. Occasionally it fell to me to be general, and during crises people took care of their responsibility and I assumed a very authoritarian role. As soon as the crises lifted there was no way I could remain in that role. People ceased to listen to my loud voice, collective decision making resumed, and although I was still the responsible father I was no longer the commander.

I have seen a number of groups fall apart because some members became seduced by temporary roles they had to assume during crises. Some people enjoy exercising control over the lives of others and once given a taste of power can't give it up.

When I quit Other Ways after three years I was initially delighted to be released from all the responsibility of struggling with the school board. I was relaxed for about three weeks and then all of a sudden I realized I didn't have any power any more, wasn't on center stage in the Berkeley education scene. I panicked briefly, had several anxiety attacks, found myself scheming and fantasizing being called back to Other Ways. Part of me knew it was all over, that I was too tired and drained to do anything but rest and think and build up new energy for other battles with other groups. Another part felt hurt, injured, rejected even though I had voluntarily left. I felt a loss of power and had to sit on my hands for several months as I recovered from that loss.

Actually I didn't sit on my hands. I took up macramé and used my hands to tie thousands of knots as I sorted out my feelings.

Another role I wanted to play was that of hermit, although it didn't fit my character very well. I needed time to retreat to my cave and write and think. Yet at Other Ways there was too much public pressure on me, too much responsibility and engagement with other people's lives to leave any energy for writing. For two years I had pretty much stopped writing and after a while felt resentful toward the others for putting me in the position of choosing writing or teaching. Of course no one put me in that position consciously—it is just that it took years for us to understand one another's most essential needs and by then we were no longer working together.

I remember feeling somewhat condescending toward Mike and his running, believing it to be something of an affectation. I didn't realize that his need to run was as deep as my need to write; that those activities are ceremonies of purification for both of us and can only be denied at the cost of great anger and frustration.

There is no way of predicting beforehand which roles members of a group will assume or what constellations of roles will develop over the course of time. In extremely structured groups most acceptable roles have clear definition and are inherited from others who had the role in the past or simply assigned. In newer groups people often assume roles that they only later become aware of when conflict arises. At Other Ways we discovered that we had chosen family roles for ourselves; we did not set out to become a family. Some of the roles that emerged in the group fit well. I didn't initially mind being the responsible father and playing the role helped me become stronger, although later the responsibilities became unbearable. However, Darryle's role of the jolly, indulged uncle supported the worst in him and eventually forced him to quit right after I left.

One of my dreams was to leave Other Ways at a time when my particular skills were no longer needed. When I actually left, there really was no one to assume the administrative and financial governance of the school who also believed in humane and open learning.

I wanted Darryle and David to take over Other Ways. But indulged uncles and people accustomed to thinking of themselves as dependent adolescents can't move into other roles overnight. I left more suddenly than anyone anticipated. One day after my writing class some of the students took me aside and told me that I seemed bored with teaching, not interested in them, and weary. They told me to take a rest. That moment I realized that the basic joy I received from being part of Other Ways— teaching—no longer existed and therefore I would have to leave. In order to avoid thinking about the future of

Other Ways I thrust the leadership of the group onto David and Darryle, who agreed to assume it and finished the semester quietly tying up my classes and avoiding all communal meetings.

A few days after I announced publicly that I wouldn't be back the next year David and Darryle went to see the superintendent to inform him that they would be responsible for Other Ways. He smiled and informed them that proposals would have to be written, the program evaluated, that he couldn't guarantee anything for the next year—he was testing their strength and they panicked. They were in the wrong roles and got no support. The next day Darryle disappeared, and I have seen him only once in the past three years and we could barely say hello.

David tried to run the school but couldn't get the superintendent to take him seriously so he quit too. It wasn't the superintendent's fault entirely; had Dave been more confident he could have forced the superintendent to acknowledge his leadership. But after three years of struggle none of us believed we would need to start all over again when I left.

The people in Other Ways never learned how to support one another or prepare for stable, long-term survival. We made mistakes all the time and some of us learned how not to make the same mistakes again in other groups. One central point I learned was that even in the most egalitarian, loving, democratic, and healthy groups people will assume differentiated roles that are rooted in basic personal as well as collective needs and instincts.

[6]

Sometimes different roles clash, or people struggle over who is to assume what role in the natural history of the group. There is a factor, however, that determines to a large degree the nature of group existence and that puts constraints on the roles that are possible if the group is to survive. This factor is the process of group centering

Just as scrutiny of the center within the individual provides one way of understanding behavior, the same is true within a group. The group is not merely a collection of discrete individuals existing independently of one another. There are purposes, intentions, goals, styles that define or separate the members of a group. The analysis of personal centering developed in the section on the individual can also be useful for looking at groups.

During the stages of development of Other Ways we passed through or manifested the symptoms of many varying forms of distorted being; we also occasionally displayed signs of being a healthy group. A specific analysis of the group center and its relationship to the roles its members assume might help others avoid some of the problems we faced at Other Ways.

Remember the typography of individual centers:

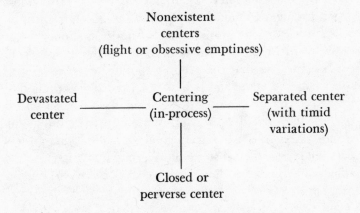

Nonexistent
centers
(flight or obsessive emptiness)

Devastated
center

Centering
(in-process)

Separated center
(with timid
variations)

Closed or
perverse center

This scheme can be applied directly to groups. For example, starting at the top of the diagram, there are groups with nonexistent centers that define themselves purely by virtue of common rituals the members perform. Others define themselves in flight from something else. The ritual group and the fugitive group are not uncommon within both the dominant culture and the so-called counterculture. They are the equivalent of the individual who completely structures his life to avoid being nothing and the individual who is always running away from life.

Imagine the following ritualized existence. People come together to form a commune. They adopt a hip style, share money and responsibilities, have collective meetings and sensitivity groups twice a day. They might set up roles within the group, or pretend there are no differences in roles among the members. It makes no difference in this context—what is characteristic is that there is an attempt made to articulate and predict everything within the context of the group's life. The whole concern of the group is itself; its members fill up their days preening one another, caring for the environment, baring their souls, worrying about the rituals of dining and waking up in the morning and going to bed and making love. There is nothing outside the group's rituals that is of collective concern. In a way the commune I'm describing is like an old folks' home or a retirement community. There is no common work, on relationship to the world outside the group, nothing to do but cultivate the rituals of daily living in order to conceal the fact that the group is bound together only in its attempt to avoid individual isolation and nothingness.

In retirement communities one senses a resignation to the inevitability of death and a need to hang on to the rituals of day-by-day living. In communes and other groups that come together just so individuals don't have to be alone, one also senses boredom invading the environment. After an initial period of excitement things settle down—small changes in ritual become causes of great concern, slight modifications in the environment lead to disproportionate outbursts.

Groups like this tend not to explode so much as drift apart. One member finds a new group, someone gets a job or goes to live with a man or woman who refuses to join the group.

Sometimes after a few months the whole group dissolves. In other cases there are individuals within the group who thrive on the structure and remain, welcoming new people, bidding old ones farewell. The commune becomes a boarding house run by a few old-maid hip people. At best these places can be tranquil rest homes, way stations for people in search of themselves. At worst they are empty dead ends in which people's lives are endless repetitions of meaningless though hip rituals.

Many people can't rest or die quietly. There are lots of people on the move in our culture. Kids running away from home, people running away from families, school, jobs, the ghetto, the law. These people feel a need at certain stages in their lives to keep on going—to crash in one place, then pick up and move. They create a new hobo class within our culture and come together periodically in what could be called fugitive groups. There are crash pads all over the country as well as groups that are bound together through smoking dope or performing acts of violence that are not politically or economically motivated as much as done to validate one's fugitive status.

People in flight are as dangerous to one another as they can be to people outside the group. Fugitive groups tend to blow up—there are fights or sudden shifts of direction since there is no center to the group's existence. People's roles within these groups might swing violently—from messiah to thug, from spiritual leader to rip-off artist. Loyalty to the fugitive life alternates wildly with loyalty to self. This fugitive existence reminds me strongly of what I imagine corporate conglomerate life must be—a group of people circling the world buying up businesses, conglomerating, acquiring, running, but not for money or power since they have more of either of those than they need. All they care about are flight, movement, acquisition for its own sake and for the violence it does to others. These corporate fugitives are known to be as explosive and disloyal to one another as any less legitimized fugitive group. The disloyalty comes from a lack of center—there is nothing in a fugitive group or within the lives of most

of the members to be loyal to other than the state of being
a fugitive and the pleasure of the flight.

Other Ways was not a fugitive group and we were not
usually obsessed by the rituals we created. However, there
were parts of all of us that needed to feel fugitive as well
as times when we used the rituals to avoid dealing with
problems of substance.

I remember the particular glee Fred, Mike, Darryle, and
I felt over seeming fugitive during a trip we took to Washington some time during the end of the first year. I was
invited to be on a Presidential Task Force whose role was
to consider the possibility of federally supported experimental schools. A few days after the meetings in Washington the Other Ways gang—Darryle, Colly, Fred, Mike, and
I—was scheduled to do a conference in Nashville, Tennes-
see. Mike, Darryle, Fred, and I decided to go to Washington together and all attend the Task Force meetings. We
were crazy enough to believe we would be listened to, but
not so crazy as to take Colly with us. He would call the
President a racist motherfucker to his face—would do what
all of us fantasized doing, but being with him in Washington, D.C., was more than we were willing to risk. The
arrangement was that Colly would meet us at the motel
next to the Nashville airport, where the conference was to
take place.

I still remember the wonderful fugitive feeling I had as
the four of us walked through the Washington airport.
We were special—black and white, big, dressed crazy—feeling fugitive and flaunting our differentness. Fred's Afro
seemed bigger than ever; I fancied that my beads shone in
the light. Darryle looked upon the whole thing as a
monumental joke. Mike was deranged and delirious with
fantasies about changing the world. A kid came up to us
in the airport and asked us whether we were a rock band
or the SDS. We were neither but acted as if we were both.

We all did manage to attend the Task Force meetings. It was a strange experience—eleven responsible men, some very nice and liberal, all believing in the need for "responsible" change, all salivating when five o'clock came around and it was cocktail time, most believing that marijuana was sinful. We crazies walked into the meetings and were greeted politely and treated as exhibits to be scrutinized during the deliberations. I was the least strange of the four of us—an intellectual from Harvard who doesn't mind sitting and talking all day.

Mike came back from the first lunch break with flowers for all the members of the group. Darryle and Fred wandered through the Washington community finding out what was going on with the schools in D.C. and bringing information about actual experiments to the committee, whose concern was mostly abstract, intellectual, or in some cases a matter of gaining power and money through a new federal program.

For a week during the days I argued and argued with people on the committee not to start a program that would create a new bureaucracy and rip off the kids once again. During the evenings we ate and drank with the members of the Task Force—tried to tell them what we were doing, to confront them with their own racism, with the power games they were playing, with the everyday pain of poor people, of third world people, of students who feel powerless. People were watching us, analyzing us, trying to find out why we looked as we did and broke the polite conventions of their culture. Occasionally some listened, or confessed their own uneasiness with the government and the culture. Our actions in the situation were determined by a serious commitment to change—but also by a secret pleasure in being part of the fugitive few. This sense of being part of a movement, of giving a peace sign or power salute to other crazies we met on the streets, in restaurants, airports, preoccupied us in ways that made our arguments and actions less effective than they could have been. We

did not unambiguously want to persuade those we fancied
enemies to agree with us. If they agreed, we would have no
claim to a fugitive life, we would not need to be special
or united. To the degree that we were unsure of our goals
and purposes for existing as a group, we escaped into the
romance of being the righteous underworld opposition
being pursued by phantom enemies. Often this self-justify-
ing flight blinded us to the real enemies, who certainly
existed and still exist. We were running to keep busy and
feel together and so didn't take time to look around, to
develop long-range strategies for change and for survival.
It was too exciting.

I remember going out to lunch with a White House
fellow the last day of the Task Force meetings. Sitting in
on the meetings, surviving and fighting twelve hours a day
to convince people that Defense Department planning was
not the way to change schools, listening to cruel idiots
referring to children as clients and to poor people as target
populations, listening to people agree with our ideas and
in the same breath retranslate them into a cold profit game
all exhausted me. At lunch I just broke and couldn't stop
from crying quietly, in despair. The White House fellow
was calm, collected, sympathetic, paternalistic, told me he
understood how hard my work was. Then he bought an
expensive lunch, promised to check up on the work of the
commission, claimed he was completely in agreement with
my analysis. He, one of the real enemies, had me—there is
no other way to describe it. In flight, playing everyone as
an enemy, I broke down not with my people (I was too
proud for that, trapped by my role as the together father)
but with someone who needed to know that I was merely
a harmless though sometimes dazzling talker.

I am no longer in flight. But it takes a long time to find
a direction and center, and consequently cease to use flight
as a weapon of self-deception.

Style and ritual were used by us on that trip in the same
way that we used a fugitive identity. We dressed differ-

ently, shook hands differently, drank to the ancestors, were Other Ways, a name that seemed richer and more meaningful the farther we got from Berkeley. All these trappings helped us pretend we already had a direction, a focus, a center, when we were merely at the beginning. The substance of change, however, was not wholly absent from our lives. We were not merely a fugitive group or a ritualistic functionless group. We were beginning to articulate a vision of new ways for the old and young to come together and to actually do what we were dreaming and talking about. Without the real work—its roots in day-to-day activity that was meaningful in many small ways, that put us in contact with young people and teachers and forced us to develop ways of bringing people out of this competitive culture and into themselves—we would have drifted apart or exploded much sooner than we did and without growing ourselves or helping others.

[7]

Sometimes a new group suffers from the overdetermination of the center rather than from its absence. There are some groups that define themselves in terms of specific revolutionary activities or in specific areas of social or economic concern. These groups have a clearly articulated ideology, a practical though usually abstractly conceived program, a defined base and area of operations, and a confidence (usually bolstered by some theory) that events in the world will turn out as the group expects them to. For example, several years ago there were groups of young white people who considered themselves the vanguard paving the way for black urban guerrillas who were supposed to be waiting in the ghettos for the proper moment to rebel. These young people structured their groups around the task of bringing about violent urban revolution. However, there were no guerrilla bands; the vanguard at that point in U.S. history was a vanguard without a following. Facing the defeat of their goals and expectations, the groups that were obsessively and totally centered on violent urban revolution had to collapse. There was nothing within the structure of many of these closed groups to allow the members to redefine goals, change structure and role, and pursue revolutionary commitment and activity while developing new strategies and reconsidering old theories.

The so-called profit motive is another perverse centering factor for many groups within our culture. The goal of most businesses is to produce excess wealth for the people who run or manage the business. Profit being the motive, the nature of the work or of the product is a secondary concern. Organizations devoted to the accumulation and concentration of wealth are naturally structured in a hierarchical way that rigidly divides those who control from those who serve. On the level of control, people needn't know much about the nature of the work or the product —management is considered a technical skill that involves principles relevant to all profit-making ventures. I remember the experience of having a large corporation buy out a former publisher of mine. The corporation saw to it that most of the creative editors were fired—their styles were too individualistic to fit the paradigms of efficient corporate managers. The experts that did come into the publishing house had no more regard for writers than for any other workers or servants they had to deal with, and looked at books as no different in essence or function than toilet paper or underarm deodorant. They felt that managing a publishing business should be made identical to managing any other business they controlled. Unprofitable lines of goods—like poetry—should be eliminated or modified to meet basic customer cravings such as violence or sentimental romance, or repackaged to look as though it met those wants.

The roles in a closed profit-making system are not communal or familial—they are technologically or hierarchically defined. Workers are not expected to give advice on how to manage or set goals; age is not respected and, in fact, is reduced to coefficients of productivity. The system is rigid and movement from role to role is difficult, frequently involving dislodging, discrediting, and destroying others.

A profit-oriented, closed group cannot respond to failure; people go out of business, sell out, run away—rather than reconsider their aims and social structure.

Nor can such an organization respond to changing social conditions other than by trying to suppress or manage anything new. When large businesses went into the Job Corps business or undertook performance contracting with schools, they set up carefully managed minicorporations that looked and felt like the parent companies. The style was stiff or, when more open, was liberal cocktail party suburban. The client populations, the inmates of Job Corps and the students in the schools, were expected to respond to the rewards of corporate management and manipulation in the same compliant way white-collar workers respond. But the young people didn't respond as planned. They were too wild, humane, funny, suspicious. They didn't like the closed, cold style of managed institutions and, besides, they did not stand to pocket the profits the operation could make. There was nothing in it for them and the corporate managers couldn't understand that. Trapped into the role of professional managers, self-fancied experts on the production of everything, ruling members of a rigidly hierarchical system, they couldn't listen to anyone below them or accept failure. In many of the more chaotic of the Job Corps camps the corporate managers turned to the military for help and many retired army officers "came on board" to help shape up the kids. Of course, more oppression just led to more overt counter-violence and so camps had to close.

In the more liberal camps the managers looked to technology instead of the military. They believed that teaching machines, reinforcement systems, developmental programs, professional counseling and guidance would help. The machines got broken, the reinforcements offered by the management systems were too paltry to matter, and the counselors were ignored. The members of the Job Corps camps did not want to be, could not become compliant consuming members of a profit-greedy and inhumane system. They needed other things—hope, a share of the wealth, power, authentic community, the possibility of a full life, the elimination of racism. None of these goals can be incorporated into a system that builds a rigid group dedicated to the acquisition of wealth. Without replacing this perverse center no change can take place.

For some groups freedom can also become a centering principle that leads to perversity, that is, to an obsessive commitment that makes human life expendable. I know some "free" schools where the teachers and parents adopt a rigid paralytic definition of freedom and center all their activities and concerns on maintaining this definition. Freedom for these people means the total, absolute ability for people, adults and children, to do what they want when they want. In a congenial setting where people know and respect one another, and have things they want to do, the rhetoric is harmless. However, freedom can become an obsession—the cement that binds the group together. In this context tension develops when two people want to do the same thing, when one person insists upon the freedom to torment another, when some individuals insist on consuming the group's resources and feel free to give nothing back to the group. The principle, the fixed center of the group, the mutual agreement over absolute freedom leads to the group version of what I called the tension of perversity in the closed person. The principle held so obsessively leads to contradictions within the group that make life continually tense and often unbearable. The roles equally rigidly set up by the principle—the absolute equality of all—lead to tension as well. Children are expected to do no more or less than adults. If infants cry, adults are free to feed them or not as they wish. If young people are destructive that is their concern. I actually know of an instance where several ten-year-olds set fire to a dry field and almost caused a forest fire while their teachers watched paralyzed because they didn't want to interfere with the young people's freedom.

The tension of perversity develops in closed groups often when pressure begins to develop from outside the group. In the corporate case, this happens when social pressures or decreasing profits demand an adjustment that the perverse centering excludes. In the case of the obsessively "free" institution, pressures often materialize in the form of financial crises, eviction notices, police harassment. There are times when the group needs to come to a decision on how to act, when roles and responsibilities have to be clearly defined, when work has to be portioned out, when youngsters and infants have to be protected. These crises will naturally cause tension—people straining to maintain the center or to redefine it in the interests of collective survival. Some groups will open up a bit, redefine the center or ignore it for a while; others will become paralyzed and wait to be destroyed; others will reject the center violently and adopt a new obsessive centering principle that more often than not will be an opposite of the previous one (a swing from absolute freedom to absolute submission is not that far when one considers that in both cases there is a submission of the person to the principle) is elevated to the center of life.

Although perversely centered groups are often dangerous and always inflexible, there are times when more open groups must deliberately make themselves temporarily perverse or provide a perverse face to people outside the group. For example, when there is a project that has to be carried out during a fixed period of time roles and responsibilities have to be assumed and rigidly kept to. If a school is given a week to bring the building up to code, materials have to be purchased, some people have to paint, saw, and so forth. Some have to deal with the building inspectors and make sure that the correct forms are filled in or that the violations have been specified in writing so that people know exactly what to fix. To hang too loose, or leave it up to chance or whim or inclination to insure that everything gets done in time, is self-destructive. The need to tighten up and become temporarily perverse often occurs in times of crisis. When Other Ways was attempting to negotiate with the B.U.S.D. for funds to continue, we found that if the group hung loose, we would be destroyed. If some of us were going to sit down to talk with the superintendent or some other bureaucrat, it was crucial that our people agreed with one another on all points, that we acknowledged a spokesman, that if someone had to get angry or make threats or walk out it was preset who would assume that role and be in a position to decide on crucial points. If an unexpected problem arose during the negotiations, it was equally necessary that we had agreed upon a procedure to withdraw and caucus rather than make snap decisions that might defeat us. No matter how loose and democratic we were internally, no matter how much argumentation and disagreement existed during our staff meetings, it was crucial that we present a unified, closed perverse face to the enemy.

Naturally we learned this lesson by acting stupidly and barely surviving our mistakes. For example, the first time we were denied money by the superintendent's cabinet we took our case to the Berkeley School Board—all of us, drastically, angrily. We had fifty or so students, the entire staff, friends, parents. We jammed the place and everyone got up to speak passionately on our behalf. There was no coherent planning. One of the students who was particularly distressed at the thought of Other Ways being destroyed came to the mike almost in tears. His voice trembled as he described how much the school meant to him. He was facing the five-person school board as he spoke. Suddenly he turned away from the board and pointed a finger at a man in the back of the room. He accused that man of taking our money, of corrupting students, of not caring. There was a stunned silence in the room—the man was a principal in the school district. The man was also the student's father. A confused mixture of personal, political, social accusations poured out. The son and father were both pained, distressed. The audience was shocked, angered— What was the young man up to? What were we up to? What had we put him up to? We just about blew our chances to survive that night; the young man was crushed and we had to help him through the trauma. We spoke to his father, who emerged with incredible dignity and compassion for his son's suffering. We were rescued by one of the school board members—but barely. Yet that needn't have happened had we just been sufficiently perverse and controlled at that moment.

At other times we learned that an easy way for a group to be defeated in negotiations is for them to show internal disagreement publicly. The superintendent, for example, is a master at turning people against one another, of shifting the focus of a meeting from himself to the group that is petitioning. Any sign of weakness can be fatal. We ended up role playing many of the meetings with people who had power over our lives. We defined roles, found ways of checking one another, of keeping some people out of meetings, of matching our strength with the strengths of people we had to deal with. If someone was a secret hippy, our negotiating team was sure to include David and myself; if someone respected or could be influenced by black people, the negotiators would come from the black staff. If women were needed, we were often in trouble, since Betsy did not feel comfortable doing formalized politics (though she was extremely skilled and effective doing person-to-person bargaining). Our inability to eliminate sexism was one of the main failures of Other Ways.

I have been lucky enough to assist one particularly well-controlled temporarily perverse group—the I.S. 201 negotiating team. I.S. 201 is the intermediate school in Harlem I mentioned earlier that was taken over by a group of community people. For several months the community leaders conducted negotiating sessions with Teachers Union leaders, representatives of the New York State Commissioner of Education's office, and the Superintendent of Schools of New York City. The negotiations were held under the auspices of the Ford Foundation and usually took place at Ford's offices. In private sessions everyone had a voice; there were arguments, lots of play, lots of struggling toward positions on local power, educational policy, structure of decision making, and so forth. Internally, different members of the group shifted roles often—sometimes one person was leader, others followers; there were different wise men or women at different times; people assumed different degrees of militancy on different issues. During negotiating sessions everything was fixed—David Spencer was the angry leader, Babette Edwards the mild leader (roles that were often reversed in private sessions). Consultants like myself were to talk to Dave or Babette but had no business saying a word during negotiating sessions. David or Babs or perhaps Bob Nicol could make decisions for the group—to leave or to break down into small groups, for instance—but nobody else could. A rigid, closed, organized, and unified face was presented to the others, the enemy, at all times. There was no way to divide the group, no way to make an appeal to some members of the community group that might set them in opposition to other members of their group. To an outsider that necessary closedness might have seemed perverse. But it worked for the community, which did achieve at least temporary control over 201 and its feeder elementary schools.

I imagine that some socialist nations have to institutionalize temporary perversity in order to deal with crises. The building of dikes, repairing of bomb damage, creating of new industries require a people to function in highly defined and circumscribed ways for specific periods of time. However, such activities do not require that people define themselves in terms of those temporarily perverse roles. A factory worker in our culture is a factory worker—an economic serf. It is possible that in other nations someone works in a factory when necessary but that the role is temporary and partial. He or she can work in the factory half time, study at the university, work in the fields, be full party to political and economic decisions, be a full member of the culture instead of a serf. It is hard for us to realize that roles which define people in our dominant culture can be temporarily assumed masks that do not define the person in other cultures.

There is a problem, however, that arises within groups that become temporarily closed for specific purposes. Perversity can be pleasing to some members of the group and therefore a tendency to keep things closed can develop. Someone who successfully speaks for the group can slip into the belief that he or she is or should be the leader all the time. Someone who has to act the thug with respect to the outside world might enjoy that role so much as to turn into a bully within the group. It is crucial that the group find a way to deal with undoing its own temporary perversity. Perhaps a celebration of equality, a banquet, a collective drunk or high, a dance, some form of coming together as equals should follow every act of necessary perversity.

[8]

Other Ways was not the only alternative learning setting developing within the Berkeley public schools five years ago. A group of teachers and students from Berkeley High began a small separate student-centered high school on the campus of Berkeley High. If Other Ways was filled with crazies impatient for change and fantasizing taking on the whole system, Community High was considered a model of responsible change. It was staffed primarily by some of the best credentialed teachers at Berkeley High, shared facilities with the more uptight main school, and was devoted to change within the regular channels of the school bureaucracy.

This liberal commitment to change within the structure put the school in a hypocritical and eventually untenable situation. The internal and external self-definition of the group did not coincide. Internally there was much talk about student governance and student initiation of classes. There were many areas in whch the students and teachers deliberated issues of mutual concern. Student decisions were often respected, and the director of the school for the first few years was elected by the students.

There were major problems, however, since the principal of the high school considered Community High to be under his jurisdiction and not an autonomous entity. Furthermore, he was opposed to the principles upon which Community High was based. He did not believe in student-developed curriculum, in student decision making, in the development of a nonhierarchical learning situation. He believed that the curriculum should be set by the adults, that "hard" learning (math, English, science) should be emphasized (instead of "soft" subjects like psychology, art, crafts, politics, self-defense), that class attendance should be compulsory and tests and grades given to evaluate the students. Community High was a bother, a sign of giving in to kids and other bad elements in the community, and he had no stake in seeing it survive, much less thrive.

The teachers at Community were under constant pressure from the principal to test, to keep the students quiet and orderly, to justify the curriculum, to keep attendance in classes—in other words, to return to the fold. This put the teachers and the director, more specifically, in a bind: the students vote no compulsory attendance—the principal demands it; the students vote no required subjects—the principal insists on them; the students vote to change the environment—the administration says the building cannot be touched. The teachers on the one hand believed in the open democratic principles of their school and yet on the other did not want to lose their jobs or break away from the high school altogether. Their lives were centered in one way internally and in another way externally. There was no way to reconcile or integrate this opposition. The position was impossible to sustain and a new director had to be found each year. The school was separated in that it attempted to please irreconcilable forces. If the students and teachers chose to leave the campus, they would have had to fight for money and survival. If the teachers chose to return to the regular school, many of the students would have dropped out.

There was no final resolution. The school drifted for three years. Some teachers did extremely good things; some of the students benefitted from the openness. Finally, however, most of the staff left—either to pursue other careers or to get off into a less hypocritical and tense teaching situation. The school now has a fourth director and a new direction, which seems much more traditional. It is hard to tell where it will emerge, however, since it is still neither fully autonomous nor fully under control of the principal. Strong leadership and new energy could probably revitalize the school.

Many groups that try to bring about change within the institutions of this culture suffer from separatedness and hypocrisy. The institution has no reason to change; in fact, the inertia of institutions in our culture seems to dictate that movement has to always involve growth and the increase of power rather than change of focus. Corporations, school systems, prison systems—and the people who control them (with extremely few exceptions)—do not plan their own demise. Therefore, when a group within the institution plans to create fundamental change and still keep the institution intact, it assumes a separated role. It is devoted on the one hand to change, on the other to preservation. This means that certain bureaucratic forms designed to control change have to be respected; that individuals' feelings must not be hurt; that protocol must be observed if one is to survive within the institution; that power games must be played, people manipulated. For example, some of the directors of Community High tried to go over the principal's head and appeal directly to the superintendent. Almost without exception they were referred back to the principal. In a few cases the superintendent indicated to the principal the need for minimal support so that the staff and students could decorate their environment and decide upon their own time schedule, for example. However, he also constantly reaffirmed his loyalty to the principal.

If a group is willing to attempt to change the prison system or school system or medical system or corporate structure from within it is crucial to realize that hypocrisy and separatedness are going to define their existence. The group will have to control members who want change to happen more quickly than the institution is willing to bear. People who want to make a break or confrontation will also have to be held in check, as will people who are fed up and want to call it quits or sell out. A crucial role in the separated group is the mediating role—the man or woman with patience.

Patience is one of the modalities of separated existence. People within the institution sympathetic to change tell groups who are actively working on change to be patient. Within the group the mediator needs to counsel the members to patience and to blunt the group conscience and pain in order to keep it operating. If members of the group feel too much pain for poor people, for oppressed people, students, then they will not be able to wait. They will want to stop the suffering immediately and therefore will no longer be patient, responsible, or within the system.

The role of the mediator—the rational, responsible, liberal, patient individual who takes the long view ("the institution will change more fundamentally if we move slowly and respect people within the system; after all, they're human beings too")—is a difficult one. The mediator must keep the hypocrisy and separatedness up, must convince people not to despair or revolt. The skills the mediator must display within the group that wants to change an institution are the same ones people within the institution use to keep the institution unchanged. It is therefore not surprising to find that many mediating people move comfortably into the system they wanted to change and become just like their enemies. The mediator is essentially co-optable, just as the separated group is potentially volatile. It is frequently a question of the group's pain threshold. A group can remain separated so long as its members can perceive possible success in the future and let this possibility outweigh suffering in the present. It can also remain separated if its members are comfortable and can deceive themselves into believing that because they are more committed to change than most people, they don't need to do more than the little they are already doing. However, separated groups do not bear well the trauma of having a nonseparated member, of having a member who refuses the hypocrisy of playing within an institution that is sick. People who refuse to conform to the nature of the group must be expelled or they will undermine the trust accorded the group by the people in power. In a separated group the mediator or another person must assume the role of executioner if the group is to survive. Separated groups must develop a mechanism to reject members who want to go beyond patience and tolerance and hypocrisy. That is why one often finds pleasant liberal groups turning viciously on some of their members. It also might explain why liberal groups tend to have so many schisms. It is a matter of the differing levels of hypocrisy the members can bear.

Loyalty is an issue that constantly comes up within separated groups. Ties to the system pull against ties within the group. One cannot be very effective within most institutions in this culture unless one is considered loyal to the people higher up in the system. What loyalty means is that one can be trusted never to betray or try to destroy one's masters. To be considered disloyal is simply to be considered capable of acting on principle even if it destroys a colleague. To be loyal, then, is to be in complicity with people in power to keep a lid on change and to protect incompetent and dangerous people if necessary. To be disloyal means to be willing to try to destroy someone in power. The paradox of separatedness within the context of an institution is that if a person is truly loyal, then he or she will have to prevent change; and if a person is publicly disloyal, then he or she will never get enough power to cause change. The only way a person or group within an institution can develop the power to change it in fundamental ways is to consciously become hypocritical and lie as a political necessity.

There is a temporary and planned form of separatedness and hypocrisy. It is possible for people or groups of people to deliberately infiltrate an institution with the intent of tearing it apart and rebuilding it according to a caring, egalitarian socialist vision. These individuals will attempt to seize power and make indispensable places for themselves within the institution they intend to tear down. They must be willing to act hypocritically at times, to live with a conscience and pain that can only be borne through the vision of a new world that informs their work. Most people who grow up in our culture and who are committed to change cannot sustain the hypocrisy required to gain power. In addition, most people do not believe that fundamental change is possible. People in this culture, especially the white middle class, are resigned to seeing at most small controlled differences in the lives of the poor. They are too comfortable in their own lives to grab hold of a vision of revolution or imagine risking their lives or, what is perhaps more difficult, working quietly for ten or twenty years to make the revolution happen. Reward is too much of an issue in all of our lives and groups want to be recognized and loved as much as individuals do.

However, it is possible that being a consciously hypocritical individual striving toward wholeness, aware that personal health is thoroughly bound up with the health of the culture, willing to work quietly and take risks when necessary might be the sanest role possible for a moral being in our culture at this historical moment.

Other Ways had its share of hypocrisy and none of us liked to face it. We pretended not to accept the authority of the superintendent, and yet we went to him for help when we were in trouble. We did not believe in tests, diplomas, grades, and yet evaluated our students' work, hustled to get them legitimate Berkeley High diplomas, and submitted transcripts listing all of their classes through the regular school district channels.

We liked to believe we responded to the needs of our students, but occasionally we responded to the pressure of parents or the school district, contrary to the students expressed wishes. Survival was always an issue, so we conformed to outrageous building codes, wrote jargon-filled meaningless proposals, entertained visitors, and made presentations to people outside the group that concealed our deep troubles and misrepresented our virtues in order to create a respectable impression.

Understanding the points at which one is being hypocritical for the sake of survival or in order to develop the power to change things does not make it any easier to accept hypocritical actions. This honesty about dishonesty can be of use, however, in tempering the overglamorous and uncritical interpretations some of us put on our work.

In addition to frequent hypocritical action any group of people committed to organizing themselves with the purpose of remaking our society and culture must face the prospect of being devastated. People who have wealth and power are not about to give them up easily and will act as harshly as necessary to prevent change. Any new group that develops power has to be wary of infiltration, provocation, harassment, and, as the case of the Black Panther Party has shown, murder.

It is difficult for a group that values openness, generosity, humanness to protect itself from being infiltrated by an agent of one of the supressive arms of our present government. Since most people in new groups do not come from the same family or neighborhood, they are all strangers brought together by a combination of chance and conviction. Some groups form at universities, others in different institutions or corporations that bring together people who have not grown up with one another. It is usually only in poor communities that groups form from people who've known and tested one another out for years.

In addition, many new groups depend on style rather than substance and allow anyone with the right cut of hair and clothes and rhetoric to join up without much questioning. It is easy to imitate a radical style, and many young people get so carried away by the excitement of being in revolt that they become incautious, easily led, and ultimately defenseless. A group has to build trust and strength if it is to survive. The people must know and trust one another well and unequivocally rid the group of anyone who betrays or sells out.

Infiltrators don't merely spy on groups and pass reports on to people in legitimate authority. They often provoke action that is careless, illegal, and usually a diversion from the long-range goals of the group. For example, agents provocateurs suggested to students during the Columbia University Insurrection of 1968 that they blow up the dormitories; the agents were willing to supply dynamite. At that time, blowing up the dorms was counter to any strategy for changing the university. Fortunately, the students were able to neutralize the agents' attempt to devastate their group. Some people, however, were carried away by fantasies of violence, of heroic struggle and death, by the whole romantic paraphernalia of unreasonable dreams of immediate unplanned revolution. It was necessary to deal with the impatient, immature, homicidal, and suicidal tendencies of some of the young people.

The pressure one has to live with in order to sustain an effort to create change often leads people to homicidal and suicidal fantasies that make them vulnerable to provocation. People naturally want to get rid of the tension and frustration that are part of being in opposition, and this can lead them to act stupidly or incautiously.

One has to be wary of individuals within the group who keep pushing for violent activity or pronounce that the final moment for revolution has arrived. Groups must check themselves constantly, must keep long-range goals in mind. People must check up on and check out one another without becoming too paranoid or consumed with hate. If an infiltrator is discovered, he or she must immediately and unambiguously be expelled. No changes of conscience on the part of the infiltrator should be considered, since it is possible that the rhetoric of changed conscience is an infiltrator's way of reestablishing his or her role. A group cannot afford to live with a member who at one time acted to betray the group and its principles.

In addition to infiltrators within, a new group might have to face harassment from outside the group. Other Ways had to fight the school bureaucracy. We also had to do battle with the juvenile bureau of the Berkeley Police Department, since the lieutenant in charge felt that youngsters did not have a right to be in the community for any purpose (including learning) between the hours of nine and three and, therefore, during our second year, students were busted for being on the streets and their student cards were confiscated without explanation. We also had to deal with the building and health departments, which evicted us from one location and kept on inspecting and turning down any other location we chose.

After a while the game of cops and robbers we were forced into began to bug the students and staff, and we were almost harassed into acting violently and stupidly, thereby destroying ourselves. As discussed earlier, the day we got evicted we were given an hour's notice to vacate the building. At the same time the paddy wagon and the police department finger-printing van pulled up across the street. The police were setting us up for a confrontation and some of the angrier kids were ready to take on the cops. There was no way we could win that battle—the kids would have been busted, the staff accused of irresponsibly provoking violence and using the students. What little support we had within the school district and the community would have disappeared. It was at that moment, when we all felt devastated and some of us were ready to act murderously and suicidally, that we decided to go to Giovanni's, the Italian restaurant, and celebrate! The cops were left watching an empty building.

That same year, the time of Laos and Cambodia, of Kent State and Jackson State, we came close to being devastated in a more direct way. We were sharing a building at that time with the Berkeley Free Clinic and Rap Center. The three groups—Other Ways, the Clinic, and the Rap Center —lived in an uneasy state of truce. The Rap Center used part of the school as a crash pad in the evening and often people were still crashed out on the floors when our students arrived in the morning. There were all kinds of conflicts between our students and the crashers—racial, sexual. The Free Clinic dealt with serious drug freakouts, with tear gassings, with all sorts of people who were torn apart physically and emotionally. Clashes with our students were inevitable. Somehow, however, we managed to deal directly with individual conflicts and divide up the space so there would be a minimum of contact between the three groups.

Although the three groups were separated and somewhat hostile, in the fantasy of some members of the police department we were thought to be cooperating in manufacturing explosives and stocking weapons. Twice during the Kent State demonstrations in Berkeley the building had been gassed by police who were chasing demonstrators. One day at noon I noticed the paddy wagon and fingerprinting van parked across the street from our building. I immediately told the students and staff and we evacuated the building and called up all the students who were due to arrive in the afternoon. We dispersed to Dave's house and Darryle's apartment and my house. I also passed on my suspicions to the people at the Free Clinic, but they were powerless to move their patients and equipment. At three o'clock that afternoon about thirty to fifty cops attacked the building looking for our stock of weapons and explosives. They wrecked our school—smashed furniture and blackboards, tore up books. The Free Clinic was treated even worse—patients were tossed out of bed and beaten, anyone who could walk, crawl, or run was chased out of the building and then gassed when he hit the streets.

We were lucky. It is possible that Other Ways could have been devastated by direct attack.

If a group doesn't acknowledge the possibility of being devastated and provide forms of retreat, withdrawal, going underground, and celebrating renewal during times of extreme crisis, it might get wiped out under the slightest assault. A devastated group is a panicked group. The center falls apart, people forget their roles and fall all over one another in an attempt to escape collective destruction. All internal cohesiveness disappears. Some people turn murderous, others suicidal, others hysterical. In panic people forget who they are or what binds them together. This culture does not prepare individuals to function cooperatively with others and therefore people tend to act as individuals during crisis and abandon one another. I have seen very warm, loving groups dissolve into a collection of unrelated, hostile individuals striving to save their own skins under pressure. Perhaps the problem is that panic causes regression and turns people who are striving to become open, sane, and loving into the competitive, violent beings they were trained to be in school and at home.

It is probably impossible to avoid assault from within or without if one is doing decent work within this culture. Therefore, it is necessary to prepare for the possibility of devastation—to rehearse panic, to entrust the role of reconvening the group to specific individuals, and to pair people and make them responsible for each other's survival in times of major stress. The new group, the new culture, must develop mechanisms to deal with the greatest strains the group might face before the problems arise; there is no afterwards if the members panic. For the center to hold, rituals of crisis must be created to remind the members of their unity and to have them reenact this unity despite the pressure.

The reenactment of unity—the celebration, the feast, the orgy, the dance, the song, the collective painting—is both a symbol of the group and the vehicle by which the symbol becomes the reality. Active fantasy can also play a role here. On a group level fantasy becomes an extension of role playing or simulation. It becomes a way for members of a group to come together and display mutual trust and therefore unity by letting their worst fears and anxieties be indulged in front of one another.

It is possible for the group to convene itself and have each member find a spiritually comfortable spot in the space, relax, and then call forth some figure or role to adopt—any figure or role that emerges. Then each person could become the figure he imagines and play out the confrontation from the perspective of a gallery of fantasy figures. This gives people the opportunity to become devilish or saintly, cowardly, murderous, weak, omnipotent—to get out in the presence of others some of the fear and some of the energy mobilizing for battle. It is difficult for people to move naturally into such archetypal simulation and sometimes fantasy play works more easily after straightforward role playing.

There are other collective fantasies a group can develop. People can switch sex roles; live in a fantasized future; play out one another's fantasies. Sometimes personal crisis can be supported through a group's giving its fantasies over to an individual's problems and acting out possible solutions for the benefit of the person under stress. This is a way of generating unexpected solutions to painful problems without forcing a solution on the person in pain and without degrading him or her.

For example, if one person tells the other that he or she is terrified of breaking off an impossible relationship, the group can get its fantasies to work setting up ways of handling the situation. I do not mean here that the group should sit together, analyze the situation, and then rehearse the reasonable possibilities, although this too might happen. What I mean is that the problem is set and then the members of the group become whatever character/ animal/vegetable/mineral arises in their fantasy and then act upon the relationships from that perspective. If someone becomes a stone, he or she can sit impassively until the other goes away, or roll over him or her; if the person becomes a pigeon he or she can fly away or shit on the other's head. A lot of the solutions that fantasy generates are absurd, funny, obscene, impractical, impossible. Many provide hints at the possible. It is up to the individual in trouble to make a decision about how to act (the decision might even be to ask others to act with him or her). However, the wider the range of possibility, the richer, funnier, more absurd the whole context seems, the easier it might be for an individual to act without feeling that his or her whole existence was being threatened or to take a risk if real threat exists. Fantasy can be a useful if somewhat uncontrollable companion to individuals and groups.

The results of the fantasy role playing can be analyzed by the group in much the same way as the more literal role playing. However, sometimes it is best not to analyze but to use the event as merely catharsis, giving people the opportunity to give in to their fear, anxiety, or anger collectively so that when they have to function in a controlled and carefully planned manner under conditions of real confrontation they will know what they are capable of and therefore be able to control themselves among strangers. I have seen a lot of groups divided against themselves by clever administrators, and seen individuals collapse into puddles under pressure or, what is equally dysfunctional, explode violently and out of proportion to the needs of the situation because fear, anger, and distrust built up and were never articulated within the group. Active fantasy is a way of allowing people to tell one another how they are feeling without losing face, and therefore it can help keep a group together throughout crisis.

[9]

So far I have been concerned with distorted and unhappy ways of communal existence. Health is much more difficult to get at. However, I believe that for the group as for the individual health is not a static condition to be attained once and then maintained in a fixed way so much as it is a continual process of *self-definition, criticism,* and *conscious reconstruction* centered on activity that is *personally fulfilling* and *collectively significant.* The healthy group strives to maintain *wholeness, openness, commitment,* and *specificness* in much the same way the individual does. This sounds very abstract, but it can be translated into the specifics of daily living.

A group needs to have an articulated center that provides it with coherence and a reason for survival. However, self-definition is not as simple a matter as it might seem. For example, suppose some people get together to form a group dedicated to developing humane schools for young people. That simple goal is not concrete enough to be translated into action. The members of the group have to be more specific and decide which schools they want to change for which young people. They have to decide where to begin, how modest or ambitious their immediate goals will be. They have to focus on numbers and concrete reality while defining their specific role as a group. This can often lead to trouble. For example, if the group fails to define itself with respect to certain realizable goals, at least as a start, and decides it wants to change all schools everywhere, it may die of abstraction. I have seen a number of educational switchboards and networks atrophy and die for lack of a concrete self-definition that would have enabled the members to assume responsibility for acting. The members of these groups all agreed on the need to change schools; they agreed on principles that ought to be embodied within healthy schools. However, the individual members struck out in every direction looking for a focus. Some people did a little work with parents, others developed a newsletter, some brought together curriculum material or planned a conference. There was no collective self-definition even though there was an agreement on principles. The members of the group worked at cross purposes because they wanted to do everything right away. The only way they could have survived was if they had focused their common commitment upon a specific goal—to change one school, or collect and distribute information in one community, or organize one group of parents.

There are other examples of overambitious self-definition. The desire for national self-definition is one of the curses the media have brought to any movement to change this culture. As soon as something interesting develops, a lot of attention is focused on it, there is a constant pushing for people to appear on television, speak to the press, speak at conferences, create national organizations. Many good people allow themselves to be seduced away from specific work in a given community, and many groups allow themselves to go national before they have developed solid local bases.

In education there is a band of superstars who play the conference circuit, talking about what should happen within the schools or beyond the schools. I used to be one of them and now, with a new book of mine on reading recently published, I'm being pressured into joining the ranks again.

The group of us created a great deal of enthusiasm and got people to start their own things all over the country. Yet for the most part we were not involved in functioning and healthy schools or communities that embodied the ideas we were hawking. Without these examples we talked a lot of abstract nonsense and gave the impression that things were easier to change than they are. I know that as I became involved in Other Ways it became harder and harder for me to give a talk on "education" or on "how to change the schools" or on "how to be as groovy or relevant as Herbkohl." What I saw and see now is the need for specific group self-definitions to develop that take into account local conditions, the strengths and weaknesses of the members of the group, strategies for beginning and for surviving, as well as the initial agreement upon principles. Beyond this and more difficult, any group that wants to develop a healthy alternative must lay down roots in a specific community. The people must commit themselves to settling down and not running away when trouble develops. People have to define their roots in space and time as well as in ideas and stop tripping from alternative to alternative, from free school to free school, commune to commune, community group to community group, place to place. Strategies must be developed that fit with the needs of specific communities at particular moments of their history. Abstract ideas must be translated into everyday realities and tempered by the failures and successes that occur during the process.

An inadequate or unarticulated self-definition can cause major problems for a group. Some groups can define themselves totally in terms of opposition. For example, they can set out to destroy the police, or the medical profession, or the capitalist-imperialist-racist society. With this negative self-definition the group is bound together by the common enemy and is in danger of collapsing if the enemy is defeated or backs off. At Other Ways the group was most coherent and together when a clearly defined enemy was applying direct pressure. Sometimes, especially during the time we were without a building, a few weeks of no contact with the police or building department or school administrators would cause a lot of anxiety in our group. The negative definition of ourselves at war with the system had taken such a hold on us that we periodically forgot our positive self-definition. During these times we would go through crises of self-identity and have to remind ourselves of our goals. Fortunately, our students never let us forget for too long that they were the only justification for our existence.

Because one can find an identity through fighting and therefore become dependent on the battle, it is sometimes hard to stop fighting even after a victory. When we won something from the superintendent we didn't know how to stop because the battle temporarily defined us. Sometimes we fought past the specific victory and right back to a position of weakness. We had to learn to function in an autonomous, self-governing way.

There are other problems with a group's self-definition. Sometimes people come together in a group because they agree upon general principles and assume that they are together on everything else.

It is almost as if fragmentation or schism is a necessary stage in the development of new forms of life. People come together seeking liberation, or perhaps more often because they believe a promise of liberation is offered to them. Then they discover that each individual's conception of liberty is rooted in his or her past life and present needs.

Some people need to express their violence, others need to control it; some need to retreat from sex, others to engage. For some people liberation can mean the ability to say no to an authority, for others it can consist of learning how to say yes and open themselves to others. These are common needs, of course, but the nuances and differences cannot be put down or looked on as secondary. People who come together must listen to one another and mold a common work and life out of personal as well as collective needs.

However, listening to others, taking their words seriously, is difficult in this culture, since language is systematically degraded in the service of making people submissive consumers. I know of many instances where a group of white and black people sit down to talk about racism and yet are incapable of hearing what others have to say. The greatest offenders are usually the whites, who refuse to deal with the possibility that they might be racist. A black person will say to a white person that he or she is racist. The white will deny it, will tell the black he does not really mean it—will do or say anything but listen and consider the possibility that the truth has been told.

If a black perceives a white to be racist, it is usually because the black is seeing something about the white's behavior that is so ingrained in white American culture that the white is blind to his or her own behavior.

When a group comes together and begins to define itself specifically as well as in terms of ideas it is essential that each individual voice be heard. People must feel free enough to describe what they want out of the group, to explain their own emphases, strategies, dreams, to say what they feel comfortable doing and what scares them or is repugnant to them. This personal and specific information is the basis upon which a healthy collective self-definition can be made. Some people might leave the group during this process if their idea of what must be done is inconsistent with the general direction of the work. That is probably better than having people go along reluctantly and then discovering that they are working at cross purposes with everyone else.

It might even make sense to ritualize the process of self-definition (which can and should also become a process of redefinition as the group functions and is forced to respond to the consequences of its behavior and the culture of the larger community in which it functions). For example, sessions can be set up where each person will pretend he or she is the group rather than an individual and will elaborate on the following statements: 1) I as a group believe that my function is to _____. 2) Within me each person has the following functions: _____ (it is important for each member of a group to articulate from personal perspective how he or she would like to see everyone else, including him or herself, function).

After several perspectives on the group are articulated, it is possible to make up a discrepancy/agreement analysis of the different views in order to focus on potential problems within the group and to determine a collective identity. For example, imagine a group of four people who set up a school—two men and two women. They all articulate the goals they perceive and the roles they perceive for each other and come up with the following:

GOALS

Man 1 Woman 1	To develop a model school where children are respected and where skills are learned freely with the ultimate goal of using that model to challenge public schools that are failing the students.
Man 2 Woman 2	To develop a school where kids are free to do whatever they want whenever they want to do it, so that a model free school can be used to show parents how they can develop their own schools outside of the public school system.

ROLES AS SEEN BY	Janitor	Secretary	Head teacher	Math	Reading	All pupils
M1	kids & teachers	W2	M1	W1	M2 M1	M1, 2 W1, 2
W1	kids & teachers	all share	M1	W2 W1	M1 M2	" "
M2	teachers	all share	none	W1 W2	M2 M1	" "
W2	teachers	all share	none	W1 W2	M2 M1	" "

Looking at this analysis, which a group should be able to make of its own functioning, it is clear that there will be problems—perhaps irreconcilable ones—over self-definition. Two people want to change the public schools, two want to bypass them. Two are concerned with the acquisition of skills, two aren't. One person wants a female secretary, the other three want to share secretarial responsibility. Two people want a head teacher, two want democratic governance of the school; two want the kids to share the responsibility for cleaning up and caring for the environment, two don't. Probably on a general level the four agree that young people must be respected, that the public schools are damaging, that young people must have considerable freedom of choice. However, it is a question of whether the general agreement will be negated by all the specific disagreements.

Most groups I have seen do not ask themselves questions of this kind at the beginning; therefore, contradictions within the group are not articulated beforehand and thus not dealt with. Rather, these contradictions emerge as the group functions, leading to factionalization, gossip, hostility, and eventually schisms or dissolution of the whole. What starts out as an exciting adventure in forging a new world ends up in a series of sordid internal clashes. I have seen many groups where things turn ugly as differences that could have easily been articulated and dealt with at the beginning emerge in bitterness.

It is possible in this context that some dreams can be dealt with collectively as indicators of self-deception and frustration within the group. For two years I conducted a class at Other Ways called the Unconscious and Decision Making. The class was centered on the question of how people make important decisions such as whom to marry, love, or hate, or what vocation to choose, or what political attitudes to adopt. We read Camus, Laing, Sartre, talked about logical and rational vs. nonrational choice, and discussed personal styles and affinities. What developed as the major concern of the class, however, was the collective interpretation of individual dreams. I started out by reading my dreams—a few that occurred during analysis, but mostly current ones. I explained to the kids that I reserved the right to keep certain dreams private (and that they should assume that right too) but that I promised not to conceal any aspects of the dreams I chose to share. The condition was that after I gave my dreams to the group they would contribute as well. The kids in the class tended to be the ones I knew best and after a while there was enough trust within the group so that dreams that seemed embarrassing or sensitive could be told without fear of their being used against people. We sat around and tried to help one another understand the meaning of the dreams in the present. There was no pretense at playing at psychoanalyzing anyone or turning the class into a therapy session. Dreams are a normal and common form of human activity that should be integrated into one's total life. There is too much association of dreams with forbidden wishes in our culture. I hoped the group could look upon dreams as spiritual guides, internal voices, indicators of feelings not fully articulated, organizers of experience.

We were able after a year to deal intelligently with one

another's dreams. Usually the reading of the dream was preceded by a short description of when the dream occurred and how the dreamer was feeling that day. For example, someone might say: "I dreamed this last night. I went to bed angry—had a fight with my mother again and wanted to leave home."

Then the dream would be read and I would say to the dreamer: "What does it mean to you?" Often just the act of reading a dream out loud to others clarifies things and gives the dreamer enough distance to form a tentative interpretation.

After my question members of the class joined in with alternative interpretations and suggestions or with questions for the dreamer. We never came to any final interpretation and didn't set as a goal getting to "the" meaning of the dream. We tried to develop many interpretations of each dream so that we could all gain insight into one another and at the same time get hold of ways of interpreting our own dreams; it was up to the dreamer to take away what he or she cared to. The dream itself was respected, left whole and slightly mysterious, never drained of all meaning, and at most partially understood. Through our sessions many of us developed an appreciation of the beauty of dreams in themselves, aside from interpretation.

It is possible for groups to incorporate shared interpretations of dreams into their existence. There is no need to turn dream interpretation into therapy—one need not be sick to dream. It is possible for a group to generate collective dreams or to have people focus on group life and dream about the group in ways that might be useful to sort out all the complex reasons people have for being part of the group as well as their unarticulated goals for the group. The same questions an individual can ask of his or her own dreams can also be asked within the context of the group, which can learn about itself and its center through the dreams of its members.

During times of crisis, for example, members of the

group can be asked to concentrate on dreaming about the group and its future. If there has been no prior cultivation of dreams as a form of learning, then people can be encouraged to fantasize all the possibilities for the future, to welcome the wildest thoughts, the most timid and cowardly ideas that come to their minds as well as the boldest and most romantic. People should be encouraged to share these fantasies, to be willing to appear scared or nervous or ready to explode. The group, by accepting the feelings, can come to support individuals unaccustomed to conflict, as well as get a psychic portrait of its collective stance at a time of crisis.

Of course, there is no need to wait for trouble to bring forth dreams and fantasies, to express fears or romantic dreams. The group has to learn to accept, support, and nurture its members or it will certainly contribute to its own dissolution.

[10]

The inability to deal with criticism is a major reason many groups fail to achieve collective self-definition. People do not like to look dumb or feel uncomfortable in front of others, and do not know how to admit mistakes publicly. They do not know how to give or take criticism without being threatening or threatened because all criticism is dealt with as an attack on the individual instead of as a way of building strength for the individual and the group. This arises, I imagine, from a basic insecurity about our own worth, which gives rise to the aggressively defensive posture most of us assume under pressure. Both men and women in our culture victimize themselves and the groups they belong to by being overfull with macho—with what many women's liberation groups call male chauvinism, but which I think could better be called me-chauvinism. Men and women may manifest their defensiveness in different ways—men by pulling up their chests, getting physical and boisterous, pretending to be powerful; women by pouting, pretending to be defenseless and weak, or in some cases by threatening to scratch and bite and kick. However, the problem manifested is the same—criticism is seen as an attack, as a form of rejection rather than a form of love.

To give criticism out of love, with the intent of building someone up and strengthening a group, is not natural in our culture. I know that I myself have to prepare to criticize someone. The act of being critical causes me anxiety— I feel my fists clenching, my brows knitting a bit—and usually I spit the criticism out hostilely even though I don't mean to. It is as if I throw the criticism at someone and prepare to duck or run. I always used to anticipate a hostile response to criticism and prepared to defend myself before I said anything.

Other people try to sneak criticism into their conversation so that their own conscience can be calmed at the same time as the person being criticized is given the out of not noticing the criticism.

It has taken me a long time to learn how to say directly and without hostility or fear of a hostile response what I perceive. Sometimes it is necessary to tell people that they are acting irresponsibly or that you think they are running a game on you or that they are assuming responsibilities they are not capable of dealing with. Sometimes it is necessary to confront people and run the risk of being attacked in return. I think one of the main problems Other Ways encountered was that some of the staff people were afraid to criticize me—especially during the first year. The fear was somewhat justified in that I often explode at people or totally withdraw from them when I feel they intend to hurt me.

None of us knew how to both give and take criticism, and that kept us in a bind. We tolerated a lot of behavior that was detrimental to the functioning of the group. We told secretive jokes about things like Mike's running, Darryle's being late all the time, Collingwood's calling people motherfucker, or my shooting my mouth off. When we realized the need to be direct with one another it was too late—the group had already fallen apart.

A lot can be learned through analyzing one's failures; however, although the past can be instructive, it cannot be corrected. I have found it useful to practice criticizing someone else—to attend to the tone of your own voice, to the tension of your muscles, to other manifestations of anxiety, to impulses to fight or run, to fear of being attacked. It might even be possible for people to practice criticism on one another by playing a version of the dozens.

The game is to make up absurd though sometimes to-the-point criticism (or possibly insults) and keep a conversational tone. Any number can play.

A sample game. Two people, A and B

A: Your toes stink.

B: O.K., but you never brush your teeth.

A: That may be, but my breath doesn't stink like yours.

B: That's nothing; your eyes never focus on another person because you're always scared.

A: That may be, but . . .

During the game it is important to stop whenever anxiety or hostility begins to build and let the other players know you feel angry or threatened. This way not only will people be able to get the tone of criticism under control, they will also begin to learn how to admit publicly that they are angry or threatened and ask others to help them deal with these feelings.

Taking criticism is, if anything, more threatening than giving it. In the game the responses given to the criticism might have helped the players. Both A and B prefaced all their responses: "That may be, but . . ." or "O.K., but . . ." It is part of the game, as I imagine it, to get people accustomed to absorbing criticism, sometimes accepting it if it makes sense, sometimes rejecting it and going about their business, but primarily attending to the content of what is said rather than the tender needs of their egos.

I have learned to take criticism, to listen to what is being

said about me and think about it. For the most part I have
learned to control my impulses to defend myself or attack.
Sometimes something said hurts so much that I regress and
pout or shout. Perhaps a technique groups should utilize
is a period of silence or reflection after a serious criticism
is made of any member. Or perhaps the group should institutionalize the separation of the feelings that surround
criticism from the substance of the criticism itself.

For example, until people are comfortable enough to be
direct with one another group criticism sessions can be
set up with the following structure:

A person, M, is chosen to criticize (or praise) others in
the group *specifically with respect to actions or attitudes
that affect the whole group.*

The criticism, however, is ritualized to take the following form:

M: I will criticize K. First I want to tell you how I feel
saying these things. I am scared/angry/annoyed, . . . Now
for the criticism.

K's response can also be ritualized: I will respond. However, I want to tell you how I felt hearing those things
about me. I was pissed/embarrassed/ready to punch M in
the face/ashamed. Now let me take a minute to think about
what was said.

A break is taken, K responds, and then a general discussion can take place or the experience can be repeated.

I know this game situation is extremely artificial and
imagine that more natural ways of practicing giving and
receiving criticism can be developed. In any case, the
ability to incorporate criticism into the ongoing life of a
group and to use it to build a sense of common purpose
as well as mutual regard is one component of a healthy
group's functioning. The criticism, however, is not sufficient. When valid criticism is made, something must be
done about it, and that leads to another aspect of healthy
group existence—the ability of a group to reconstruct itself while still functioning, to rebuild itself on the open
seas.

Many crises and problems develop in group life and survival often depends upon the way these are dealt with. Sometimes these problems come in a disarmingly pleasant form. For example, I know of a number of alternative schools that after two or three years of near poverty are all of a sudden offered a lot of public or foundation money under the condition that they make slight modifications in their functioning. There are many different ways these offers can be dealt with, all of which, however, require the schools to redefine and reconstruct themselves on the basis of their changed circumstances.

Here is an imaginary portrait of such circumstances that approximates some of the conditions faced by Other Ways and other alternative schools in the Berkeley School District the years after I left. The New Harvest Free School developed out of the collaboration of some white college students and some parents within the black community of a large university town. The school's philosophy was that the students should all have an opportunity to develop freely and at their own rates, and the parents and staff should develop the political power within the community to protect and nurture the school. The staff and parents were overtly and unambiguously radical in politics and became a source of problems to the local city government. However, the school went very well, was picked up by the media, and became something of a national model for the blending of politics and open education. On the basis of the school's work the Experimental Schools Branch of the Office of Education offered the local school district a large grant under the condition that they incorporate the New Harvest Free School into the public school system and expand on its good example. Naturally, since money was involved, the local superintendent approached the board of the New Harvest School and offered them full support under the following conditions:

1. That the school hire at least one teacher presently in the public schools.

2. That several teachers from New Harvest get state teaching credentials.
3. That city and federal evaluators be allowed to study and evaluate the school.
4. That overt political activity be dropped.

On the positive side the school district was willing to:

1. Grant the director of New Harvest principal's status within the school district.
2. Allow the educational functioning of the school to remain in the hands of the parents and teachers.
3. Provide money for salaries, supplies, and repairs to the school building to bring it into conformity with the state education code.

Each of the conditions provides real problems that the members of the school community must deal with thoughtfully, collectively, and in detail. To leap at the offer of money without considered redefinition and restructuring is to court certain (though maybe prolonged) death. The degree to which the community will be able to deal with these issues will depend on the explicitness of its previous self-definition and on the way criticism is dealt with internally. If the group has a strong set of priorities, if, for example, giving up political activity would cause many people in the community to leave, then taking the money is not wise. If, however, the community values the work with the kids more, then the political activity can be redirected to the arena of the school district rather than to the community at large.

The conditions for getting money must be seen in the light of priorities the group has set for itself. If no such priorities exist, an offer like this will create factions, the group will probably split up, with some of the people remaining outside the system in politics and some within the system running the school. Or two schools, one within and one without the system—hating each other—might result.

Each condition, however, will call for a restructuring of the group and some members might not survive the windfall.

The rewards also have to be considered, for they might potentially be dangerous. Let's suppose that up to the time of the offer New Harvest School had no single director but was run as a collective. The school district does not recognize or understand collective functioning, nor does the federal government. The district must have a principal if it has a school, just as the federal grant must have a project director. Here the new world and the old world meet on collision course. If New Harvest refuses to designate a principal or project director, one will be appointed from outside the group to act for them. If they do choose someone, then despite themselves responsibility will be distributed unequally within the group, and only the authority of the head person will be recognized by local and federal authorities.

There might be other unexpected problems with getting the money. For example, bringing the building up to code might lock the school into a building it doesn't want. Getting salaries from the school district might force each paid member of the school to define his or her salary in a way consistent with school district pay scales. If everyone in the collective was getting the same salary in the past the district might force inequality in pay so that New Harvest conformed to the rest of the school district's policy.

There is a feeling of excitement and relief that members of poor groups feel when the possibility of being supported arises. There is a temptation to take the money and run—to deal with the consequences of changed status later on. In my experience that's always been a mistake. Mechanisms have to be established so that the group examines the consequences of changed status rather than becoming its victim. A lot of hard fantasy has to be used. Everyone must sit down and speculate upon, imagine, act out if necessary the foreseeable consequences of changed status. If someone disagrees with the general feeling that person must be attended to and not put down. Once again every voice must be heard if the group is to survive its reconstruction.

Perhaps everybody ought to be asked to speculate on the following themes in front of the group:

—If we accept, the best that can happen to us is _____.

—If we accept, the worst that can happen to us is _____.

—If we do not accept, then our options are _____.

—If we do accept, we are betraying the following principles of our functioning: _____.

—If we do not accept, we are betraying the following principles of our functioning: _____.

—Is there reason for us to continue, split, or go out of business?

There are often more painful situations that lead to a need for reconstruction:

—An infiltrator has been discovered.

—Members of the group have been killed or jailed.

—Members criticize one another and changes have to occur on the basis of these criticisms.

—A schism is about to take place and the group might fall apart.

—The group is being harassed out of existence.

—The group has failed to achieve its goals.

—The goals of the group are beginning to seem wrong.

—The analysis upon which the group's action is based appears to be incorrect.

In all of these cases the only healthy thing to do is bring everyone together, restate the original self-definition or clarify it, do a critical analysis of the present and future possibilities, and work toward reconstruction. This is extraordinarily hard work. The easier routes are to drift apart, split up, sell out, act without thought or preparation, and in general let things happen to the group instead of the group's assuming power over its own future.

[11]

In order to mobilize the energy required for survival members of a group must get something that is personally fulfilling out of their participation in collective activity or the group itself will fall apart.

As a new group develops, it is very important for people to pay attention to one another's personal needs and pleasures; to watch faces and bodies and offer support when the pressure of life within the group seems painful, humorless, and futile for someone. It is important to prevent people within the group from becoming alienated from one another and feeling used or exploited. There are a number of ways people can learn to support one another. First, people within a group should find out what one another's personal needs are, both within the group and in their private lives. For example, at Other Ways I needed time to prepare my classes and concentrate solely on teaching and writing. Betsy needed time away from the nagging, small administrative problems, as well as time away from us. Colly needed to be protected during his depressive phases and allowed to vent his hatred and bitterness in a safe environment. Mike had to have time to train. Like fools, we laughed at Mike, hung around Betsy all the time, indulged the worst in Colly. We only realized when we were all exhausted the need to protect one another's personal pleasures and rewards as much as possible.

As well as our personal needs, each of us got different kinds of fulfillment from work within the group. I needed to feel that people were learning and playing with words and numbers. David got fulfillment from helping young men and women learn to move independently throughout the city and woods. Betsy nurtured many of the students most seriously in trouble and needed that nurturing experience. If the group had failed to provide the opportu-

nity for these different needs to flourish, it would have
fallen apart even more quickly than it did.

However, there is a major danger here—forgetting the
students because of obsession with our needs as adults.
Groups that function to serve others—schools, businesses,
legal or medical aid collectives, etc.—can become so consumed by the process of their own growth and the struggles of their staff that the people they serve are ignored.
At Other Ways the students were frequently irritated by
the staff's obsessive concern with working out its problems
of organization and of the distribution of power. And we
did forget the young people occasionally and directed our
attention to internal staff policy or political battles on a
district level. Fortunately the students never let us get
away with those indulgences too long—they demanded to
be taught, to be heard, and to remain where they belonged
—at the center of our concern.

There are times when the needs of the group have to be
dealt with obsessively and individual concerns have to be
put aside. This must be articulated collectively and explicitly. If twenty-four-hours-a-day politicking has to take
place to get money or win an election or deal with the
police or renovate a building, then people must take the
time to tell one another what they wish they were doing
and to commiserate with one another. It might even
be possible for people to spell one another so that each
individual is protected and given time to do what he or
she needs to keep together. For example, I could have been
relieved of all but teaching responsibilities one week a
month; we could have all agreed to stay away from Betsy
after five o'clock or give Mike an hour a day to run. If a
crisis came up that demanded we give up these personal
needs temporarily, we could have rewarded ourselves with
a holiday and an orgy of self-indulgence when the pressure
lifted.

It is possible to ritualize statements of personal satisfaction and need with respect to collective activity at group meetings. For example, once a month each person can elaborate for the others on the following statements:

—Of all the things we do the ones I feel finest about are _____.

—I can't stand doing _____.

—If I can't do _____ I'll go crazy.

—Doing _____ makes me want to quit.

—Not being able to spend some time doing _____ drives me up the wall.

A group that avoids dealing with the personal fulfillment of its members will probably not survive long. However, a group that ignores its relationship to the world outside the group and does nothing but satisfy its members' needs is cruel and unhealthy and likely to consume itself.

I know of a number of so-called countercultural groups —communes, collectives, free schools, cooperative businesses—that are dedicated solely to satisfying the personal needs of the individuals involved and providing the opportunity for each person to do his or her "own thing." They claim that racism, oppression, poverty are not their concern and rationalize that by purifying themselves they will begin to purify the world by example. These groups frequently end up nurturing and eventually being destroyed by individual petty selfishness. One person's "thing" doesn't leave room for another's, nobody feels any responsibility for doing anything for or with the others. The group comes to resemble a traditional madhouse, with each individual wrapped in his or her own obsessions, talking only in soliloquy and letting the physical environment degenerate.

It is a short step from doing one's own thing to believing that other people must also do it. A number of originally hang-loose groups turn not so surprisingly into extremely fascist organizations where one member starts organizing and directing others. Instead of developing collective responsibility selfish groups turn into slave–master groups, the more passive members becoming the slaves and the more aggressive ones the dictators. Doing "one's own thing" frequently disables a person for collective functioning: when one becomes bored with that thing, one becomes susceptible to doing someone else's thing and becoming a slave.

[12]

Ignoring the outside world is another form of group selfishness. Splitting from the city or buying a group of houses and setting up fences and guard systems to keep out the world exacts a great moral cost from the members. Closed groups become mean groups, constantly on the defensive, ready for battle. I remember the hostile stares I got visiting some of the closed free schools in California, the sense that I brought the infection of the world into a pure place. For my part I was struck by the smugness, the sterility, and emptiness of many of these places. The reception I received made me want to strike out at the group much the way I suppose many black people feel when they pass through a hostile white neighborhood.

The claim of blissful neutrality and complacency felt by groups that separate themselves from the world is complemented by hostility from the outside. The rich can seal themselves off from the poor and build walls and hire guards. That doesn't prevent the poor from knowing that the rich exist and are consuming wealth and resources. On the contrary, it sets the poor to scheming to gain those resources with whatever means are available to them.

I remember the Lower East Side of New York eight or nine years ago when there was an invasion of young white disaffected middle-class people who wanted to live simply in voluntary poverty, wanted to be left alone to do their own things. About the only possessions they allowed themselves were expensive stereos, hundreds of phonograph records, and lots of dope. It shouldn't surprise anyone that local people who were involuntarily poor resented the invasion and tried to rip off the white kids whenever and however possible.

Getting ripped off in the city impels some groups and individuals to flee to the hills—the countercultural equivalent of the middle class fleeing to the suburbs. Often the flight is specifically from blacks, Chicanos, poor whites. Racist and elitist sentiment is as prevalent in the counterculture as in the dominant culture—of which it is often an inverted reflection.

To remain healthy and in contact with the world a group must define its work with respect for the resources and needs of all people. Internally the group has to find some collective identity and externally it must in some way contribute to the undoing of exploitation and oppression. Significant activity of this sort can take many different forms, depending upon the circumstances of the group. Farming communes can assist ghetto food cooperatives; free schools in the hills can develop urban branches and maintain urban and country locations to be shared by poor and rich people. Profits from hip business can be fed back into community activities. A single group does not have to assume the responsibility for changing the whole world, but it should stretch itself to make some specific changes. If not, it is no different in substance from a large corporation or exclusive social club or restricted community and deserves the same fate that they deserve—to be pulled down and rebuilt to meet the needs of all the people.

Relating to the world outside the group, having responsibilities and obligations beyond a small circle of friends can keep a collective cohesive and honest. If deadlines have to be met, assistance given, products exchanged, the group has certain clearly defined areas where specific goals and deadlines are set, making it less easy to slack off or become lazy. If produce has to be delivered to hungry people, if ward workers or media experts have to perform in a political campaign, if doctors have to deliver babies and give health checkups, if voters have to be registered and then brought out to vote, the group cannot devote its time to overindulgent psychologizing of all of its actions and fall into nonfunctioning.

Recently I received a survey in the mail that asked the following questions:

—What in your opinion is the best open school in the country?

—What is the best book on free schools?

—What is the finest magazine devoted to alternative education?

—What is the finest teacher training institution?

etc.

At first I was tempted to answer the questions, but then I caught myself. The "best," the "finest"—there are a lot of schools, books, magazines that try to deal with the passage of our young to adulthood in this culture—but "best?" "finest?" The questions betrayed a competitiveness that seems unavoidable in even the most radical ventures in this culture.

I remember the times at Other Ways when we bragged about being the best alternative school in the Bay Area—and remember how it cut us off from our most natural allies, the other alternative schools we were putting down. They acted the same way toward us. There is no conception in most alternative groups of the whole, of a collective struggle that goes beyond the individual group and reaches through all levels and functions in this culture. Instead, there is jealousy and competition, the inability to forge alliances or respect and support other people's work. Some people act as if they could make a revolution all by themselves, and they pout, despair, and quit fighting when they fail. This is just another way our schooling causes us to neutralize change—by turning it into a competitive activity. As long as so-called radicals are competing with one another, forgetting their individual and modest roles in the whole struggle to remake this culture, there will be no major threat to the people who control our lives.

It is crucial that we learn how to forge alliances and look at our own work in the perspective of the whole. We must support other people who are struggling. It is foolish to claim, for example, that it is better to struggle within the public school system, or outside the system, to develop a community controlled school, or a deschooled learning network. We must, each of us, as individuals and as small groups, pick our own spots to do healthy work and support others who are working for similar goals.

It is easy to forget the whole and feel that only one's own struggles are significant. There are rewards for being the "best," "chicest," most popular radical in your field. The media will pay attention to you, graduate students will study you, people will offer you money to give speeches and write books. You will probably be imitated, replicated, funded, and evaluated to death—and you will probably lose your allies and whatever base in a particular community you have developed.

People involved in the struggle to change this culture cannot afford to forget, ignore, or put down their brothers and sisters who are struggling in different places and possibly different ways. We have to become attuned to how different groups perceive their own roles in their own communities with their own constituencies. And we must be prepared to come together if the moment ever arises when enough strength has been built to tear the house down.

Some groups seem to be involved in more glamorous activities than others and glamour sometimes is taken as a measure of radicalness. For whites, developing an open or socialist classroom in a ghetto is more glamorous than doing it in the suburbs; working in a fugitive free school located in a storefront is more glamorous than working in an alternative school within a public school system; func-

tioning in a legal or medical collective is more glamorous
than trying to change a public hospital. This is all crap.
In his account of the Cuban revolution Che Guevara
talked about the guerrilla bands in the hills and their
support groups in the unions and the professions who
functioned within the cities. He said that each served a
function, that each was necessary, that revolution was not
possible without both preparing an army in the hills and
infiltrating the schools and transportation and communica-
tion and business operations in the cities. Both groups had
to be prepared and willing to work together if the revolution was to succeed.

For America, at this moment in our development, the
bands in the hills would be involved as much in glamor-
izing themselves and putting down the urban fighters as
in preparing the way for a different world. And the people
struggling in the cities would respond in kind, everyone
forgetting too often and too easily the common enemy.
To succeed in changing this culture we must pull together, support one another's struggles, and keep a vision
of the whole before us. This means, for the group as for
the individual:

—Keeping in mind the oppression others are experiencing and the subtle ways in which one's group's actions are
in complicity with the oppressors;

—Constantly being aware of how one's way of living af-
fects the lives of others;

—Caring for the health of the world, having a vision of
the whole and one's place in a struggle involving many
groups;

—Being aware of the interrelationships within the life
of the group of the physical, spiritual, collective, personal,
ritual, and generally cultural aspects of everyday functioning.

[13]

There are some characteristics of group life that give
rise to contrary tendencies within the group and often

lead to conflict and under extreme circumstances perversity. Within every group there is:

—A need for stability as well as a need for newness and change;

—A need for structure and a need for flexibility;

—A need for collective action and a need for personal independence;

—A need for unanimity and a need for disagreement;

—A need for logical planning and a need for spontaneity.

Under pressure many groups choose to emphasize one aspect of these contrary pairs and legislate the other out of existence. Some groups decide to be stable, rigidly structured, demanding of absolute allegiance, and completely predictable. Others choose the route of personal whim, spontaneity, flexibility, independent action. The former type of group turns fascist, the latter chaotic. For a group to remain open the complex interplay of both terms of the contraries has to be integrated into its common life. Flexibility has to be balanced by enough structure so that people know what they are responsible for; spontaneity is needed to respond to new situations; logical thought often prevents group suicide. Personal independence must be respected, but binding collective action sometimes has to be taken.

There is no final balance a group can set with respect to the contraries—sometimes more structure is needed, at other times flexibility is crucial. A school has to set classes at regular times and teachers who commit themselves to show up must be held to that responsibility. On the other hand, if the students fail to show up or complain that the whole business of regular classes does not meet their needs, then the group must be flexbile enough to examine the structure itself and change it.

The only way I know of to deal with the contraries on an ongoing basis is for the group to learn from its failures and have a clear sense of where such failures began.

Suppose a certain group began by defining itself as:

—Stable, with set specific goals;

—Structured, so that each member had a definite role to play;

—Collective, in the sense that all activity had to be agreed upon by the group;

—Unanimous, in that all decisions were made by consensus, with all dissenting voices needing to agree before action took place.

Suppose, more specifically, that the group was a medical collective of six doctors and six medics whose goal was to set up a people's health clinic. They agreed that all medical and economic decisions would be made collectively, that they would all work out of a storefront, and that doctors would do all surgery and medics could take care of health checkups, superficial wounds, colds, flus, and other less serious ailments.

The first week of functioning the following problems arise:

—A person requiring surgery comes to the storefront when only medics are around, so they perform the surgery.

—There is a need for an emergency home visit, and since only one person is around he or she must decide independently whether to leave the storefront or refuse the home visit.

—The health department condemns the storefront, but in a liberal gesture offers space in a local private hospital in another, richer part of the community for the collective's use.

These three problems question the group's goals and specific plans as well as the pre-agreed-upon function of the collective in decision making and the differentiated roles of the doctors and medics. The group must deal with these issues if it is to survive. Of course, it is possible to wait and see what happens—to ignore the decision to make a home visit or to operate without a doctor. But these problems will come up continually and must be dealt with before they factionalize the group (e.g., medics vs. doctors; individual decision advocates vs. consensus people, etc.) and possibly destroy it.

The medical collective might hold to its original scheme and come down heavy on the medic who operated. It might decide on no home visits, might demand twenty-four-hours-a-day availability of all members so that emergency collective decisions could be made. It might hold itself rigid and make life intolerable for its members. And with all its internal conflict it might forget that it existed to serve people. The patients coming to the clinic might find themselves forced to take sides or shunted off while the staff discussed itself. The very center of its existence might slip away.

It is also possible that the group could keep sight of the needs that had to be served, accept its own failures and its inability to predict the problems of everyday functioning. Then it could reconstruct itself, holding to the central goal of developing people's medical service, while resetting the balance of the contraries to satisfy the needs of everyday functioning. It could decide that teams consisting of one medic and one doctor should be available at all times and work together; that only some emergencies merited home visits; that individual decisions (or decisions agreed upon by the teams of two) could be made in cases of emergencies; that the storefront shouldn't be abandoned until another place in the same part of the community is found. A group such as this medical collective learns about itself if it is open to deal with failure and the unpredictability of events in people's lives. Openness to the constantly shifting relationships of contrary tendencies within the group keeps the whole healthy and coherent. It enables the group to react in new ways when old ways have failed, as well as to hold together when the unexpected occurs.

[14]

To become part of a group that endeavors to confront this culture and dares to change requires strength and commitment. People must be willing to take risks, give up a secure and predictable life, and cut off many options that give them a safe out. I know many people who claim to be radical or countercultural and yet are constantly hedging their bets on the future in good old competitive and capitalist ways. They put money away, buy investment property, in some cases stocks and bonds, and then in public denounce liberals who are cautious in the same way. I hedge myself but at least do not pretend I don't worry about my own personal and family security. I think I would be able to throw myself into certain ventures and risk being wiped out—but it would have to be at a time when there seemed to be a possibility of victory. At this moment I am committed enough to changing the schools and culture to risk making many enemies and to cut myself off from the possibility of working within any public system whatever. However, I have to have two years in the bank to feel secure enough to take those risks. I do not look upon money in the bank in terms of objects or properties so much as time. With two years saved, I can risk being wiped out with any group I become part of and still be able to lick my wounds and regroup.

It is important for people not to overromanticize their commitment and then later panic at the possibility of being cut off from what they want to do. It is possible to commit oneself to violent action—but one has to understand the consequences of the commitment. If you bomb a police station, you will not be loved or forgiven by most people. If you confront a politician or bureaucrat in public, you can expect him to try to destroy you. If you become part of a group with certain goals, you had better be committed to them, for you might be hanged because of them.

Many people are not accustomed to assessing the commitments they have made to groups or to their own work. They are even less clear about commitments to change the whole culture. A loose commitment to overcome racism, oppression, exploitation, sexism is meaningless unless it functions in specific everyday ways. At Other Ways we all talked a lot about commitment to the kids, to one another, to all of suffering humanity, but many people faded when the money was tight or external pressure developed or more attractive opportunities materialized.

Glib statements about commitment are a common form of radical self-deception. I have to see how individuals or groups function over a period of time, how they deal with defeat (or, for that matter, success), how they respond to new problems and pain to see what commitment is embodied in their actions. In this culture, where the words of individuals or groups are not to be trusted, it is only over time that something as crucial as commitment can be assessed.

Honoring one's own words is a first step toward having one's words honored within a group. Before embarking on any activity affecting the lives of others it is essential to qualify commitment by asking oneself:

—Under what conditions will I quit?

—How long do I usually keep at things? Can I (do I want to) stay that long this time?

—What else am I committed to?

—What do I feel most strongly committed to?

—Why am I getting into this in the first place? What needs of mine are being satisfied?

—How do I customarily deceive myself? What are the signs that I'm lying to myself? Are there any present now?

The group must air these questions collectively. Commitment is not to be played with, involving as it does one's whole self and the lives of others. To build trust in a group based upon mutual statements of commitment and then to opt out of the commitment and betray that trust as specific demands upon one's time and energy become painful is a form of murder. To commit oneself to battling exploitation and then decide it isn't worth the effort is to value one's personal discomfort over the miseries of the greater part of humanity. It is in the worst sense a form of being a good American—it is a disease. The demands of a specific and healthy commitment involve one's whole life over one's whole lifetime and promises cannot be lightly made.

Recently I've begun to teach again, and I have become involved in a community-oriented education group called the Center for Open Learning and Teaching. Before joining the group I asked and answered these questions and shared the answers with the other members of the group, who were also able to specify their commitments. My answers to these questions were:

—I'll quit if I end up administering and hustling for money instead of teaching.

—Three years is my cycle and that's all the time that can be expected of me as a definite commitment.

—I have to and will continue to write.

—My family and my writing are as central to my life as teaching or affecting the ways others teach.

—I need to do well what we almost did well at Other Ways; to make a sane and healthy place to see my children and other children grow in; to believe that I can die surrounded by younger people who care for the world and not be abandoned like the old people I know.

—I want to succeed badly, have never fully freed myself of the need to be on top, best, first; and I deceive myself when I talk most positively. My praise, especially for things I am involved in or want to succeed, has to be scrutinized cautiously.

[15]

It is difficult to characterize a personal or group center or to describe the process of centering. I find myself at times talking about "the center" as if it were a stable configuration of vocation, sensibility, and style, while at other times talking about "the process of centering" as if growth and self-modification were the crucial components of health. This shifting seems unavoidable, since the center —centering image encompasses many sets of contraries: stability and change; focus or direction and self-modification; commitment and criticism; structure and freedom; ritual and spontaneity. In the everyday lives of individuals and groups there is a complex interplay of these contraries, often determined by political, economic, and social constraints on behavior. The center is the theme that runs through all the behavior of the group and individual; it is like glue or cement or oxygen or soil or water—it is the binding factor, the nurturing element. When the center does not hold or when people become alienated from the center or forget about its existence, things fall apart. Yet the center or the process of centering is elusive, cannot be defined in words. It differs so much from group to group (although certain general principles probably hold) that no single description can be adequate. However, even though the center cannot simply be described, or perhaps because of this, people develop representations of the center, images to guide them and put a name to what they are living through. These images often assume a life of their own. Beginning as representations, as condensations of complex combinations of structure and process, they become autonomous and often affect the group in unexpected ways. People need to name the unnameable, to hang on to images of their own lives and use these images to help them with decision making and self-definition. Sometimes these images enrich thought and keep people in contact with the center. At other times they are traps that lead people and groups away from themselves into behavior based on the power of the image rather than the necessities of a healthy life. This can be made clearer by examining a few traditional images of the center.

In some nations the king or shah or emperor is the image of the center. In our democracy the royal person is replaced by the royal cloth. To define oneself or a group as loyal to the flag is to assume an abstract moral loyalty that can lead to attitudes such as those expressed by slogans like "My country, right or wrong." The impersonal center reduces the power of the individual, who through blind loyalty becomes a slave. There is not very much difference between an individual who says (and believes) "I am a slave of the emperor—he defines me, uses me, and can dispose of me however he sees fit" and one who replaces the word emperor by the word "flag" or "country."

The flag is not the only image of the center that appeals to many people in this culture. There are others—the dollar, the astronaut, the pioneer. Each of these images presents a way of thinking about how the country is to go about centering itself, and unfortunately few of them bode well for a healthy future.

The name "Other Ways" always confused people outside our group. People were constantly calling us "The Other Way," "Another Way," "The New Way," missing the point. We were Other Ways—many other ways, not just one other way. We prided ourselves on developing lots of alternative ways of teaching and learning and tried to avoid falling into the trap of adopting only one form of behavior or a single style. When confronted with seemingly impossible problems—like functioning without a building or money—the image of Other Ways was very useful. Instead of following the old, unsuccessful patterns of behavior, we asked ourselves what other ways, no matter how crazy they seemed might be available to solve the problems. We entertained opening a book store, a restaurant—we actually made and sold books and posters, did theater and poetry, ran conferences, and hustled in a lot of other ways.

The image of Other Ways helped us deal with contrary tendencies within the group. For example, there was always a structure-freedom argument within the group. Some people believed the students should have maximum freedom, others that our work had to be carefully planned and well structured. The argument was futile as long as acceptance of the bogus opposition between freedom and structure was the precondition of our discussions. It was necessary to reformulate the issue and ask the question

"What kinds of structure allow what kinds of freedom?" to come to some fruitful resolution of the problem. The issue was not freedom or structure as much as what kind of alternate structure was necessary to allow our students the maximum choice consistent with collective survival.

Reformulation and mediation of the contraries was the idealized form of collective functioning at Other Ways. Our logo, which Allan Kaprow and I created, represented this notion. The logo was:

This symbol was created by the fusion of two classical alchemical symbols that Allan and I came upon in a book of symbols: ∾ is the alchemical symbol for sublimation, for raising something to a higher level, for exploding something or setting it free to fly. ≂ is the symbol for precipitation, for the fertile rain, for bringing things down to earth, for teasing something valuable out of a solution.

The symbols fused ≋ represented the unity of the opposites, of sublimation and precipitation, of building and destroying—in other words, of the process of replacing an old culture by a new one while preserving whatever was of value in the old one.

The logo and the name were images of the process of centering we underwent. They served as guides, as signs and symbols of our unity and identity. They became charged with energy and meaning when we were under pressure. At certain moments I held an affection for them that was quite mystical. At other times (for example, right before I quit) they repelled me, so that I got nauseous at the mention of the words "Other Ways."

Images have the power to appear to embody the nature and dreams of a group or an individual. They can be used as a guide to collective thinking (What is Other Ways' answer? How should a Weatherman act? A Communist? A Minute Man?) especially when the problems being dealt with are matters of moral decision. Questions of whether to fight or retreat, lie or tell the truth, compromise or refuse to budge, change direction or continue to function in the same way—all these can only be answered within a group by reference to moral principles, many of which are not explicitly articulated until the crisis arises. These principles are often embodied by the image the group created in the act of self-definition, an image freely chosen by the group that represents some collective imagination or vision—healthy or sick—that satisfies the needs of the group's members. I have known groups that didn't feel comfortable until they found the right name or logo or symbol; they needed that image of self and only when they discovered or created one did they feel that they were a "real" group.

This doesn't mean that every group must develop an image of its center or that a group without an image is deficient in any way. Nor does it imply that the image plays only a positive function within the group, for many images trap people into believing they are stronger or cleverer or more powerful than they actually are and therefore lead to stupid behavior. What it does imply is that images play a much more central role in moral thinking than this rationalistic culture credits them with. The image often serves as the mediator of the contraries—the weighing and balancing mechanism that determines the relative proportions of honesty/dishonesty, destruction/creation, activity/passivity, compliance/defiance in the life of the group. It can be the embodiment of the first principles of the group, the abbreviation of that complex of action and principle that I have been calling centering.

Images have to be treated carefully and intelligently. One has to consider why they are chosen—what they mean within the group and what they are meant to convey outside the group. This is especially true when one is under pressure and the tendency to overidentify with the image and become defensive and uncritical is greatest. I remember times when some of us acted and felt as if the mere invocation of the name Other Ways justified our existence and proved our strength.

As powerful as images can be, they are manufactured and can easily become devoid of meaning and turned into clichés. A year after I left, the Other Ways name and logo lost energy and meaning. Only one student knew what the logo represented. For the rest it was a bunch of lines on a piece of paper, a design someone thought up, nothing to think about, a visual cliché. The name was equally arbitrary to the students, who in what I fancied was a final insult (but there was no hostile intent) named the school paper *The Other Way*.

[16]

At the turn of the century a number of mathematicians set out to create the perfect mathematical system. They dreamed of being able to set out the axioms and rules of proof needed to generate all of the true theorems of mathematics. They wanted to prove that this system was consistent (i.e., free of contradictions) and complete (i.e., every theorem formulated within the system was either provable or disprovable based on the axioms and the rules of proof). Their final desire was to discover or create a universal calculus or decision procedure that would automatically tell one whether a given theorem was provable or not.

This utopian mathematical dream has social counterparts. People dream of creating the ideal social system, the system free of contradiction and pain, well-ordered and containing a universal human calculus that automatically resolves all social and personal conflict. Such utopian thought is current among many people who define themselves as revolutionary or countercultural. Ironically it is also current among reactionary social scientists committed to behavior control and behavior modification.

A consideration of the fate of this mathematical dream

of perfection and completion has a lot to teach people who have similar social dreams.

Gottlob Frege, a 19th century German mathematician and logician, was one of the first men to construct a logical system that claimed to be able to generate all number theory. His system was extremely elegant and had a small number of axioms and a few basic notions like "set," "not," "all," and so forth. Upon first examination the system seemed to do what Frege claimed for it. The natural, rational, and real numbers could be generated by the system and most mathematical theorems seemed to be provable within the system. Upon closer scrutiny, however, the system was found to have unexpected contradictions. For example, Bertrand Russell pushed the notion of set to its limits and discovered what is usually called the Russell paradox. He considered the set of all sets that do not contain themselves and asked whether that set contained itself. The answer led to the paradox:

> If the set contains itself, then it does not contain itself.
>
> If the set does not contain itself, then it does contain itself.

This paradox may seem puzzling to nonmathematicians. However, it depends on self-reference (i.e., a set that refers to itself), which leads to other simple paradoxes that might clarify Russell's argument. Consider the following sentence:

> (i) This sentence is false.

Now, is sentence (i) true or false? If it is true then according to the meaning of the words it is false. Similarly, if it is false then it is true. This paradox is generated because the word "this" in the sentence refers to the sentence itself and not to some other sentence. Russell created a mathematical contradiction in Frege's system using the device of self-reference.

The existence of one contradiction is fatal for mathematical systems. If one statement and as well its negative can be proved, then the system becomes inconsistent—i.e., every statement can be proved from the axioms and therefore the system collapses by being unable to distinguish true and false mathematical statements.

Russell did not throw out Frege's whole system when he discovered the contradiction. Rather he threw out the bad set (i.e., the set of all sets that do not contain themselves) and set out to patch up the system. Other logicians and mathematicians also set out to patch the system in different ways. For a while Frege's dream remained alive even though his particular system was changed, often beyond recognition.

However, in the 1930's, the dream was dealt a fatal blow by Kurt Godel, presently a fellow at the Institute for Advanced Study at Princeton, who proved what at the time was counter to the intuition and desires of most mathematicians—that is, that no system could ever be created that could be proved complete and consistent, and account for all the true theorems of mathematics.

Let me elaborate on this a bit, for Godel's conclusions have interesting social analogies. What Godel showed was that if you have a system that claims to generate all and only the true theorems of mathematics (there are an infinite number of such theorems), then the following will be true:

1) The system will be incomplete in the sense that there will be an infinite number of statements within the system that can be neither proved nor disproved by the axioms of that particular system. This means that any such system will leave an infinite number of mathematical questions undecided. There is not even a theoretical possibility of developing a universal calculus or procedure for automatically proving all mathematical theorems. *Systems created by man have unforeseen constraints upon what they are capable of doing.* The shock and initial disbelief of Godel's results that the mathematical community experienced came from the stunning fact that the most

sophisticated creations of mathematical imagination are
imperfect by their very nature.

2) The system might be consistent, but you can never
prove it within the system itself. To prove the consistency
of a system that generates number theory a stronger system
has to be used—i.e., one that contains the system to be
proved consistent as well as other axioms. Absolute consistency is an impossible dream. The best one can hope for
is relative consistency and then the consistency of the
stronger system remains an open question.

Since the acceptance of the validity of Godel's theorems
mathematicians have revised their dreams and developed
new intuitions about systems. There is no longer talk about
one universal system or of magical computers that can
solve all mathematical problems in an instant. People expect the unexpected, and a whole new branch of mathematics, metamathematics, has developed that studies the
nature of systems. It is no longer felt that if the axioms
and rules of reasoning are set down the resulting system
will be predictable and controllable. The system must be
studied in detail and most likely will have properties that
confound our expectations and invalidate our intuitions.

There have also been attempts to create perfect social
systems, and these systems too have given rise to unexpected contradictions and are incomplete in many ways.
The dream of a free world economy and of free competition among people has given rise to economic exploitation,
the concentration of wealth and power, and the development of economic slavery throughout the world. Plans for
technological development and dreams of a post-scarcity
world failed to consider the depletion of the world's resources and the danger of cancerous overdevelopment.

Obsession with economic man and the redistribution of
wealth leaves a social system open to sexual and racial exploitation and to power struggles that exist despite economic equality.

Plans for a world full of peace and love have turned

sour and in many places communities based upon an ideology of love have turned fascist.

When people encounter social contradictions in the form of unexpected conflict, misery, or disaster, their tendency is the same as Russell's—i.e., to patch up the failing system, throw out the bad set, and still cling to the dream of a complete and perfect social order. A wide range of variations on the original system develops, each dealing with some contradiction or incomplete component that has arisen during the natural history of the system. Sometimes so much patching is done that nothing remains of the original dream but a collection of patches. Corporate capitalism has as much resemblance to a free market as Soviet communism does to a classless society. Perhaps what is wrong is the very idea of a perfect social system that can be completed once and for all times. It is possible that there are constraints on building any social order as fundamental as those Godel uncovered for mathematical systems.

I believe that there are such fundamental constraints on the development of social systems that people involved in changing culture and society must accept. These constraints can be thought of in Godelian terms.

First of all, social systems are bound to be *essentially incomplete*—that is, not capable of prescribing automatic solutions to all problems that arise among people. Some systems, at the cost of freedom and mobility for most people, can attempt to legislate all conflict out of existence. Marriage can be arranged, vocation predetermined, leisure managed, thoughts and feelings controlled. However, time usually slips in—the unexpected occurs from outside the group, or a new type of conflict arises, or an unexpected blessing befalls some people.

Furthermore, human beings cannot withstand the pressure of total control and collapse into uncentered being—that is, into psychosis—when there is no space or time for individual development. A totally controlled completed social system is probably not possible because its members would not reproduce or survive. When the system attempts to control all behavior, an underground culture usually grows in opposition to the dominating culture. This underground culture might be revolutionary in character and attempt to overthrow the dominant order. But more likely it will be gossipy and divisive, consisting of the secret and small things individuals under pressure do to retain their uniqueness and pretend to power of their own.

Most systems are not so total—many areas of life are left to individual preference. Other areas of life are not dealt with at all until circumstances force people within a culture to make new decisions. For example, places with no substantial nonwhite populations have to deal with racism all of a sudden if there is a large nonwhite immigration. Cultures accustomed to redistributing a small amount of wealth collectively sometimes are forced to deal with a sudden overabundance of wealth whose existence is contingent on breaking up the old social order. Gifts of money and resources from the United States, for example, are intimately bound up with conditions leading to the cultural dissolution of the seeming beneficiaries.

Because social systems are incomplete, there are always new problems for people to face as individuals or groups. Cultures have to be responsive to the unexpected in order to survive. Mechanisms of social reconstruction have to be invented suddenly and under pressure or members of a culture will turn destructive and suicidal, will do nothing, have nothing of value to remember and therefore nothing to give a new generation, have no good reason to reproduce or work. When old dreams of perfection fall apart, they can be replaced by new equally incompletable and inevitably frustrating dreams of perfection or perspective can be shifted: dreams of perfection can be replaced by a sense of the essential incompleteness of any social order and therefore a commitment to continual reconstruction.

What is probably hardest to do and yet most necessary is to give up the idea that some final perfect stage of human society is attainable. The best we can expect is a continuing and shifting constellation of human needs, habits, and resources centering on eliminating oppression and nurturing individual and collective growth.

The second point is that as well as being incomplete a social-cultural system cannot be proved consistent from within the system.

Let me define the concept of the consistency of a social-cultural system in the following ways: a system is consistent if the roles people play are complementary and do not lead to direct and inevitable conflict. The rules and laws and customs are consistent if they do not imply contradictory behavior—i.e., if they do not counsel people to do and not to do the same thing. Some examples:

—In a pseudo-democratic culture everyone is told he has an equal voice. Some people try to exercise that voice and other people in power evoke laws that take the voice away while still claiming to be democratic.

—In a "liberated" group of men and women it sometimes happens that one person's liberation inevitably leads him or her into conflict with other people who conceive of their own liberation in a different way. For example, at Other Ways there used to be violent unresolvable clashes between so-called liberated males and females, each group conceiving the other as an oppressive force. Conflict was unavoidable at that moment. Later on, mutual adjustments of positions were made so that we could survive as a group.

It is difficult for people within a culture to know explicitly all the rules and roles and customs that govern their social life and thought. Even for specialists in the preservation and recording of the culture there is no way to know whether all historical and natural circumstances the group might face can be dealt with without contradiction.

In fact, contradiction within a culture is often an occasion for explosion or redefinition. I can think of a number of contradictory situations within our culture that must lead to redefinition:

—Young people are prepared for roles within a technological system that has no jobs available.

—Overabundant wealth leads to post-scarcity planning while some people remain hungry.

—Schools preach honesty while adults accept corruption as the nature of man.

—Children are told they are loved, then given roles as slaves and treated with hostility when they step out of those roles.

There is another consequence of the inability of people to know the consistency of the social system in which they function. When a new rule is made, a new role assumed, a new ritual or custom adopted, it is not possible to foresee all the consequences of that act of reconstruction. Frequently new groups lay down rules or laws that lead to consequences the members are incapable of dealing with. For example:

—A rule is made that no one can be expelled from the group, and someone within the group is acting in a way that will lead to the group's destruction.

—It is agreed upon that everyone should love everyone else equally, and people find themselves unable to feel that way.

—People are allowed to choose roles freely, and everyone chooses a dependent role and nothing gets done.

—People are allowed to choose roles freely, and everyone chooses a managerial role and nothing gets done.

—Consensus is needed for all decisions and it cannot be reached on major issues of survival that must be dealt with.

It is not that every way of organizing human lives is necessarily inconsistent. Rather, we will never be able to know with certainty whether it is consistent or not.

Because of the incompleteness of social systems and because of the many unexpected consequences of creating new cultural forms (or being trapped within old ones), it is crucial that we look upon the enterprise of remaking our culture as a continual process consisting of action, evaluation, and reformulation. We must give up the notion of a final solution to human problems. We must become accustomed to remaking our lives, and because of this we have to develop ways of understanding and evaluating the groups we are part of or which affect our lives. We need to develop coordinates for social perception, techniques for studying groups that will enable us to modify group life while maintaining the struggle for a healthy existence. We must come to understand that social creativity is as important as technological ingenuity.

Many of the ideas and concepts I discovered in rethinking my experiences at Other Ways have led me to develop a profile that might be useful to others for understanding group life and for pinpointing problems that can be anticipated or contradictions that might arise. During the process of self-analysis it is useful to consider the following coordinates concerning the roles people assume within the group:

—Do people assume *familial roles* with respect to one another? Do they act as mothers, fathers, children? Are these roles explicitly acknowledged or are they assumed unconsciously and allowed to develop without formalization? Are the roles permanent or fixed, or do roles change as different situations develop? If familial roles are assumed, does the family structure seem viable or does it seem likely to give rise to contradictions (as, for example, when everyone plays child, or everyone plays father, or mother)?

—Does the group have *power roles?* Is there a social class, an economic class, a pecking order? Are these roles institutionalized, or is power constantly fought over, with the pecking order constantly shifting? How are decisions made? How do people say decisions are made? Does the way people say decisions are made describe what actually happens or are there contradictions in the structure of power and authority within the group?

—Are there *tribal roles* within the group? That is, are there factions, clans, subgroups, caucuses? How do these groups relate to one another? To the whole? Are these groups formalized and publicly recognized, or do they function as secret societies and covert factions? Do any of the subgroups function at cross purposes with the supposed direction of the whole? What are the power roles within the subgroups? What is their role with respect to one another? Is there a group order of dominance and submission?

—Are any *archetypal roles* operative? How do clowns, fools, jesters, wise people, seers, prophets, demons, hermits, shamans function within the group? Are these roles formalized or covert? Are they temporary or permanent? How do members of the group regard one another's roles?

—How do the roles match the work the group sets out to do? Are there special *work roles?* Do the different roles overlap? How will the different roles function in times of crisis? Under external pressure? Are the roles consistent with one another, or do they create a mismatch? How is responsibility allocated and how is nonperformance dealt with?

—What are the *sexual roles* for members within the group? What relationships are approved, sanctioned, prohibited by the way sexual roles are established within the group? How much of the sexual life within the group is overtly acknowledged? How much is hidden? What contradictions are likely to arise from hidden sexuality? How do sex roles relate to power roles, work roles, familial roles, and so forth?

Some general questions can be asked with respect to roles within the group:

—How are roles assumed or changed?

—What are the signs that people are assuming certain roles?

—Does the group define roles rigidly or flexibly?

—How much of what goes on is public knowledge, private knowledge, unthinking and unanalyzed behavior?

The typography of group centers can also be used to understand groups. One can ask:

—Is the group closed or perverse? This must be spelled out in specific terms. How is it closed? Is the state temporary or permanent? Do members of the group perceive of the group as closed or do they act one way and talk another way?

—Is the group devastated? How does this devastation manifest itself? What is the source of devastation—internal or external?

—Is the group separated and hypocritical? What are the specific forms of hypocrisy that determine the group's life? How do members perceive their own hypocrisy? Is it acknowledged publicly? Dealt with? Ignored? Is there a resignation to hypocritical existence?

—Is the group without a center? Is it in flight or totally bound up with meaningless rituals?

There are some more general questions that can be asked about the center:

—How does the group define itself in terms of vocation, style, sensibility, ideology? What is the relationship between these components of centering? Does the group strive for health? Even more specifically:

—What is the process of *self-definition?* How much is articulated? Does the group let things happen to it or does it try to control its destiny?

—Is *criticism* a part of group life? What are the occasions for criticism? Who is expected to criticize whom? Is the act a hostile or supportive one? What forms of covert criticism (e.g., gossip) exist? Does criticism by a member of the group involve self-criticism as well? Is the critique direct or indirect, encouraged, avoided? What is the level of anxiety for people who give or receive criticism?

—How is criticism acted upon? Is there any form of *conscious reconstruction* that the group assumes responsibility for? Do things actually change or are the same mistakes repeated neurotically and the same hostilities never resolved? What are the mechanisms of reconstruction—how do people support each other? How do they learn to change their behavior? Do they change it? How is fear dealt with?

—What does each member get out of participating in the group? Is the functioning of the group *personally significant* for all the members? Some? None? What seems to be the threshold of personal dissatisfaction that drives people out of the group? Do people know one another's needs well enough to make adjustments so that personal misery is avoided?

—Is the group's functioning *collectively significant?* Does it relate to a wider world or is it solipsistic? Do people within the group function together or do they go their own way? Do people pull together or fall apart under pressure? Do they like being with one another or do they stay together out of obligation, or fear, or boredom? Which people work well and easily with one another? Which ones don't? What is done about the people who have trouble collaborating?

—Does the group have a humane vision of the *whole,* of the world outside of itself? Does it place itself in any larger struggles? Does it feel sympathy or pain or compassion or solidarity with others? Is it an isolate?

—Is the group *open* to change, to newness, to changing direction, to creating alliances and coalitions, to rethinking problems? How are contrary tendencies within the group dealt with? Are people able to resolve conflict without legislating it out of existence? Are they open to one another or do they turn away, repel one another when mistakes are made or failure seems possible?

—What *commitment* have the members of the group

made with respect to one another, to the work? How is this commitment articulated? What reservations do people have? Is there apathy within the group or overly romantic commitment so that some people are likely to burn themselves out quickly? Does the actual work done match the verbal statement of commitment? Is the question of commitment avoided so that people do not know what to expect or demand of one another?

—Finally, how does the group's commitment and self-definition translate into *specific* everyday functioning? What does the group do other than talk? Is it effective? What is the quality of daily life like for each member? How does the group plan its work? Is there an over-all strategy? Do people agree upon tactics and then carry them out? Do plans get followed? Are ideas translated into actualities?

It is useful to examine the images a group uses to define itself. How did the images develop? Does the group have a name, a totem animal, sacred object, sign, handshake? How do images, ideas, styles affect the individuals within a group? Do they set members of the group off very clearly from outsiders? Are they meant to separate the group in this way?

What power and autonomy do the images have? Do group members think and talk in terms of the images they have identified with?

All of these questions can be raised with respect to family groups, work groups, communal groups, schools, unions, collectives, businesses, and so forth. They provide a general profile of how things work, of what might go wrong, and of how things might be changed within a group. They do not provide a total picture of group life. They do, however, provide a way—one of many possible ways—of giving oneself an analysis of social functioning that is somewhat comprehensive and yet practical enough to lead to social invention and the resolution of some unnecessary conflict. I find that they help me keep from repeating mistakes I made in the past, make me stronger, more committed, wholer, more able to integrate my individual needs with collective functioning.

Of course, all of this is hard work.

Many people ask whether it is worth beginning again after the fate of the civil rights movement, the disenchantment with alternative schools, the resignation and conformity of many university students, the general amnesia about our role in Vietnam, the cynicism and harshness the federal government and large corporations manifest when dealing with the needs of poor and powerless people, the crises that seem manufactured to confound and exploit the middle class. The answer is, What choice do we have? Either we struggle to create a sane world or destroy ourselves and the earth through greed and thoughtlessness.

Bibliography

For people who wish to pursue some of the ideas in this book here is a short list of works that deal with group and personal change as well as the problem of centering:

Adams, Henry. *The Education of Henry Adams* (Modern Library, 1931).

de Bono, Edwards. *New Think* (Basic Books, 1967).

Henry, Jules. *On Sham, Vulnerability, and other Forms of Self-Destruction* (Vintage, 1973).

————. *Pathways to Madness* (Random House, 1971).

Jahn, Janheinz. *Muntu, the New African Culture* (Evergreen–Grove Press, 1961).

Jung, C. G. *The Archetypes and the Collective Unconscious* (Princeton University Press, 1968).

Laing, R. D. *The Politics of Experience* (Pantheon, 1967).

Levi-Strauss, Claude. *The Savage Mind* (University of Chicago Press, 1966).

————. *Structural Anthropology*. Especially pages 167–185 (Basic Books, 1963).

Plato. *The Republic* in the revised Jowett translation (Oxford University Press, 1955).

Richards, M. C. *Centering* (Wesleyan University Press, 1970).

Sennett, Richard. *The Uses of Disorder* (Knopf, 1970).

Stevens, Wallace. *Opus Posthumous*. Especially the essay on pages 183–201 (Knopf, 1957).

Wittgenstein, Ludwig. *Philosophical Investigations*. 2d ed. (Macmillan, 1958).

About the Author

Herbert Kohl is the author of *Reading, How To; 36 Children;* and *The Open Classroom.* A graduate of Harvard and a former director of the Teachers and Writers Collaborative, a group that attempted to revise the curriculum in elementary and secondary schools, Mr. Kohl taught and directed an open school in Berkeley, California, called Other Ways, within the Berkeley Unified School District. He is a former columnist of *Grade Teacher Magazine* and was involved with parents in Harlem and East Harlem who are engaged in the struggle for community control of schools. Presently he is teaching kindergarten and first grade in Berkeley.